CR[...]EORY

THIRD EDITION

CRIMINOLOGICAL THEORY

A Brief Introduction

J. MITCHELL MILLER

The University of Texas at San Antonio

CHRISTOPHER J. SCHRECK

Rochester Institute of Technology

RICHARD TEWKSBURY

University of Louisville

Prentice Hall

Boston   Columbus   Indianapolis   New York   San Francisco
Upper Saddle River   Amsterdam   Cape Town   Dubai   London   Madrid
Milan   Munich   Paris   Montreal   Toronto   Delhi   Mexico City   Sao Paulo
Sydney   Hong Kong   Seoul   Singapore   Taipei   Tokyo

Editor in Chief: Vernon R. Anthony
Acquisitions Editor: Tim Peyton
Editorial Assistant: Lynda Cramer
Director of Marketing: David Gesell
Marketing Manager: Adam Kloza
Senior Marketing Coordinator:
  Alicia Wozniak
Marketing Assistant: Les Roberts
Operations Specialist: Clara Bartunek
Creative Art Director: Jayne Conte
Cover Designer: Bruce Kenselaar
Manager, Visual Research: Beth Brenzel

Manager, Rights and Permissions:
  Zina Arabia
Manager, Cover Visual Research &
  Permissions: Karen Sanatar
Cover Art: SuperStock
Full-Service Project Management:
  Shiny Rajesh/Integra Software
  Services, Pvt. Ltd.
Composition: Integra Software
  Services, Pvt. Ltd.
Printer/Binder: Courier Companies, Inc.
Text Font: 10/12 Palatino

Credits and acknowledgments borrowed from other sources and reproduced, with permission, in this textbook appear on appropriate page within text.

Library of Congress Cataloging-in-Publication Data

Miller, J. Mitchell.
    Criminological theory : a brief introduction/Mitchell Miller, Christopher
    J. Schreck, Richard Tewksbury. —3rd ed.
       p. cm.
    Includes bibliographical references and index.
    ISBN-13: 978-0-13-507151-9 (alk. paper)
    ISBN-10: 0-13-507151-8 (alk. paper)
    1. Criminology.   2. Crime.   I. Schreck, Christopher J.
II. Tewksbury, Richard A.   III. Title.
    HV6018.M545 2010
    364.01—dc22

                                        2010001093

10 9 8 7 6 5 4 3

Prentice Hall
is an imprint of

www.pearsonhighered.com

ISBN 13: 978-0-13-507151-9
ISBN 10:   0-13-507151-8

CONTENTS

CHAPTER FIVE

The Social Ecology of Crime   93

CHAPTER SIX

Learning and Cultural Transmission Theories of Crime   118

CHAPTER SEVEN

Strain Theories of Crime   142

CHAPTER TEN

Evaluating and Integrating Theory   215

PREFACE

There are several criminological theory texts that address crime from a certain viewpoint; for example, a critical, feminist, life-course, or biological perspective. Others offer a common theme, engaging crime theory from an international, cultural, or historical approach. In this third edition of *Criminological Theory: A Brief Introduction*, we alternatively feature a balanced social science orientation. We have sought to emphasize and further the objectives identified in the previous editions—to portray explanations of crime from selected theoretical traditions and to survey leading classical and contemporary theories of crime in a straightforward, ideologically neutral manner in a conversational voice that students will actually want to read. We have sought to demonstrate the applicability of criminological theory to everyday life by offering real-world, contemporary illustrations and examples, as well as hypothetical scenarios relevant to society, generally, and college life, specifically.

NEW TO THIS EDITION

This new edition features several improvements, including the following:

- Chapter 2, "Classical and Neoclassical Criminology," has been restructured and largely rewritten to better reflect the evolution of the classical perspective to modern deterrence and rational choice theories.
- Chapter 3, "Biological Theories of Crime," and Chapter 4, "Psychological Theories of Crime," place greater attention to the growing and quickly diversifying aspects of individual biological and psychological criminogenic factors.
- Chapter 5, "The Social Ecology of Crime," offers considerable new information on social disorganization theory, and Chapter 6, "Learning and Cultural Transmission Theories of Crime" highlights discussion of Akers' social learning–social structure theory and Anderson's code of the street.
- Chapter 7, "Strain Theories of Crime," and Chapter 8, "Control Theories of Crime," provide expanded coverage of

Agnew's general strain theory and Hirschi's original control theory, respectively.

- The critical perspective covered in Chapter 9, "Theories of Social Conflict," has been enhanced and now better emphasizes the contemporary significance of labeling theory and the lingering relevance of restorative justice and reintegrative shaming theories.
- The authors have attempted, across all of the chapters, to (1) increase coverage of the level of empirical support that exists for the numerous theories presented and (2) consider criticisms so that readers may determine which perspectives are viable and yield implications for criminal justice practices and policies with scientific backing.

The authors are committed to engaging criminology from a strong social science orientation, bringing distinct theoretical preferences and insights that, hopefully, will motivate students to carefully consider the range of alternative explanations offered for the same crime realities and outcomes. A social science orientation necessarily means a theory–methods symmetry; in the case of criminological theory, this means consideration of proposed theories according to the level of observed empirical support, that is, research evidence.

While maintaining social science as a standard by which to assess whether individual theories are "good," this new edition identifies recent advances in the field which modify, advance, and affirm the nature of theoretical criminology as it continues to evolve. Criminological theory necessarily follows real-world crime trends, and, while new theories are not crafted overnight and research confirmation when a new theory is developed is a slow process, new criminal behaviors and unprecedented forms of older crimes have emerged to capture the national conscience since the last edition. Few, if any, of us anticipated almost three years ago that new forms of white-collar crime would appear in terms of predatory lending that nearly collapsed the U.S. housing industry, or the Bernie Madoff ponzi scheme, which cost thousands of Americans billions of dollars and their life savings. Fewer still would have imagined a renewed subcultural presence. While we've largely narrowed the relevance of the culture and crime relationship to either inner-city minority or rural poverty contexts, the shocking mass removal by state officials of over four hundred children from the Yearning for Zion ranch, a reclusive Fundamental Latter Day Saints compound in rural Texas, has again made relevant consideration of social learning influences on crime and deviance.

Our intention is not to persuade adoption of any particular theory, but rather to familiarize the reader with leading theories, generally. Along the way, we hope that conceptual, analytical, and critical thinking skills are developed as readers compare and contrast the different and sometimes conflicting explanations illustrated. The various supportive ideas and criticisms offered across the theories examined will ideally prompt scrutiny and reconsideration of existing assumptions and beliefs. By engaging an analytical and critical approach to the text, it is also our hope that students will come to view the nature of crime, the development of the criminal law, and the criminal justice system's prevention and reduction efforts more like criminologists do. Such an approach goes beyond a mere assessment of various criminal and deviant behaviors as right or wrong and considers outcomes and events in a broader light, wherein explanations reflect a myriad of factors, such as individual, environment, social structure, culture, and group processes represented throughout this text. Last, we invite both student readers and instructors to feel free to contact any of the authors with comments or suggestions on how we might further improve the text; given the vast nature of criminology and its ever broadening and interdisciplinary nature, we may have unintentionally failed to include some important research suggesting level of support for various perspectives or perhaps newer criticisms of specific theories. This input is valuable for improving the book and ensuring that it better meets the needs of classroom instructors.

Several colleagues facilitated revision of the second edition. We appreciate the detailed comments and the identification of related empirical support for theories they provided.

The authors offer sincere thanks to the following reviewers for their insightful suggestions: Holly Ventura Miller, University of Texas at San Antonio; Brenda Chaney, Ohio State University; Stephanie Manzi, Roger Williams University; Elicka S.L. Peterson, Appalachian State University; and Xln Ren, California State University, Sacramento.

CHAPTER 1

THEORETICAL CRIMINOLOGY
An Introductory Overview

The threat and fear of crime are constant concerns that seriously impact modern life. Television programs and newspapers remind us daily of violent acts and threats to our personal property. We are entertained, if not mesmerized, by crime, both through the glamorization of criminal genius and the bravery of law enforcement. We watch intricate plots accentuated by high drama unfold in the movies, on reality television policing shows, and during live court coverage of highly publicized trials. Crime also heavily impacts our daily lives by affecting our routine choices in ways that are so customary they seem altogether normal. Our daily patterns reflect the concern about crime in terms of where we park, how and with whom we interact, which school to attend, and the constant need to secure property. These and similar quality-of-life matters are directly attributed to both the perception and reality of crime. The safety of neighborhoods and schools, as indicated by crime rates and fear of crime, is a major consideration in choosing where to live. In short, crime is a major force in contemporary society and a leading social problem that demands a considerable portion of our public resources.

The problem of crime is addressed on many levels by the criminal justice system, ranging from prevention and awareness efforts to rehabilitation of offenders. While it is essential that law enforcement, the courts, and the correctional system work to maintain a safe and orderly society, the criminal justice system is logically more effective when informed by a scientific knowledge base on the causes, patterns, and nature of crime and delinquency.

Whereas criminal justice is concerned with the actual practices of law enforcement, legal process, and corrections, **criminology** is focused on the processes of making and breaking laws (Cressey, 1978, p. 3). Criminologists seek to understand how the creation of criminal law defines misbehavior according to different and sometimes competing interests and how the criminalization of behavior interrelates with culture and class status differently throughout society. More importantly, criminologists are concerned with the

1

various causes of crime. It is vital to understand the underlying reasons for crime in order to best inform criminal justice practices and policies. Criminal justice science and criminology are different in that the former seeks to identify "solutions" to the crime problem while the latter is more focused on discovering the basic nature of crime and its many complex forms. The knowledge generated by criminology is an important component in society's understanding and response to crime and deviance. Anticrime strategies, for example, are ideally designed in sync with the extant knowledge base on criminal behavior and the distribution of crime throughout society.

Numerous facts are known about the causes and nature of crime, and criminologists often disagree about the reasons for crime and its relationship to other social problems. Some contend that the focus should be on individuals and their behavior—particularly the factors involved in the decision-making process leading to crime. Others look, instead, to social factors largely external to the individual, such as poverty; the quality of obtainable education; and the age, gender, racial, and ethnic composition of the population. Regardless of the particular perspective, criminologists attempt to discover, arrange, and make sense of facts about crime in a systematic manner. This process requires the creation of theory, wherein facts about crime are examined in relation to other facts—the major focus of this text.

In the following chapters, the major theories about the complex causes of criminal behavior are presented and discussed, with attention given to each theory's implications for responding to specific types of offenses or offenders. The specific theories examined across these chapters are all unique in that they identify or situate the cause or responsibility for crime in a distinct source. Accordingly, each chapter has something additional to offer in terms of furthering our understanding of crime. The various theories that will be examined address different types of offenses (such as violence, property crime, and morality infractions), the role of various internal (such as biological and psychological) and external (such as social disorganization and culture) factors, and the effects of formal (such as the production of law and enforcement initiatives) and informal (such as shaming and peer effects) social control mechanisms. An effort has been made to illustrate these theories in terms of their relevancy and applicability to everyday life.

Before examining the diversity of theories presented in this book, it is useful to establish a frame of reference or common background against which the individual theories can be considered and compared. In the context of social science theorizing, this framework consists of the following elements: (1) the origins and evolution of criminological thought leading up to the point of formal theory construction, (2) the nature of theory, (3) the criteria for assessing the quality of theory, and (4) the role of theory for criminal justice practices and policies.

THE ORIGINS AND EVOLUTION
OF CRIMINOLOGY

Attention to crime can be traced back to ancient Babylonia and the Code of Hammurabi, as well as the Judeo-Christian perspective presented in the Bible. Beyond these edicts of infraction and punishment, contemporary criminologists typically recognize the origins of criminality in the Enlightenment period of the late eighteenth century, particularly the social and intellectual reforms in Western Europe. Philosophers from this period, such as Voltaire, Rousseau, and Locke, observed the superiority of reason based on direct experience and observation over the blind faith and superstition that characterized social life during the previous feudal era. Before this emphasis on reasoning, crime was first dealt with informally within and between families, with great emphasis placed on the realization of revenge (Larson, 1984).

The family-revenge model of justice—for example, multigenerational feuds between Scottish clans—presented social-order maintenance and governing problems for feudal lords, whose solutions were trial by battle and then trial by ordeal. Under trial by battle, either the victim or a member of the victim's family would fight the offender or a member of his or her family; under trial by ordeal, the accused would be subjected to some "test" that would determine guilt or innocence, such as running through a gauntlet or being repeatedly dunked in water while bound by rope. Both approaches were vested in the spiritual notion of divine intervention. In battle, God would grant victory to the innocent side and likewise protect the falsely accused during trial by ordeal, as in the biblical report of protection afforded the prophet Daniel in the lions' den.

Clearly, these methods failed to effect justice relative to a person's guilt or innocence, instead yielding outcomes specific to a person's fighting ability, the capability to withstand various kinds of torture, or simply luck. Although the Enlightenment period introduced a new way of thinking that provided an alternative to the logic of spiritual explanations, spirituality continued to affect interpretations of both crime causation and systems of justice for several centuries. The idea of being controlled by an evil spirit or that one's criminal behavior is attributable to the influence of the devil or some other "dark" force has long been a default logic to account for the unexplainable. Primary examples from early U.S. history include the Salem witch trials, in which crime problems that could not be solved were attributed to witchcraft and demonic possession, and the origins of "correctional" institutions in Philadelphia by Quakers who believed that isolation, labor, and Bible reading would result in repentance—essentially a spiritually based form of rehabilitation. The very term *penitentiary,* which referenced institutions where society's crime problems were addressed through religious conversion, illustrates continuation of the belief in spirituality as the source of and solution to crime. Today there is renewed endorsement of the spirituality argument, evident in the Bush administration's development and implementation of "faith-based" initiatives, many of which are crime related or crime specific (Allen, 2003).

While the Enlightenment period did not completely end the belief that spirituality affects crime, the momentum of experience-based reasoning led to a general view of social order that served as a forerunner to criminology. One of the primary concepts from this era that was important for the development of criminology is the idea of the **social contract**. First introduced by Thomas Hobbes (1588–1679), the social contract involves the sacrifice of some personal freedom by endorsement of governmental law enforcement in exchange for protection and the benefit of all. For example, it is likely that there is someone on campus each day from whom, either alone or with the aid of a friend, you could forcibly take personal property such as a wallet, purse, or textbook. Similarly, there is likely an individual or group that could forcibly take your property. Despite these obvious probabilities, everyone comes and goes in relative peace and safety. By sacrificing your ability to take what you might from others, you are protected from such a loss—this trade-off of loss of potential gain in exchange for law and order is an oversimplified example of the social contract.

As a result of the Enlightenment period, then, superstition- and spirituality-based orientations to crime were exchanged for innovative ways of thinking that emphasized relationships between criminal behavior and punishment. This newer approach, exemplified in the writings of the Italian Cesare Beccaria (1738–1794) and the Englishman Jeremy Bentham (1748–1832), is known as the **classical school of criminology**, a major point of origin from which criminological theorizing would develop (see Chapter 2). Grounded in the concept of deterrence and emphasizing free will and the dimensions of punishment (certainty, severity, and celerity), the classical school is significant for the development of criminological thought in at least two respects: (1) Crime was no longer believed to be a function of religion, superstition, or myth that placed the problem beyond the control of humankind, and (2) crime was seen as the result of free will. Viewing crime as a function of free will, essentially decision making, meant that it could now be explained as an outcome of rational choice. The notion of rational thought (a determination of gains versus risks) suggests that the crime rate is logically related to the elements impacting the decision to offend, such as the amount and relative value of criminal proceeds and the likelihood of getting caught in the act. The principles of the classical school, revised by legal reformers and now referred to as *neoclassicism*, continue to influence the nature of formal social control (the criminal justice system continues in the attempt to achieve deterrence as one of its primary objectives) as well as the study of criminal behavior.

Another perspective on social life began to emerge in Europe during the nineteenth century that first emphasized the application of the scientific method. This perspective, known as **positivism**, stressed the identification of patterns and consistencies in observable facts (Bryant, 1985). By examining known patterns, it was believed that causes of behavior could be determined, which would enable predictions about outcomes when certain conditions exist. For example, we can ascertain a pattern of comparatively high criminality among the lower socioeconomic class. Given the absence of other intervening factors, we can predict a rise in lower-class criminality if a sharp increase in unemployment affects unskilled laborers. Regardless of whether this relationship is true, this line of thinking differs from the classical school's attention to freewill decision making, positing crime instead as a manifestation of **determinism**.

Determinism takes the position that human behavior is caused by factors specific to the individual, such as biological and psychological issues (as discussed in Chapters 3 and 4, respectively) or the environment (as discussed in Chapter 5). Perhaps the most famous figure associated with determinism in the context of criminality is Cesare Lombroso (1835–1909), whose "criminal type" illustrated in his influential work *Criminal Man* (1863) suggests that some people are born criminals. Lombroso's work, along with that of Edwin Sutherland (1883–1950), was essential to viewing crime in a newer, more scientific light.

In the evolution of American criminology, positivism began replacing the classical approach to crime during the 1920s, largely due to the rise of the **Chicago school**, a movement resulting from a series of seminal studies conducted by the University of Chicago Sociology Department. From the 1920s through the 1940s, the Chicago school demonstrated that crime is a product of social ecology, particularly the disorganization that characterizes urban life.

The social ecological approach to crime is less concerned with the ways in which criminals and noncriminals differ in terms of intelligence, physical characteristics, and personality and more attentive to economic disadvantage, community cohesion, and social stability. The Chicago school crime studies of Shaw and McKay (1924), Merton (1938), and Sutherland (1939) grounded U.S. criminology in sociology and established a dominant *paradigm*, or model of inquiry, oriented toward environmental causes of crime. These works (discussed in Chapter 5) represent some of the first American criminological theories and, more importantly, established a context in which the majority of future theories (presented throughout this text) would be developed. At this point, we need to examine more closely the nature and role of theory.

THE NATURE OF THEORY

What exactly is **theory**? A one-word definition of theory is "explanation." Too often, theory is erroneously thought of as philosophy or logic that has little relevance for real-world situations. In reality, theory is a part of everyday life, an attempt to make sense and order of events that are otherwise unexplainable. Think, for example, about the following common scenario. After dating for two years, a college couple's relationship is suddenly ended by one of the parties. Shocked and upset by news of the unwanted breakup, the rejected person will often consider, at great length and with the advice of friends, the reasons or causes leading to the outcome. Even if knowing *why* will not change the reality, we still want to know the answers, perhaps because making sense of seemingly random events reassures us that the social world is not chaotic and arbitrary. On a more pragmatic level, knowing why things happen enables us to modify our behavior or change relevant circumstances for a more preferable outcome in the future.

Developing explanations for everyday events, then, is a common practice that entails mentally sorting causes and effects, which is a form of theoretical expression. Academics, on the other hand, often refer to scientific theory. Simply put, scientific theories are a means of explaining natural occurrences through statements about the relationships between observable phenomena. Observable phenomena are specified as either a cause or an effect and then positioned in a relationship statement. The causes and effects are termed *variables* (a variable is simply something that varies and is not constant). These formal statements, which are often presented as a hypothesis, are formed in order to explain or predict how some observable factor or a combination of factors relates to the phenomena being examined. These relationships, which form specific theories of crime, are developed according to the logic of *variable analysis*. This analytic strategy specifies causal elements as *independent variables* and effects as *dependent variables.*

In criminology, not surprisingly, crime itself is the foremost dependent variable. It is vital to note here that the strategy of variable analysis is not interested in explaining crime per se; that is, the objective is not to explain what crime is in a definitional or legal sense. Rather, the variable analysis process seeks to account for *variation* in crime. Most theories conceptualize crime as a generic dichotomy—that is, the separation of phenomena into one of two categories. When crime is the dependent variable in a theory, further scrutiny usually reveals that theorists are actually referring to either **criminality** or **crime rate**. Criminality denotes the extent and frequency of offending by a societal group, such as the young, minorities, noncitizens, the unemployed, or people from a certain region. Crime rate, on the other hand, denotes the level of crime in a given locale. The focus on either criminality or crime rate is observable in the framing of different research questions: Why is there more homicide in Memphis than in Phoenix? Why are more males than females involved in crime? Again, the goal is not to explain the crime itself, but rather to account for the fluctuation in behavior across time, place, or social group.

After specifying causal and dependent variables, criminologists consider the nature of the relationships to determine inference and possible implications. The information revealed from a theoretical proposition is interpreted by the condition of **correlation**. Correlation speaks to the *covariance* of variables, the direction and strength of fluctuation in a dependent variable attributed to one or more independent variables. Directional correlation refers to either a positive or negative relationship. These terms do not carry the same connotation as when normally used in everyday language. The expressions "The running back rushed for positive yardage" and "She has a negative attitude" are value laden and indicate desirable and undesirable conditions. In the social sciences, a positive correlation means that an independent variable and dependent variable fluctuate in the same direction, such as a group's level of drug use and criminal involvement. A negative correlation means that independent and dependent variables covary in different directions, such as educational attainment and crime (with the obvious exception of white-collar offenses).

Consideration of the relationship between school grades and the status offense of truancy provides a good example of directional correlation. Suppose a researcher gathers data on both absences and grades from a large sample of randomly selected middle and high school students. Findings supporting the logical hypothesis that increased absences cause lower grades would be a negative correlation, as would better grades covarying with a decrease in absences. In the latter scenario, the correlation, though negative, is also the desirable outcome.

The strength of correlation, on the other hand, specifies the degree of covariance between independent and dependent variables. For example, a gang awareness program delivered to middle school parents (in this case, the independent variable) may effect a minimal decrease in gang membership (the dependent variable). This relationship suggests an undesirable outcome, not because the correlation is negative but due to the finding that the independent variable generated only little change in the dependent variable—perhaps because the parents of gang members are less likely to participate in an awareness program in the first place. The strength of a correlation is ascertained through statistical analysis enabling the exact determination of covariance between variables, a calculation related in terms of statistical significance.

In order to analyze theoretical propositions, independent and dependent variables are respecified from a categorical and conceptual level to a measurable level, a process known as *operationalization.* Operational definitions, then, enable empirical examination of cause-and-effect relationships by specifying measurable indicators for variables. How a variable is defined will affect the nature of a relationship and yield different (and possibly undesirable) implications for addressing crime. The following example of measuring recidivism demonstrates how important the measurement process is and how easily measurement error can occur.

Recidivism (repeat criminal offending) is one of the most common theoretically based dependent variables used in criminological research, especially as an indicator of effectiveness for criminal justice program evaluation. Depending on whether an evaluation is being conducted in a law enforcement, court, or correctional context (all three of which conduct deterrence and rehabilitation programs whose success is largely indicated by recidivism), the act of reoffending is likely to be operationally defined differently according to the immediate context. Repeat offenses are typically measured in a law enforcement context—for example, as the rate of rearrest. While it is seemingly natural and understandable that rearrest could be used as a measure of police activity, it conveys the false assumption that everyone who is rearrested will be convicted and thus overestimates or exaggerates the perceived level of reoffending. Court-based operational definitions more accurately measure repeat offending as reconvictions, which is technically more consistent with legally determined official realities, but in correctional contexts reoffending is often calculated as reincarceration. Measuring reincarceration as an indicator of recidivism can also distort the true level of reoffending by not including those convicted whose sanction did not include jail or prison time.

The strength and direction of correlations, then, serve the objective of determining *causation,* that is, whether the independent variable(s) prompt change in a dependent variable and, if so, in what manner. In order to have confidence in observed causal relationships, there must also be both specificity and accuracy in the measurement process, referred to by researchers as *operationalization.*

ASSESSING THEORY

What makes a theory scientific? And what makes a scientific theory good? As mentioned before, theorizing is a natural part of everyday life. We all need and attempt to make sense of what happens around us; it is just human nature to want to understand. If a one-word definition for theory is "explanation," we can argue that a one-word definition for untested theory is "opinion." Just as multiple opinions often exist as to why certain events occur in social and business contexts, alternative and competing theories often attempt to explain the same types of crime. How do we know which theories are accurate and which ones are mistaken?

Characterizing theory as scientific means that inferential claims about relationships (the observed correlations) can be falsified. Research entails gathering data according to the operationalization process so that the theory is framed for systematic observation of cause and effect. The analysis and conclusions concerning the existence and nature of relationships are then compared to the conceptual logic of the theory itself. When observations are inconsistent with the basic premises of a theory, the theory is falsified. Observations that are consistent with a theory's statements about the relationship between cause-and-effect statements are often deemed more credible, but this does not mean the theory is necessarily true, as alternative theories might explain the same relationships.

Criminologists especially seek the answers to a wide range of research questions that focus on causality: Will increasing the severity of punishment lower the amount of crime in society? Do fines levied against the parents of truant children increase levels of parental responsibility and ultimately result in less truancy? Does a substance abuse treatment program in a correctional setting impact prisoners' rate of recidivism and drug relapse? These and similar questions reflect the desire to specify causal relationships that, in turn, may yield implications for criminal justice practice. Causation, in the context of scientific theorizing, requires four main elements: (1) logical basis, (2) temporal order, (3) correlation, and (4) a lack of spuriousness.

Scientific theory, just like any type of accurate explanation, requires sound reasoning. There must be a logical basis for believing that a causal relationship exists between observable phenomena. Criminologists are not concerned with offenders' hair or eye color when attempting to account for their behavior, for example, because there simply is no logical connection between these physical traits and criminal behavior.

A second necessary element for scientific theory construction is *temporal order*—that is, the time sequence of cause-and-effect elements. In short, causal factors must precede outcomes, as in the relationship between religious involvement and morality crime. Faith-based initiatives are vested in the belief that religious-based programs will better social conditions, including a reduction in crime. If offenders participate in religious programs (the independent variable) and subscribe to the convictions of religious doctrine condemning behavior such as gambling, commercial sex, and recreational substance use and abuse, a reduction in their commission of these vice crimes (the dependent variable) would appear to be a causal relationship because the religious programming both preceded and logically prompted the decreased involvement in the specified behaviors. Another example involves a scenario in which parents' concern about a child's misbehavior involves discipline. Theorists would not hypothesize that discipline caused the misbehavior, because it was applied after the fact.

Correlation, described earlier in this chapter, is a third required element of a scientific theory. Correlation, again, indicates the presence of a relationship between observable phenomena and the nature of the relationship in terms of direction and strength.

The last essential element for scientific theory development involves the condition of *spuriousness*. Some theorists argue that internalization of subculturally defined values (the independent variable) causes or influences involvement in crime (the dependent variable). Many subcultures, however, are also characterized by poverty. Poverty confuses the causal relationship between subculture and crime, as it may be poverty that causes crime, and subcultures simply emerge within impoverished groups. So the relationship between subculture, poverty, and crime is spurious because cause and effect cannot be determined. Theorists, then, must frame relationship statements that reflect an absence of spuriousness.

By incorporating these elements, theorists increase the likelihood or probability that relationship statements are accurate, but this does not mean a theory is certain or necessarily true. Also, it is important to observe that these elements neatly align with the logic of variable analysis, reflecting a positivistic inquiry strategy to theory construction.

THE INFLUENCE OF GENERAL SOCIAL PERSPECTIVES ON THEORIES OF CRIME

Criminological theories identify causes of crime at different levels of social realities and interactions. *Micro-level theory* focuses on individual and small-group behavior, such as face-to-face interaction. A decision to rob one person instead of another based on perception of ability to resist or parental role modeling, regardless of whether it is positive or negative, is an example. *Macro-level theory* looks to the structural properties of society, such as social inequality, culture, and demographic characteristics of the population (such as age, gender, race, educational attainment, and citizenship).

Specific theories of crime are framed within larger conceptual frameworks or theoretical traditions. Because criminology is typically considered a specialization within the discipline of sociology, the three leading perspectives of social life significantly condition the development of crime and deviance theories (see Table 1.1). These three perspectives are functionalism, social conflict, and symbolic interactionism (Collins, 1985).

Functionalism is a theoretical perspective developed by the famous sociologists Emile Durkheim and Talcott Parsons, which contends that social

TABLE 1.1   Criminological Theories Grouped by Social Perspective

FUNCTIONALISM	SOCIAL CONFLICT	SYMBOLIC INTERACTIONISM
Classical criminology	Labeling theory	Differential association
Deterrence theory	Marxist radical theory	Learning theory
Rational choice theory	Feminist criminology	Routine activities theory
Subculture theory	Peacemaking criminology	Social control theory
Social ecological theory	Cultural criminology	Reintegrative shaming theory

order is realized because people reach a general *normative consensus;* that is, they agree on what is acceptable. Though norms can be either formal or informal, functionalist criminology categorically accepts formal norms as stated in the criminal law as a point of departure for theoretical development. Classical, neoclassical, and many positivistic theories of crime reflect the functionalist tradition of seeing crime as nonconformity.

The *social conflict* perspective does not view norms as representative of societal consensus, but rather as expressions of the interests of those in power. Crime is considered less a violation of normative behavioral standards and more a reflection of conflicting values between social groups and classes, ideas put forth by Karl Marx and Friedrich Engels. The conflict perspective is evident in a number of critical and radical criminological theories, including Marxist criminology, feminist criminology, left-realism, and cultural criminology, all of which view crime as a by-product of social alienation stemming from social inequalities.

The third sociological theoretical tradition influencing criminology is *symbolic interactionism,* an approach developed by the twentieth-century American sociologists George Mead and Herbert Blumer that focuses on shared meanings of social life determining communication and a range of human interaction, including crime. This perspective has shaped the development of several prominent theories including learning theory, reintegrative shaming theory, and routine activities theory.

The Role of Theory

Theory is vital to criminology for several reasons. It provides a scientific orientation to the phenomenon of crime, in which observations of facts are specified and classified as causes and effects. It grounds several styles of inquiry in a logic of systematic analysis. More importantly, the relationships between causes and effects can be identified, thus composing a knowledge base to guide decision making and planning concerning how to best address the problems presented by crime. Some theorists examine the relationships between observable phenomena to simply find out for the sake of advancing knowledge, the goal of *basic* or *pure research.* Most criminological theorizing, however, generates practice and policy implications and, as such, is *applied research.* Even the pure theorists, who may have no particular interest in addressing a specific crime or delinquency issue, may generate the knowledge necessary for others to modify the criminal justice system's efforts.

There is, then, a connection between theory and policy. Theoretically based research may, for example, shed light on a better way of doing things, meaning that new programs should be developed and implemented or that existing programs are not working. Different theories may suggest similar or quite alternative practices and policies, often depending on what is proposed as the root cause of criminal behavior. The leading theories of crime described in this text suggest various paths of action. This is to be expected because it is only natural that the identification of a problem's source and its defining attributes will affect the solution. As you become familiar with the different perspectives in the following chapters, notice that each unique theory indicates different directions for how society should address crime.

SUMMARY

Criminological theorizing is vital to both the study of and response to crime. It is illogical to solve the problem of crime without first fully understanding its complex nature. Theory furthers this understanding by identifying factors associated with crime and examining causal relationships. Ideally, criminological theory is based in logic and is temporally ordered in terms of causes preceding effects. Also, good theories must exhibit correlation and a lack of spuriousness. Criminological theory is diverse, having identified multiple sources of crime over time that are reflected in a sequence of philosophical perspectives: spirituality and superstition, free will, determinism, and positivism. Theories reflect both macro- and micro-perspectives on both criminality and crime rate, as illustrated in the subsequent chapters of this book. In a sense, the various theories surveyed in this book affix responsibility for crime to a wide range of sources, and students sometimes view theories as "blaming" groups of people or certain social policies for either contributing to or failing to adequately address the crime that exists in society. Accordingly, it is important to approach the various theories with an attitude of objectivity and openmindedness rather than attempting to identify perspectives that reinforce existing attitudes. Doing so will enable a greater understanding and appreciation for the multifaceted nature of crime and its many causes.

KEY TERMS

Chicago school an important movement influencing the social sciences that was concentrated in the University of Chicago Sociology Department during the 1920s through the 1940s; demonstrated that crime is a product of an area's social ecology, particularly social disorganization in urban areas

classical school of criminology a movement accentuating rational thought as the major influence on human behavior; major theorists include Jeremy Bentham (1748–1832) and Cesare Beccaria (1738–1794), whose works emphasized the concepts of free will and deterrence in the context of crime and punishment

correlation the presence of a relationship between observable phenomena, usually characterized in terms of strength and direction

crime rate the level of crime attributable to a geographic locale such as a city, county, or country

criminality the extent and frequency of criminal offending by a group of people

criminology the study of the various factors and processes of making and breaking laws; a social science address of crime characterized by a theoretical–methodological symmetry

determinism   a philosophy contending that human behavior is caused by biological and psychological factors specific to individuals and/or structural factors composing the environment

positivism   a philosophy contending that scientific inquiry should focus on the study of relationships between observable facts

social contract   the sacrifice of individual freedoms in exchange for protection and social benefit; first introduced by Thomas Hobbes (1588–1679)

theory   a systematic explanation composed of statements indicating an outcome's causal and associated elements

DISCUSSION QUESTIONS

1. Theory is a systematic way of developing explanations—something we do in everyday life to solve problems and to better understand the social world around us. What are a couple of problems or issues that you've dealt with recently that have involved theoretical thinking?

2. How does criminology differ from criminal justice?

3. What are the basic assumptions of the three leading perspectives (classical school, determinism, and positivism), and how do they contribute to the development of criminological theorizing?

4. How are the general social perspectives of functionalism, social conflict, and symbolic interactionism important to the construction of criminological theory?

REFERENCES

Allen, M. (2003, September 23). Bush presses faith-based agenda. *Washington Post*, p. A10.

Bryant, C. G. A. (1985). *Positivism in social theory and research*. London: Macmillan.

Collins, R. (1985). *Three sociological traditions*. New York: Oxford University Press.

Cressey, D. R. (1978). *Principles of criminology* (10th ed.). Philadelphia: Lippincott.

Larson, C. J. (1984). *Crime—justice and society*. Bayside, NY: General Hall.

Lombroso, C. (1863). *Criminal man*. Turin, Italy: Fratelli Bocca.

Merton, R. K. (1938). Social structure and anomie. *American Sociological Review, 3*, 672–682.

Shaw, C., & McKay, H. D. (1942). *Juvenile delinquency and urban areas*. Chicago: University of Chicago Press.

Sutherland, E. H. (1939). *Principles of criminology* (3rd ed.). Philadelphia: Lippincott.

CHAPTER 2

CLASSICAL AND NEOCLASSICAL CRIMINOLOGY

Have you heard anyone lately, say a politician, a friend, or even yourself, complaining that the laws against crime are a joke and that criminals simply do not fear the system? We can all readily think of at least one crime that is often committed but rarely enforced. Are you surprised at how long it takes simply to find someone guilty? Do you believe that the system is such that the rich can easily commit a crime and get away with it? Many Americans believe that there is a "price-tag" of justice in our system today that unfairly benefits the advantaged. If you agree with these notions, then your belief about the criminal justice system and how it ought to work shares many similarities to what criminologists refer to as the *classical school,* one of the oldest and most enduring perspectives of crime.

This chapter surveys some basic assumptions about human nature and related conceptual elements that shape *classical criminology,* both in its original and revised theoretical forms. After acknowledging the seminal classical theorists and their major contributions, *deterrence theory*—the criminological theory descended from the classical school—is explained and discussed. Deterrence theory is critically considered and its limitations are indentified. Theoretical revisions addressing these shortcomings lead to *rational choice theory,* the leading deterrence perspective today in both science and real-world applications. The chapter concludes with examples of research testing deterrence and rational choice theories in various contexts as this theoretical tradition continues to unfold. Thinking about classical criminology in chronological terms, then, the theoretical lineage and development of the perspective is comprised of three connected phases (classical, deterrence, and rational choice), with the second and third phases reflecting increasing influence of social-ecological and situational factors. The incorporation of deterrence and rational choice elements constitutes what is often referred to as neoclassical criminology.

THE CLASSICAL SCHOOL

Classical theory is one of the oldest explanations of crime and certainly the oldest continuing to influence law and social control in modern society. Following only older supernatural explanations that date from the earliest attempts to account for evil acts in a demon-haunted world, classical theory derives from the ideas and writings of early Greek philosophy. That is the reason for the "classical" label—because its roots are in the classical period of Greek rationalism (the so-called golden age of Greece). Thus, while we identify classical theory below as formally originating in the eighteenth century (as the fulfillment of the seventeenth- and eighteenth-century Enlightenment movement), it actually has a much older lineage (e.g., Hobbes, 1651). At the same time, the classical model is also among the "latest and greatest" theories of crime, rediscovered by modern criminologists in the 1970s and elaborated as the logical foundation for contemporary rational choice theory (Morris, 1966; Walters & Grusec, 1977). In these terms, it simultaneously represents very old and very new thinking about crime.

The *classical school of criminology*, obviously, wasn't really an actual school but rather a general philosophy regarding crime and human nature. Though philosophical in nature, classical criminology was very much pragmatic in that its proponents sought to reform the criminal justice systems of their day. Revised or neoclassical perspectives today typically emphasize deterrence and punishment and are identified with conservative public policy, an interesting reversal of perception from the original version, which was characterized as progressive social activism.

Classical theory in criminology formally began in 1764 with the publication in Italy of *Dei Delitti e Delle Pene (On Crimes and Punishments)* by Cesare Bonesana, Marchesa de Beccaria. This small document of slightly more than one hundred pages was a protest piece, arguing against a system characterized by unwritten law, secret trials, hideous punishments, and arbitrary methods of adjudicating guilt based on religion and superstition. Beccaria desired a more enlightened, rational system for controlling crime. Initially published anonymously to avoid possible prosecution and reprisals for its criticism of the existing political and religious order (Beccaria's book was in fact banned by the Catholic church for more than a century), it was the only significant publication its author ever produced. However, the influence of this publication, which you have probably never heard about before, was such that it bears great responsibility for much of how our justice system looks today and how we think crime ought to be addressed.

Beccaria drew on the newly developing ideas of the Enlightenment movement in Europe (shaped by such figures as Rousseau, Voltaire, Locke, and Hobbes) to outline a model of criminal law, punishment, and justice that would be free of the unpredictability, brutality, and inequality of the existing legal systems based on a supernatural or spiritual view of government, law, and human nature. Adopting a utilitarian framework that viewed the establishment of governments and legal systems as "social contracts" among free citizens (rather than divine grants imposed by God), Beccaria's theory identified social harm prevention rather than moral retribution as the legitimate function of criminal law. According to Beccaria (1764/1963, p. 93), "It is better to prevent crimes than to punish them. This is the ultimate end of every good legislation, which, to use the general terms for assessing the good and evils of life, is the art of leading men to the greatest possible happiness or to the least possible unhappiness." For Beccaria, the **deterrence** of crime (through rational, enlightened administration of legal punishments) was the central purpose of criminal justice.

In *On Crimes and Punishments,* Beccaria elaborated the features of a rational, enlightened justice system that would effectively deter crime while correcting the injustices of the existing system, protect the liberty and dignity of individual citizens, and achieve the greatest good for the greatest number. Such a system would embody the ideals of the Enlightenment movement, including such now familiar concepts as presumption of innocence until proven guilty, equality of all people before the law, guarantee of due process, public and impartial trials, adherence to rules of evidence and procedure to ensure fair judgments, right to a jury trial of one's peers, and equal punishment for equal crimes.

According to Beccaria's model of justice, the prevalence of crime in a society reflects irrational and ineffective law, rather than the presence of evil or abnormal human natures. Thus, legal reform implementing a more rational and fair justice system, which would effectively deter people from choosing criminal acts, was the answer to the problem of crime. Clearly, this perspective is rooted in the fundamental assumptions that (1) people are generally good but need negative motivation, (2) behavior is calculated, and (3) crime control is an attainable goal.

Another seminal figure whose writings heavily shaped the classical perspective was Englishman Jeremy Bentham. In opposition to the operations of eighteenth-century legal and penal systems, Bentham also developed reformist propositions that were based in rationality in his famous work *An Introduction to the Principles of Morals and Legislation* (1789). Bentham is credited with developing the principle of utility, which is based on the central assumption that people inevitably pursue pleasure and avoid pain. He identified the elements by which individuals could calculate the value of pleasure or pain according to the level of intensity, duration, certainty, and extent. It is from these basic observations that later and very consequential deterrence-based models of justice and more elaborate criminological theories rooted in free will and the nature of the criminal calculus were shaped.

The contributions of Becarria and Bentham constitute the foundational tents of classical criminology that, in subsequent conjunction with mechanisms factoring the complexities of human behavior, mark the development of both pure and applied criminological theory more so than any other general or specific perspective. Prior to moving on to deterrence and other theories derived from the classical school, it is important to first consider in greater detail basic assumptions about human behavior on which virtually all classical and neoclassical theory is based.

Classical Criminology Assumptions

Theories have to begin with an idea about what people are naturally like. Are we naturally criminal or do we naturally obey the law? Also, does behavior result from rational decision making or is it a function of external forces and conditions largely beyond our immediate control? The answers to these two seemingly simple questions profoundly affect our outlook on crime and how we should respond to it.

Beccaria's assumptions of human nature were based on the Enlightenment image of human nature developed by Hobbes and Locke. The classical model holds simply that people deliberately do things because they expect to benefit from them in some way. In fact, just about everything that people do is oriented around anticipated pleasures and benefits either directly or indirectly (the classroom experience, for example, is sometimes painful, but most plow on toward the future goal of earning a degree and realizing a higher salary). According to the classical perspective, you read this chapter or even show up for class solely because you anticipate doing so will provide some advantage. Maybe you wish to gain an insight about human behavior (we professors are such optimists), so the costs of spending time reading required assignments appear to be a worthwhile sacrifice. Or maybe you fear failing a test. But crime as well as conformity to the law occurs because we get something out of it and we don't sacrifice too much either. The model of human nature assumed by the classical school is that (1) people have **free will** (to choose what to do), (2) people exhibit **hedonism** (they seek pleasure and avoid pain) and egoistic (self-seeking) behavior, and (3) people have **rationality** (to anticipate the consequences of different actions and to calculate the most beneficial outcomes).

The classical perspective dominated enlightened thinking about crime through the beginning of the nineteenth century, with the above concepts shaping law, sentencing, and crime prevention efforts. As mentioned before, no other theory has so consequentially affected law, justice systems, and crime prevention efforts. Today, as we shall soon observe, the classical approach and its basic assumptions regarding human nature are alive and thriving after a dip in popularity in intellectual and academic circles.

Given its long history and lasting prominence, it is a little surprising that the classical perspective had to rebound after being gradually supplanted in the nineteenth century by the alternative philosophy of *positivism* that pointedly rejected several key classical model premises, namely, the assumptions of free will and rational choice. The newer positivist perspective, which based its analysis of behavior on empirical research and experimentation, rather than logical deduction, was critical of the "mere philosophy" of the classical model (Akers, 1994). Critics noted that the classical theory was an idealistic philosophical doctrine that based its conclusions on universalistic assumptions about rationality and free will. It presumed that all people had free will and all behaviors were the result of rational calculation. Interpersonal differences in free will and rationality were minimized or ignored; criminals were not regarded as physically or mentally different from noncriminals—both were rational, hedonistic choice makers.

In contrast, positivism embodied a scientific perspective in which events were explained in causal rather than volitional terms—as the result of cause-and-effect dynamics rather than free-willed choices. The natural causal framework of positivism presumed that there must be a causal reason for every event—including criminal acts. We can really understand and explain an event only when we can identify scientifically what caused it to happen. The assumption of free will was viewed by positivists as incompatible with the scientific principle of causality and the idea of general causal laws. If a behavior were explained as entirely the result of identifiable causes, then there was no room left for free will. Moreover, free will was generally identified with the *soul*, which was an inherently unobservable and unscientific concept.

The growth of positivism was spurred by dramatic scientific advances during the nineteenth century, especially in biology, botany, and the medical sciences, that illustrated that science applied to all natural phenomena—living systems as well as inanimate objects. In these terms, scientific knowledge based on careful empirical research, measurement, and experimentation has more validity than philosophical doctrines based on abstract speculation and argumentation. Thus, to be fully modern and enlightened, the study of crime must adopt a rigorously scientific perspective and abstain from explanations based on philosophical argument and intuitive appeal.

Thus, by the end of the nineteenth century the classical model came to be regarded as a "prescientific," philosophical construction—imaginative and enlightened, but ultimately to be replaced by more scientifically rigorous theories of behavior. Through the middle of the twentieth century, classical theory receded from criminological view, eclipsed by positivist theories for explaining crime. While the classical model continued to provide the philosophical rationale for the American legal system, even here the positivist framework made substantial modifications to fit with scientific analysis. These changes included the widespread adoption of the rehabilitation model of corrections (based on treating the scientifically diagnosed causes of criminal behaviors rather than punishing moral/legal transgressions), the implementation of the juvenile justice system (developed at the start of the twentieth century as a rehabilitative alternative to the criminal justice system), and the expansion of the insanity defense during the twentieth century (Andenaes,

1974; Barnes & Teeters, 1951; Gibbs, 1975). The latter evolved in this period from a limited neoclassical exemption in rare cases where rationality was clearly absent to a wide-ranging defense applicable to all cases where mental illness was present in some form. Such innovations represented a fairly radical movement away from the deterrence-oriented vision of the classical theory.

As with an eclipse, which is not a permanent condition but an event of limited duration in which what is hidden during the eclipse reemerges into view, the classical theory also reemerged with a renewed focus on deterrence. By the 1970s positivist domination of criminology and criminal justice was declining, as scholars and administrators began losing faith in the social engineering model of crime control and the rehabilitative model of corrections, along with the underlying causal models of crime on which they are based. Crime rates were steadily increasing during the 1960s and 1970s, as more and more positivist-based crime control policies were enacted with little apparent effect on the crime trend; recidivism rates of "corrected" prisoners remained depressingly high; and researchers were beginning to conclude that "nothing works." Public concern and fear translated into political pressure on policymakers to generate demonstrable results in terms of lower crime rates, in general, and recidivism reduction by social (i.e., rehabilitation) programs.

This resulted in an ironic reversal of fortunes; the classical perspective was replaced by positivism in the nineteenth century because its punishment-oriented policies were seen as ineffective in controlling crime (Vold, Bernard, & Snipes, 2002). That is, as more states and nations instituted governmental and legal systems based on Beccaria's models, the crime rates in most European countries continued to rise (along with the recidivism rates of punished criminals). While this largely reflected the rapidly changing social conditions in Europe during this period, it led to a questioning of the underlying classical theory as unrealistic or misguided, and it supported a movement to replace the classical ideas with a more scientific theory of criminality. Ironically, the revival of classical theory in the United States during the 1970s represented exactly the reverse pattern. As more states implemented legal and correctional policies based on positivist theories of causality and rehabilitation, crime rates continued to climb alarmingly. Many criminologists viewed this as evidence of the failure of positivist theory and of the need to reconsider other theoretical perspectives, which notably included the classical model of rational choice.

DETERRENCE THEORY

The renewal of classical theory in the 1970s was a combination of a number of different developments. In his well-known requiem article affirming the failure of rehabilitation policy—that is, "nothing works"—Robert Martinson (1974) questioned the viability of positivist explanations for criminality and suggested that the traditional idea of deterrence should be seriously reconsidered. As crime rates continued to rise in the 1960s and 1970s, criminologists had been giving increased attention to the impact of sentencing policies on crime rates. Although most of the initial attention had been on variations in capital punishment—concluding that there was little systematic evidence of a deterrent effect of executions on capital crime rates—additional research was done on the effects of more frequent and ordinary forms of punishment, including imprisonment (Gibbs, 1986; Sherman, 1993). This latter research found that such ordinary criminal punishments often did show deterrence-like correlations with crime rates, consistent with classical theory (Moody & Moody, 1994).

Coincident with the increasing uneasiness about the growing crime rates was a widespread "postmodern" rejection of the assumption of causal determinism as a reasonable premise for explaining human actions. This came with a renewed openness to volitional or voluntaristic models of behavior, which necessarily contained elements of free will or indeterminacy. The growing omnipresence of computers toward the end of the twentieth century brought with it a growing interest in artificial intelligence and cognitive models of information processing, which also prompted a renewed interest in decision making and an emphasis on rationality in human behavior (Becker, 1968). Thus, a variety of different factors all pointed toward a revival of interest in classical theorizing.

A final factor facilitating the reemergence of classical theory is recognition that it is not necessarily incompatible with scientific theory and research (Cook, 1980). The traditional argument portraying positivist and classical perspectives as antithetical were based on idealized and exaggerated premises. That is, original positivist assumptions about causal determinism were as overstated and scientifically untenable as were the original classical assumptions about universal free will and rational thinking. Contemporary theories depict people as having limited free will (in which many external and internal factors limit the options people have) and their behaviors as being shaped by a "soft" causal determinism (in which causal variables influence behavioral outcomes but do not completely determine them).

A slightly modified version of the original perspective emerged during the 1970s and was quickly dubbed *neoclassical*. Changes were subtle but very important. For one thing, it synthesizes the original philosophical argument with a more scientific orientation, expressing the original philosophical concepts as measurable variables and behavioral hypotheses. For another, this neoclassical model—or *postclassical*, as Roshier (1989) calls it—moderates the original universalistic assumptions, allowing for individual differences in motivation, rationality, and free will, and allowing these to be situationally variable as well. Rather than universal free will, the new model assumes a "bounded free will" (acknowledging some environmental and biological constraints on behavioral choice) and a "bounded rationality" (presuming only that most people *usually* behave in a "mostly rational" manner). However, while the new version allows for individual differences in motivation, it regards such variations less significant than external structures of rewards and punishments. The primary focus of neoclassical theory, however, is on deterrence—in fact, most contemporary criminologists refer to early neoclassical work as simply deterrence theory.

HOW DETERRENCE WORKS

To understand how deterrence works, you must at least momentarily accept basic classical ideas about human nature. You are someone who loves pleasure and hates pain, who is egocentric, and who can anticipate the consequences of your actions. Now pretend you are at a party at someone's home, and you have the opportunity to sneak into a bedroom and steal some jewelry. The advantages are obvious—you can use the stolen items yourself (wear them or share with significant others as gifts) or you might pawn them for some quick money. But what would make you stop yourself in spite of potential advantages? This is the fundamental question for deterrence, and Beccaria's ideas offered insights about how to get people to not selfishly gratify their desires at the cost of the happiness of others.

At the root of the problem is that crime feels so *good*. And because criminal acts are frequently beneficial—yielding pleasure or monetary gain at less effort than noncriminal actions—there is a naturally occurring, universal motivation to engage in prohibited acts. Thus, crime has to be controlled by negative means (such as by ratcheting up the costs). It must be legally discouraged by increasing the likelihood that its outcomes will be unpleasant (e.g., painful, disgusting, embarrassing, or aversive), at least more unpleasant than the potential rewards of the criminal act. Once the advantages are offset by the costs, then one should have no desire to commit crime. Everything so far is pretty straightforward.

Beccaria also argued that the deterrent effectiveness of criminal punishments will depend on three characteristics of how punishments are administered: (1) **certainty** (the probability that a misdeed will be detected and punished), (2) **celerity** (the swiftness with which punishment follows the criminal deed), and (3) **severity** (the painfulness or unpleasantness of the punishing outcome). To achieve maximum deterrence, a punishment needs to be unpleasant (at least more unpleasant than the benefits the act would yield), certain, and swift.

Beccaria argued that of the three characteristics, maximizing certainty and swiftness is more important for deterrence than severity. The latter, if disproportionate, may result in irrational brutality and have counterproductive effects on crime, inciting revolution, defiance, revenge, and even martyrdom. This is perhaps one aspect of deterrence that most students have a hard time grasping. If the punishment for selling drugs is death, then woe to the police officer who tries to arrest the drug dealer! Woe especially if the justice system is imperfect and has a habit of arresting and condemning the innocent. Put differently, you might reason that it is better to kill others to protect yourself from the excessively severe legal consequences of your actions. Ideally, a punishment should be just severe enough to offset the pleasure attained from crime. In effect, in the cost-benefit analysis performed by a potential offender, the cost must now weigh heavier than the benefit.

Another, less extreme, problem with severity has to do with relativity. Deterrence functions through the criminal law, which must necessarily make assumptions about which crimes are to be punished more severely and what degree of harshness in sanctioning will move people to realize that committing a crime being contemplated is simply not worth it. The problem here is that criminal statutes, such as the United States sentencing guidelines, affix penalties to the severity and associated characteristics of criminal offenses, not the characteristics of individual offenders. This seems fair, democratic, and seemingly minimizes factors that a judge or jury might otherwise use as bias against individual offenders (e.g., race, religion, social class, or sexual orientation), because all offenders, in theory, are punished based on the crime. This is also why offenders receive harsher sanctions for repeat offenses, because it is assumed that, under this "let the punishment fit the crime" model, a previous punishment did not deter and must be increased to discourage further offending. In a general sense, this philosophy views all offenders as equal—it is their criminal behavior that varies and the severity of punishment must also vary accordingly.

Deterrence Theory Limitations

The cost-benefit conceptualization of deterrence theory is often referred to as *the economic model* or *objective deterrence* because the trade-off elements comprising gains and losses are calculated through accounting for the most apparent variables. As noted above, costs and benefit calculations are actually based on a number of factors, not all of which are always known to potential offenders. Additionally, different offenders do not engage rational decision making in a monolithic or uniform way, rather as variable as human behavior itself. Moreover, deterrence theory assumptions are exposed as faulty in practice. A model of justice such as sentencing guidelines, for example, assumes that for each crime there is an average punishment that will deter most potential offenders. To set a sanction at a level that is appropriate to effect deterrence but not so severe that it is blatantly unfair assumes that most offenders generally weigh the costs and benefits of crime similarly.

Our society, however, is quite diverse, stratified, and pluralistic. Is an offense punishable by a fine—littering or speeding, for example—really an equal punishment for all? Certainly the wealthy are impacted less than the poor by loss of an equal amount of money. Yet, the law penalizes both the same. The threat of incarceration is another good example that also likely varies according to class status and socialization environment. Middle- and upper-class people may opt out of a potentially rewarding property crime due to the threat of violence in prison. If they have never been incarcerated, this threat may be heightened by media portrayals of prison gangs and sexual predators, an understandable fear of the unknown. Others who have been in and out of the system and previously incarcerated have firsthand knowledge of the correctional system, an understanding of its subculture, and may be less afraid. Therefore, it is the perception of the costs of punishment as well as the actual costs themselves that matter. Unfortunately, the costs are not the same for everyone, but, according to the deterrence model, the penalties are fairly uniform.

The variability of the true severity of punishment across the offender pool also has an intangible element. A third grader from a mainstream American suburb caught shoplifting may suddenly be socially ostracized ("Don't invite Johnny to the birthday party—he is a bad influence!") and the penalty may also extend to negatively impact the delinquent's family. Such a youth may choose not to shoplift because doing so may render a threefold negative effect: (1) the direct punishment for the offense, (2) indirect punishment from both family and peers in terms of shame and embarrassment, and (3) indirect penalties attached to the family such as damaged reputation.

Of course, this assumes that the family and peer group disapprove of shoplifting and that negative informal sanction will occur. What if they do not? In a different neighborhood in the same town, another juvenile's shoplifting arrest may be viewed as little more than bad luck by both the family and community. If so, there are less costs associated with choosing to offend—again demonstrating the variability across offenders in calculations of the costs and benefits of crime.

In response to these numerous problems and shortcomings of the economic deterrence model, then, scholars recrafted the deterrence perspective to better emphasize the boundedness of decision making and the role and variability of perception resulting in what criminologists recognize as *bounded choice* or *perceptual deterrence theory*. There have been many recent updates in the classical-deterrence perspective, but the account of deterrence provided by Beccaria (1764/1963) remains a primary theoretical cornerstone affecting justice policy. Beccaria provided a surprisingly modern analysis that clearly identified the subjective or psychological nature of deterrence and the critical role of perceptions as determinants of behavior. The rise of **rational choice theory** further accentuates the environmental, social, and individual variables shaping perception and decision making across social-ecological contexts. The emergence of the lifecourse perspective, emphasizing the points of criminal birth—entry to criminality/onset of criminal activity, criminal life—period of offending, and death or desistance from crime, couples nicely with rational choice approaches and enables criminologists to better focus on how offenders assess costs and benefits at various life stages.

People's decisions to engage in criminal behavior will be shaped by their *perceptions* of what the punishment would be, how likely they *think* they are to get caught, and how personally unpleasant they *expect* the punishment to be. The objective properties of the punishment are far less relevant to these decisions than what people think these properties are. Deterrence occurs when perceptions of likely punishments for criminal acts cause would-be offenders to refrain from committing those acts (even though they are otherwise motivated and willing to do so). The specific mechanism that inhibits would-be offenders from criminal actions is their *fear* of punitive consequences. Thus, the process of deterrence is inherently psychological, based on an aversive emotional response to what people think will occur.

Recent modern analyses of deterrence have mostly affirmed the ideas developed by Beccaria but also have noted that things are a bit more complex than he could know. For one thing, deterrence effects are divided into two distinct types, reflecting two distinct ways in which punishments may influence people's behaviors. Beccaria implicitly recognized these but did not recognize or discuss the importance of the distinction. In *specific deterrence,* the offender is inhibited from repeating criminal behavior by the unpleasant experience of being punished for the original misdeed. It involves the direct experience of punishment by the offender (who experiences the punishment).

In *general deterrence,* punishing offenders has a discouraging effect on other would-be offenders (i.e., members of the general public, other than the person getting punished, who witness or hear about the punishment). This kind of deterrence involves the indirect or vicarious experience of punishment through seeing others receive unpleasant outcomes for their actions, which provides an example of what might happen to other would-be offenders if they were to commit the same acts. These two deterrence processes seem very similar (and Beccaria lumped them together), but they refer to different psychological events and may occur quite independently of each other. Moreover, they represent separate problems in crime prevention as revealed in different patterns of criminal behaviors. Specific deterrence involves reducing recidivism (repeated offenses committed by convicted, punished offenders), while general deterrence involves reducing general crime rates (offenses committed among the general public that have not been punished).

Let's consider a couple of examples that help distinguish between specific and general deterrence. Posted speed limit signs serve as a form of general deterrence and are frequently reinforced in a public fashion, as we've all seen motorists stopped for speeding and receiving citations. The speed limit has far more impact on us, however, when applied as specific deterrence—that is, when we are the ones to be pulled over. Perhaps the most frequent and controversial debate over the effectiveness of deterrence concerns the use of capital punishment. Most criminologists observe that there is very little empirical evidence to support the argument that the death penalty effectively deters additional homicide. This is a complicated issue, but a primary reason that homicide is not responsive to harsher penalty is because it is a highly emotive crime (most of the time people are very angry and out of control and the degree of violence happens as a result). According to deterrence theory, offenders consider the benefits and costs, but these are not weighed or weighed sufficiently in the context of extreme emotional states wherein people act based on impulse and adrenaline. Arguably, their anger would have led to the same outcome regardless of the level of punishment, because the punishment is simply not considered in a rational manner. Homicide statistics and empirical examinations of the use of capital punishment tend to reinforce this argument that there is little general deterrent effect of capital punishment. On a more basic level, however, it is hard to argue that capital punishment does not have a specific level deterrent effect, as the executed are no longer capable of reoffending.

Research on Deterrence Theories

As a scientific theory, the validity of the deterrence notion depends on the ability to conduct empirical research that provides empirical tests of the key premises (hypotheses). While considerable efforts have been made in the past three decades, research to persuasively test deterrence theory has been surprisingly difficult to accomplish. A large number of studies, encompassing a broad assortment of different types of research, have been carried out on this topic, but they have yielded an ambiguous and inconclusive pattern of findings (Nagin, 1998; Sherman, 1990).

Part of the difficulty in many of these studies may be simply their failure to fully express deterrence as a scientific theory with clearly defined (measurable) concepts and fully specified (testable) hypotheses. But the most fundamental difficulty is that deterrence is not directly observable; it can be inferred only from observable events. Quite literally, deterrence refers to *nonevents* (i.e., a person does *not* commit a crime). Moreover, these occasions when "nothing happens" occur because of a psychological process not observable to an outside observer (i.e., an expectation of punishment accompanied by a feeling of fear or aversion). Failure to act is meaningful information about deterrence only if we clearly expect that the action *should* have occurred but did not, as in Sherlock Holmes's famous reference to "the dog that didn't bark."

We can infer deterrence only when we know that the person would have acted criminally but refrained because he or she considered the likely consequences of the act and feared the legal punishments that might result. People may refrain from committing a crime for lots of reasons other than fear of legal sanctions. They may simply have no desire to assault another person, sexually abuse their children, steal someone else's property, set fire to a building, drive 80 miles per hour on a busy highway, or inject heroin into their veins. They may find such actions uninteresting, uncomfortable, too much work, personally unattractive, morally offensive, physically risky to personal health and safety, likely to produce strong negative reactions from their friends and family, or sure to cause their eternal damnation. If so, then deterrence is irrelevant, no matter how severe the legal punishment, since they would not have committed the crime anyway.

The obvious difficulties of trying to study something that did not happen for reasons we cannot see means that almost all research on deterrence has involved studying only the *failures of deterrence*—that is, occurrence of criminal acts, which we *can* observe (at least in theory). But even here, we do not directly observe even deterrence failure, but must still infer it. We can observe when people commit crimes, but whether this indicates a failure of deterrence depends on what they knew and thought about before committing their crimes. To infer a failure of deterrence, we must know (or assume) that they were aware of and considered the punitive consequences of their acts before deciding to act anyway; otherwise, it is not a failure of deterrence but rather a thoughtless behavior oblivious to its possible outcomes.

In the face of these difficulties, how can researchers prove the scientific validity of the deterrence theory? A large body of deterrence studies have accumulated that employ a variety of research procedures, yielding a diverse array of findings. Findings range from strongly supporting deterrence theory to strong refutations, with the vast majority being in the ambiguous or inconclusive middle of these polar positions. These studies include four broad types of research, each with its strengths and weaknesses for informing us about deterrence effects: (1) anecdotal studies, (2) crime rate analysis, (3) natural/field experiments, and (4) self-report surveys.

First are anecdotal studies that rely on qualitative interviews, observations, and impressions of serious criminal offenders for evidence that their actions did or did not embody deterrence processes. Katz's (1988) qualitative analysis of the "nonrational seductions" of crime provided insightful evidence that rational calculations may not cover the thought processes of real criminals very adequately. Tunnell's (1990) excellent in-depth interview study of incarcerated repeat property offenders amply documented that most of the offenders studied did not really think about the likely legal consequences of their actions. They had unrealistic perceptions about the likelihood of being caught and irrational expectations about what would happen to them if they did get caught. However, while such anecdotal studies are insightful and revealing about the perceptions and feelings of criminals, they are also selective and difficult to replicate or generalize from. For this reason, even though they may tell us a lot about the phenomenology of crime and punishment, they cannot provide a very definitive test of deterrence theory.

The second type of research involves ecological studies of aggregate crime and justice statistics, such as correlation of imprisonment rates and index crime rates across states or counties in the United States. *Index crimes* refers to the eight major commonly occurring crimes reported annually in the uniform crime reports, which are compiled by the Federal Bureau of Investigation. These crimes include: homicide, aggravated assault, arson, theft, robbery, motor vehicle theft, forcible rape, and burglary. These range from the original simple bivariate correlation studies in the late 1960s to the latest elaborate multivariate, multiple-equation econometric analyses. In this approach, the deterrence prediction is that punishment and crime rates will be negatively correlated, even after controlling for other social factors that may be confounded with crime and punishment patterns. Many of these studies show results consistent with a deterrence prediction, but these correlations vary considerably in size and direction, making interpretation ambiguous. The difficulty with this approach is its indirect assessment of deterrence events. It deals only with aggregated events and does not measure individual perceptions or correlate perceptions with individual behaviors. Thus, the findings of the ecological studies are, at best, suggestive but inconclusive.

The third category of deterrence research has involved what are called natural experiments or field experiments—that is, tracking patterns of crime levels before and after a dramatic change in punishment or enforcement policy (Nagin, 1978, 1998). The change or intervention that constitutes the experimental treatment may be a political event—such as a reinstitution of the death penalty, a statutory revision of the criminal law to provide mandatory prison terms for certain crimes, a judicial moratorium on death sentences, or a police strike. The change might also be a deliberately targeted intervention—such as a scheduled police crackdown on DUI drivers or implementation of a mandatory arrest policy for domestic violence cases in some precincts—that creates a kind of natural experiment. In all such cases, the deterrence prediction is that crime levels will be higher after an interruption that lowers the risk of punishment (such as during a police strike or a judicial moratorium on death sentences). Correspondingly, crimes will be lower after an intervention that increases the risk of punishment (such as reinstituting the death penalty or instituting random roadblocks to catch drunk drivers). This kind of research design seems more rigorous than the ecological studies, which are merely correlational. However, it still provides only indirect assessment of actual deterrence events, since individual perceptions and behaviors are not measured in these studies. Although they seem more scientific, the findings from these kinds of studies have shown only mixed evidence for deterrence. Some of the studies show a definite deterrence-like effect. Some studies show an opposite pattern from the predicted deterrence effect—one in which more punishment seems to lead to more crimes (sometimes termed a *brutalization* or a *facilitation effect*).

The fourth type of research relies on sample surveys of the general public using self-reported measures of people's punishment perceptions (such as perceived likelihood of getting caught or expected harshness of punishments) and their criminal behaviors (Williams & Hawkins, 1986; Zimring & Hawkins, 1973). Here again, deterrence predicts a negative correlation between people's perceptions of the certainty and severity of punishment and their reports of actually doing the illegal behavior. Alternative versions of the surveys have asked people not about their actual perceptions and behaviors, but about their predicted reactions in hypothetical scenarios. This type of deterrence research has the obvious advantage of dealing much more directly with perceptions and with directly correlating individual perceptions and behaviors. However, two weaknesses limited the ability of this kind of research to yield conclusive tests. One is the cross-sectional nature of surveys, which make the time ordering of variables somewhat ambiguous. The other limitation is the hypothetical nature of the questionnaires, which deal with abstract predictions about what people would do in hypothetical situations rather than their actual responses and behaviors. Thus, even though they deal more directly with the psychological aspects of deterrence, perceptual surveys provide suggestions, rather than definite conclusions, about deterrence effects (Ross, 1982).

After considering all the research carried out on deterrence, most scholars agree that it is impossible to assign a simple "true" or "false" to the deterrence doctrine (Paternoster & Piquero, 1995). It is clear that the general question, "Does punishment of criminals deter crime?" is too simple to be answered meaningfully. It is clear from the considerable research carried out over the past three decades that punishment of criminals can and does have deterrent effects. However, the effects are generally weaker, and far more variable and inconsistent, than classical theory predicts. Thus, while there is considerable support for classical theory, the explanation it provides for crime is by no means complete and final. Classical theory remains a viable and useful theory for explaining many crime patterns, as well as for developing crime control policies, but it does not replace or eliminate any of its theoretical competitors—at least on scientific grounds.

Overall, it is clear that the dominant appeal of the theory is not entirely an outcome of scientific progress. The appeal of classical rational choice theory is substantially ideological rather than utilitarian. That is, it agrees with other values and beliefs people have about human nature, law, and morality; it fits with other things they believe about human nature and moral philosophy. Classical theory "works well enough" in terms of empirical research and policy evaluations, but it does not work demonstrably better than its more positivist theoretical competitors. And it does not work as well—as invariably and universally—as the theory claims it will. We know from research and criminal justice policy analysis that legal punishments provide an effective deterrent for crime in many circumstances. However, we also know that the effects of criminal punishments are limited and variable across situations and individuals. They are not universally and invariably effective; they do not always work as our philosophy prescribes.

SUMMARY

The classical school of criminology is the first general perspective on crime that attempted to understand its complex nature in a systematic and scientific nature. The perspective has had lasting impact as a leading explanation of crime for well over a century and has been vital in influencing the very nature of criminal justice systems around the world and, especially, in the Western Hemisphere. The daily efforts of law enforcement, the sanctions delivered through our court system, and certainly the deterrence and rehabilitation programs of our correctional institution all directly reflect ongoing efforts to lower the crime rate generally, and recidivism rates especially, by manipulating the criminal calculus. Deterrence theories and similar neoclassical perspectives incorporate deterministic and environmental factors that mitigate the decision-making process, but crime is ultimately seen as an outcome of free will and ineffective deterrence.

KEY TERMS

celerity the swiftness with which punishment follows a crime

certainty the probability that a crime will be detected and punished

deterrence prevention of a certain act or acts (such as crime)

free will humans' ability to control their own actions and destiny

hedonism humans' tendency to maximize pleasure and minimize pain

neoclassical theory a revised version of classical theory that acknowledges individual and situational differences in motivation, rationality, and free will (i.e., bounded free will)

rationality humans' ability to anticipate the consequences of different actions and to calculate the most beneficial outcomes

severity the painfulness or unpleasantness of a sanction

DISCUSSION QUESTIONS

1. How did the Enlightenment period influence classical theories?

2. Identify some of the classical theory's key assumptions about human nature. Do you think that humans generally behave according to these assumptions?

3. Why did classical theory come under fire from the positivistic school of criminological thought?

4. What are some modifications of the neoclassical movement that influenced the resurgence of deterrence theory?

5. Discuss some of the ways criminologists test deterrence theory today. Can you envision a study that would also test modern deterrence theory?

REFERENCES

Akers, R. L. (1994). *Criminological theories: Introduction and evaluation.* Los Angeles: Roxbury.

Andenaes, J. (1974). *Punishment and deterrence.* Ann Arbor: University of Michigan Press.

Barnes, H. E., & Teeters, N. K. (1951). *New horizons in criminology* (2nd ed.). Upper Saddle River, NJ: Prentice Hall.

Beccaria, C. (1963). *On crimes and punishments* (H. Paolucci, Trans.). Indianapolis: Bobbs-Merrill. (Original work published 1764)

Becker, G. S. (1968). Crime and punishment: An economic approach. *Journal of Political Economy, 76,* 169–217.

Cook, P. (1980). Research in criminal deterrence: Laying the groundwork for the second decade. In N. Morris & M. Tonry (Eds.), *Crime and justice: An annual review of research* (Vol. 2, pp. 211–268). Chicago: University of Chicago Press.

Gibbs, J. P. (1975). *Crime, punishment, and deterrence.* New York: Elsevier.

Gibbs, J. P. (1986). Deterrence theory and research. In G. B. Melton (Ed.), *The law as a behavioral instrument* (pp. 87–130). Lincoln: University of Nebraska Press.

Hobbes, T. (1962). *Leviathan.* New York: Macmillan. (Original work published 1651)

Katz, J. (1988). *Seductions of crime: Moral and sensual attractions in doing evil.* New York: Basic Books.

Martison, R. (1974). What works? Questions and answers about prison reform. *Public Interest, 35,* 22–54.

Marvell, T., & Moody, C. (1994). Prison population growth and crime reduction. *Journal of Quantitative Criminology, 10,* 109–140.

Morris, N. (1966). Impediments to penal reform. *University of Chicago Law Review, 33,* 627–656.

Nagin, D. (1978). General deterrence: A review of the empirical evidence. In A. Blumstein, J. Cohen, & D. Nagin (Eds.), *Deterrence and incapacitation: Estimating the effects of criminal sanctions on crime rates* (pp. 95–139). Washington, DC: National Academy Press.

Nagin, D. (1998). Criminal deterrence research at the outset of the twenty-first century. In M. Tonry (Ed.), *Crime and justice: A review of research* (Vol. 23, pp. 1–42). Chicago: University of Chicago Press.

Paternoster, R., & Piquero, A. (1995). Reconceptualizing deterrence: An empirical test of personal and vicarious experiences. *Journal of Research in Crime and Delinquency, 32,* 251–286.

Roshier, B. (1989). *Controlling Crime: The Classical Perspective in Criminology.* New York: Open University Press.

Ross, H. L. (1982). *Deterring the drinking driver: Legal policy and social control.* Lexington, MA: Heath.

Sherman, L. W. (1990). Police crackdowns: Initial and residual deterrence. In M. Tonry, & N. Morris (Eds.), *Crime and justice: A review of research* (Vol. 12, pp. 1–48). Chicago: University of Chicago Press.

Sherman, L. W. (1993). Defiance, deterrence, and irrelevance: A theory of the criminal sanction. *Journal of Research in Crime and Delinquency, 30,* 445–473.

Tunnell, K. D. (1990). Choosing crime: Close your eyes and take your chances. *Justice Quarterly, 7,* 673–690.

Vold, G. B., Bernard, T. J., & Snipes, J. B. (2002). *Theoretical criminology* (5th ed.). Oxford: Oxford University Press.

Walters, G. C., & Grusec, J. E. (1977). *Punishment.* San Francisco: Freeman.

Williams, K. R., & Hawkins, R. (1986). Perceptual research on general deterrence: A critical overview. *Law and Society Review, 20,* 545–572.

Zimring, F. E., & Hawkins, G. J. (1973). *Deterrence: The legal threat in crime control.* Chicago: University of Chicago Press.

CHAPTER 3

BIOLOGICAL THEORIES OF CRIME

Explaining how and why some persons become criminal can be an especially challenging endeavor sometimes. Although most people have their own ideas about what causes criminality, the answers are sometimes difficult to see, and unexpected. Consider the case of Andrew, a nine-year-old, who lives in a Midwestern, middle-class suburb with both of his parents, goes to a good school, has a number of friends, and is active in sports and school activities. For most of his life, Andrew has been a good child, listening to his parents, rarely getting into any trouble, and being popular with his friends, teachers, and everyone in his neighborhood. The only thing that seemed to make Andrew stand out among his friends and peers was that he was physically smaller than most other boys his age, and he was always very skinny. As Andrew approached his ninth birthday, his behavior started to change. He became withdrawn, began to resist going to school, talked back to his parents, saw his grades drop in school, and soon began to be in fights with a number of other kids in his school. At first Andrew's parents were not too concerned, thinking that this was just normal behavior, and most probably just a phase he was going through. They thought maybe he was just entering puberty a bit early, and his change in behavior was normal adolescent rebellion and change. But, his behavior continued to deteriorate; he became more and more withdrawn from his old activities, and his fights with other children became more frequent. As Andrew's ninth birthday approached, his mother took him to the doctor for his annual checkup, and mentioned to the doctor that the bruises on his arms and chest were from a recent fight he had at school. Andrew's mother told the doctor that they did not know what was causing this change in behavior and were starting to get worried. The doctor did not have any suggestions for Andrew's mother, and told her not to worry too much, unless Andrew's behavior continued to get worse.

As part of Andrew's physical, the doctor drew some blood and did some normal tests to make sure that Andrew was healthy. When the test results came back, the doctor noticed that Andrew had very low levels of several important vitamins, most notably vitamin B_{12}. This stood out to him as somewhat rare for nine-year-olds, and he called Andrew's mother and asked her to come back in for a follow-up appointment. When the doctor met with Andrew's mother, he asked questions about both Andrew's behavior and his diet. Andrew's mother reported that his behavior had not changed since the last appointment, and that Andrew seemed to eat well. However, she also mentioned that the family ate a strict vegan diet, in an effort to be healthy. The family ate only fruits and vegetables, and avoided all meat, fish, dairy products, and eggs. The doctor pointed out to Andrew's mother that this could be the source of Andrew's socially withdrawing, apparent depression, and increasing violence. The very low level of vitamin B_{12} in Andrew's body was a result of his diet—B_{12} is typically found in meat, dairy, and eggs. And, B_{12} deficiency has been shown to be related to the development of depression, withdrawal, and aggressive/violent tendencies. The doctor suggested that Andrew (and in fact his whole family) either start to take vitamin supplements or add foods to their diet that would provide high levels of vitamin B_{12}. The family soon added three meals a week of eggs to their diet, and within a couple of months Andrew returned to his old self, being social, friendly, and no longer getting into fights at school. The cause of Andrew's behavior change had been identified and solved with a simple solution of a change in his diet.

Do most people ever think that simple things like what we eat can have such a profound impact on what we do and how we act? Probably not. However, as this simple story shows, sometimes the answer to the question of what causes our behavior can be very simple, if we just know where to look. Biological issues, including those stemming from our diet, are important for both our overall health and our mental and emotional states, which are often directly tied to our behavior. Biological issues are important for many aspect of our lives, and as criminologist have argued for nearly 250 years, parts of our biological and physical makeup as persons may be the causes of criminal behavior. These ideas, having their foundation in some of the original criminological theories, are today being recognized once again as important and potentially very influential theories about crime and criminal behavior.

Biological theories of crime focus on identifying and understanding unique qualities or characteristics of individuals and showing how the presence (or absence) of some chemical, hormonal, or physical structure in our bodies is related to participation in illegal activities. The connections between criminal activities and biological aspects of individuals have gained a great deal of attention in recent years, as seen by the growth in popularity of forensic evidence in crime fighting in popular culture. For several years, the television shows *CSI*, *CSI-Miami*, and *CSI-New York* have dominated television ratings and fascinated viewers. Recognition that biological evidence can be a determining factor in solving criminal cases and leading to convictions for criminals has spawned a generation of students who find biology interesting and directly relevant to their career goals. By examining crime scenes for the smallest traces of biological or physical evidence of who was present and how violent crimes occurred, we have come to see that social and psychological approaches to crime and criminality are not the only ways of both solving and understanding crime. However, forensics is only one aspect of the biology–crime relationship. From a theoretical perspective, we need to look at a number of issues, including the physical size and appearance of our bodies to our hormonal and genetic makeup, as well as how the substances (including food) that we put into our bodies may influence our thinking and behavior. As we will see throughout this chapter, there actually are a number of explanations for crime, and in fact for most of our behaviors, that focus on some aspect of our physical bodies.

When we seek to explain crime and criminals with a biological perspective, one of the intriguing differences from most other explanations is that we are largely removing "blame" from the discussion. Such an approach, focusing on physical traits of individuals essentially, says that criminals really are not responsible for their actions, but instead they are "victims" of their own bodies. When we can point to something specific and tangible about a person and see this as the cause of behavior, we remove all (or at least much of) the blame and grayer areas of social influences. Although it might not seem to fit with what most of us have been taught throughout our lives, this approach usually does make logical sense. It is fairly easy to think of different parts of people's brains, bodies, or chemical makeup that we could point to as explanations for why people are the way they are. Biological theories also allow us to look at crime and criminals in less judgmental ways; after all, if someone commits crime because he is "programmed" or "born" that way, it really is not right to blame him for his behavior.

However, if someone engages in crime, especially violent crime, because of some characteristic that she was born with, it also makes sense to look for ways to correct or change that characteristic which may cause her criminal behavior. When explaining crime with biological theories, the obvious policy implication is that we need to identify what exactly is wrong with her body or brain, and then come up with a way to "fix" or "cure" that problem. In the case of Andrew, this was fairly easy to do. But, this is not always easy, if at all possible. Approaching the issue of crime this way is called a medical model view of crime and behavior. In this view, criminality is not something that people choose to do, nor something over which they have any (or much) control. Instead, being a criminal is similar to having a disease or a birth defect. And the way we can, and should, respond to crime is similar to how we can and should react to people with a disease or birth defect. The appropriate response is to use medical science so as to intervene or "fix" what is wrong with the body. However, just as with some diseases and birth defects, it may not be possible to cure or fix what is wrong. In these cases, then, it may be necessary to segregate, quarantine, or in extreme cases, permanently remove the sick person from society (so he or she does not infect or harm other people).

The medical model view of crime, based on biological theories for explaining why crime occurs, suggests that the responsibility for changing behavior falls on society, most especially experts such as doctors, who have the responsibility to try to help correct the biological/physical problems that cause the behavior. Or, in cases when the biological problem cannot be fixed, it is the responsibility of society (again through experts, but not necessarily doctors) to remove criminals from society so as to protect others. Just as our nation's public health system has the responsibility for controlling the spread of disease, a medical model view of crime charges the criminal justice system with controlling the spread of the "disease" of crime. Biological theories of crime are among the oldest explanations for why people break the law. Although this perspective has roots in ancient history, it has only been in the last three decades that a number of theories and research evidence have emerged that suggest a link between biology and criminal behavior (see Fishbein, 1990). Explanations for crime that point to the size and shape of criminals' bodies and family trees (heredity and genetics), scientific "facts" that show differences in genetics and chemical composi-tions of individuals, physiological consequences of what we eat and drink, and even the ways that humans have evolved have all been suggested as reasons for our behaviors, including crime. Some of these theories date back several centuries, and some have emerged in the last couple of years.

Biological theories for explaining (criminal) behavior appeal to many people because they seem to make sense when we look at the explanations. We can all think of times when we have made assumptions about other peo-ple and their actions based on something about their size, looks, or even eat-ing habits. Our popular culture is also full of images and messages that reinforce these ideas. Think about how crime and criminals are often pre-sented on television or in the movies. Frequently, the "bad guy" looks differ-ent from the "good guys," and has something distinct about him. While this is certainly not a universal aspect of crime television/movies, the influence of such messages on our thinking can be seen very easily by doing a simple experiment. Ask a group of 10 or 15 people you know to "describe a crimi-nal." Many, if not a majority of people, will give you answers that include physical descriptions, typically including suggestions that criminals are large, muscular, and mean-looking. Or, just think of what type of person most of us would be more likely to fear in a dark and deserted alley—a five-foot-tall, hundred-pound individual wearing thick glasses, or a six-foot-tall muscular individual covered in tattoos? How many of us as children were warned by our parents to stay away from other children because their par-ents "look weird"? The point is, many of us already act on information that is rooted in biological theory assumptions; therefore, it is easy to see how these types of theories could have wide appeal.

These views are not just the product of modern media or teachings for our children. Biological theories of crime and criminal behavior have been with us for a long time, but they have also seen a number of very significant and important changes over the years. In their earliest forms biological theories emphasized the idea that some people had a visible biological/physical trait or condition that led them into crime, regardless of their social environment or other factors. More recent biological theories have expanded to recognize the importance of social environments, and today these types of theories suggest that criminals (all or maybe just some) have some variety of biological/physical characteristic that can be "turned on" or that makes the individual more likely to commit crime. As one set of observers and commentators on biological theories suggest, the more recent biological theories are "most useful when looking at how such environmental influences as isolation, neglect, abuse, and other conditioning variables are imprinted into individuals to cause predictable, incorrigible behavioral disorders years later" (Knoblich & King, 1992, p. 2).

THE POSITIVIST SCHOOL OF THOUGHT

The foundation for biological theories of crime is a positivist way of thinking. **Positivism** is the idea that it is possible to identify specific causes of behavior using scientific approaches. The positivist school of thought has its roots in the scientific revolution of the sixteenth century. This means that when we say we can use scientific means to identify specific causes of criminal behavior, we need to think of science in a very broad way. Obviously, what we think of as science today (use of DNA, sophisticated medical procedures, and so on) is not what was meant by this idea 500 years ago. Scientific investigation conducted by the early positivist thinkers and biological theorists compared the characteristics of known criminals with others in the population. If it could be shown that all (or at least most) criminals had a particular characteristic—such as large ears or pointy chins—and noncriminals did not have this characteristic in large numbers, it was assumed to indicate one's criminal ways. Science in these early theories was based on observation and simple comparisons; sophisticated tools, analytic methods, and advanced statistics are all modern developments.

Positivist thinking in criminology is based on three core assumptions about individuals and how their bodies relate to their behavior. First, it is assumed that all individuals are biologically unique and different from all other people. Second, these differences in our individual makeup are believed to account for our differences in behavior. Third, criminal behavior is assumed to be a result of specific differences in physical constructions and characteristics of individuals that can be identified through observation or other scientific means.

One of the most important changes in thinking about behavior to arise from the positivist school was the rejection of the idea of free will. No longer was it assumed that people chose their behavior. Rather, behavior was a part of the individual over which he or she had little (if any) control. Our behavior, including whether we committed crimes, was simply another result of our physical development, much like the color of our hair, how tall we are, or whether we are male or female. Just like our physical traits, early positivist thinkers believed our behavior was determined for us. Individuals were really not free to determine their behavior, but rather were simply carrying out predetermined roles and actions.

Early positivist biological theories focused on identifying distinct characteristics of criminals' faces, sizes, shapes and bumps on their heads, and overall physical size and shape. Over time these ideas developed and were refined, remaining a part of public debate and influencing public policies and laws well into the twentieth century.

PHYSIOGNOMY AND PHRENOLOGY

The earliest biological theories of crime focused on the study of facial features and the size, shape, and contours of people's heads. The focus of these scientific investigations was to locate features that could be found among criminals but not among noncriminals, and then use these features to identify who is (or would be) a criminal.

Physiognomy, made popular by Johan Caspar Lavater during the 1770s, was an early form of science that sought to identify distinct facial features of people who committed crimes. The ideas of physiognomy were well received by society and caused people to watch out for people with a wide range of facial features believed to be associated with criminal behavior. Included among the indicators of dangerousness were men without beards (and, interestingly, women *with* beards), weak chins, and "shifty" eyes. Although today these types of traits clearly are not seen as indications that someone is dangerous or a criminal, it is most important that such "scientific" conclusions were considered important and prompted further development of the search for criminal characteristics in the faces and bodies of individuals. And, physiognomy encouraged people to protect themselves by watching out for others who showed signs of being dangerous. In this way, although criminals might not be able to be blamed for their behavior, victims could be held responsible for associating with criminals who had obvious and easily detected signs of being criminal.

A second, and similar, form of science closely followed on the heels of physiognomy and focused on the shape and contours of the head (assumed to be indications of the shape and development of the brain) and the relation of such to behavior. **Phrenology,** as this science was called, was popular in the

1790s and early 1800s. The basic idea of phrenology was that different parts of the brain controlled different types of social activities and thinking, and when particular areas of the brain were more developed, they would be larger and therefore create bumps or protrusions on the skull. Based on beliefs about what behaviors or characteristics were located in different areas of the brain, it therefore was believed possible to feel an individual's head and know what areas of his or her brain were more developed and, consequently, what his or her behavior was likely to be. As we will see later in this chapter, some of the core ideas of phrenology—that different areas of the brain control different forms of behavior and that the size and development of these areas of the brain are important for criminal behavior—have once again become important in biological theories. Phrenology and physiognomy, however, were rather short-lived scientific endeavors. They largely passed from influence and acceptance because they could not be verified. In other words, they simply did not prove to be very scientific.

LOMBROSO AND ATAVISM

While physiognomy and phrenology had limited influence on public policy and theory, they did set the stage for a more fully developed and influential set of ideas that came about in the latter half of the nineteenth century. Probably the best known of the early biological theorists was **Cesare Lombroso** and his ideas of **atavism.** Lombroso became widely known following the publication of his book *The Criminal Man* (1876), in which he argued that criminals are essentially less evolved forms of humankind. As he explained it, criminals tended to be "throwbacks" to a lower form of humans, more similar to our apelike ancestors than to noncriminals. Building on the growing influence of evolutionary science, Lombroso referred to such individuals as atavistic and argued that as less-evolved examples of humans, criminals were likely to display a number of physical characteristics that were common and pronounced among apes but not among "evolved" people. And, most important for our discussion here, Lombroso initially argued that atavistic people were criminals because of their less-evolved nature. Many people attribute the idea of a "born criminal" to Lombroso; however, this reference was not used until coined by Lombroso's son-in-law and student Enrico Ferri. The visible features of atavistic people were referred to as "stigmata," suggesting that they were clear signs of something being "wrong" or less developed in the person. Among some of the more common of the atavistic characteristics that Lombroso said suggested one's lower status—and greater likelihood of criminality—were the following:

- an overly large head
- facial features in which one side differs from the other

- protruding lips
- large jaw and/or cheekbones
- very narrow forehead
- a large number of wrinkles (especially very noticeable ones) on the face
- long arms, fingers, or toes
- pouchlike cheeks
- eyes or ears that stand out from the head
- large nose

This is only a partial list of Lombroso's characteristics. Lombroso and his followers identified several dozen characteristics, many of which they associated not only with "criminals" in general, but with particular types of criminals.

The science used to validate these characteristics initially suggested that there was some truth to these claims; numerous researchers were able to document at least some of the stigmata among known criminals. However, this should not be surprising. Consider the individuals that we all encounter in our daily lives. How many of the people we know could we identify as having one or a few of the list of characteristics listed here?

The fact that many of these characteristics are fairly common among people, and the fact that it was fairly easy to identify noncriminals possessing some of these characteristics, led Lombroso to eventually modify his position and add to his theory social and environmental influences. In this line of modified thinking—combining biology with social/environmental forces—Lombroso argued that criminals need to be examined not as a universal group or class, but more productively on a case-by-case basis. In this way, he suggested that criminals existed in three basic forms: born criminals, insane criminals, and criminaloids. The first type of criminal, the born criminal, is his original idea of an atavistic individual: less developed physically, mentally, and socially than "normal" people. The insane criminal commits crime(s) because of a mental deficiency or due to alcohol and/or drugs. The third group, the criminaloids, is a general class of people who do not have special physical characteristics or mental disorders, but who, under certain social conditions (such as an emotional event or a "need" for some item), may engage in some type of crime. In this way Lombroso's revised theory could pretty easily be applied to crime. Criminals were either born bad, mentally ill, intoxicated, or had some social force that pushed or pulled them into crime. With these as our options, it really is fairly easy to explain just about any crime and criminal.

Enrico Ferri, one of Lombroso's most notable protégés, built on Lombroso's work and added in a sizable component of social, economic, and political factors as contributors to crime. Ferri also proposed a categorization of types of criminals, arguing that offenders could be identified as either born, insane, occasional, or criminal by passion. The born and insane criminals are essentially Lombroso's ideas. Occasional criminals and criminals by passion were categories that refined Lombroso's criminaloid category. Ferri, however, believed that to understand the causes of crime it was necessary to look at physical characteristics of both people and environments, anthropological issues (including an individual's age, sex, and physical conditions), and social aspects (culture, religion, economic and political structures, and so on) of the environments where criminals lived. Ferri's ideas fit well with the socialist thinking of the time in Italy, and he was a political activist who was asked to chair a committee charged with rewriting the criminal laws for Italy following the end of World War I. However, with the rise to power of the Fascist political party his efforts were put aside, and his ideas did not become codified into law.

A third influential early positivist to come from Italy was Raffaele Garofalo. He also believed, like Lombroso and Ferri, that scientific approaches were necessary to understand the cause of crime and focused his efforts on developing a "universal" definition of crime. Garofalo referred to this as "natural crime." The idea of natural crime is infused with many psychological influences, showing a break in thinking from that originally put forth by Lombroso and modified by Ferri. In fact, Garofalo rejected any association with Lombroso or Ferri and at times was quite critical of their theorizing.

The thinking of Lombroso (and subsequent others) gave rise to an often unrecognized development in the study of crime: the field of criminal anthropology (see Rafter, 1992). This line of thinking began in Europe and developed in the United States in the 1890s. In 1893, Arthur MacDonald introduced the term *criminology* in the United States. This was the first use of the term in the United States, and MacDonald was the first American to be identified as a *criminologist* (a specialist in the study of crime and its causes). The focus of this work and of the criminal anthropological work that was published in the United States through 1911 was on the underdeveloped nature (or "degeneracy") of criminal offenders. As a specialized field, criminal anthropology never gained a stronghold in American intellectual thinking, and the field failed to soundly define itself. As a result, it faded from importance and influence (see Rafter, 1992). But, it is important to note that criminal anthropology was largely based on the idea of observable physical characteristics of offenders. The passing of criminal anthropology was really the end of the period of influence for theories based on the idea that criminals were less developed or evolved than "normal" people. However, both core ideas—that criminals have distinct physical features and evolution—would resurface in subsequent biologically based theories.

The ideas originally put forth by Lombroso and added to and modified by Ferri and Garofalo were popular in Europe for several decades (and in the United States for a shorter time) and inspired numerous followers, as well as those who sought to test and/or refute Lombroso's ideas. The end of

Lombroso's influence was most pointedly brought about by the work of **Charles Goring** in the second decade of the twentieth century. Goring (1913–1972) took Lombroso's ideas and tested them using a comparison between imprisoned recidivist criminals in England and a group of non-criminals—university students. Although some have argued that Goring was too determined to prove Lombroso wrong (rather than seeking to do a truly objective assessment of Lombroso's ideas), the result was a convincing showing that most of Lombroso's identified physical features could not be associated with criminality. However, Goring did show that people who experienced frequent and long imprisonments were physically smaller (in both height and weight) than others. Beyond this, however, Goring argued that physical features were not associated with one group or the other, but there was actually a greater degree of variation within each group than between the groups. In simple terms, Goring largely disproved Lombroso's ideas, and as a result Lombroso's theory lost both support and influence.

BODY TYPE THEORIES

The idea that biology and our physical traits may predispose us to a greater likelihood of being criminal is continued, and actually replaces the idea of biological determinism, in the work of biological theorists in the twentieth century. It is interesting to note that although some new theories and slightly different points of focus are presented, some of Lombroso's basic ideas re-emerge in many of these theories. Some of the more influential of these ideas and views are summarized next, including those that center on body types.

Looking at the size, shape, and form of the human body and correlating these issues with our likelihood of engaging in crime was reintroduced to criminology by the German psychiatrist **Ernst Kretschmer** and, later, the Americans **William Sheldon** and Sheldon and Eleanor Glueck. All of the propositions of these thinkers focus on the idea of somatotypes. Their argument is that our body build is associated with our behavioral tendencies, life expectancy, likelihood of disease, and temperament. The science of **somatotyping** involves categorizing individuals based on assessments of their physical traits and then looking for correlations between certain types of bodies (the categories) and those individuals' behaviors. Basically, somatotype theorists believe that people of differing body types think and behave differently; for criminologists, it was important to identify the types of bodies that are most often involved in crime.

Kretschmer (1921/1925) first proposed these ideas and presented three ideal types of bodies (later adding a fourth) found among people. The three body types are the asthenic, the athletic, and the pyknic. The asthenic body type is thin and tall with narrow shoulders. The athletic type, much as the name suggests, is muscular and well developed. The pyknic type tends to be "softer," also described in a less flattering way as "short and fat." Within each category of body type, this theory says, are found different varieties of thinking patterns and mental disorders, which in turn are related to different types of criminal behavior.

So Kretschmer contended that each body type was related to a greater propensity for engaging in different forms of criminal behavior. The asthenic body type individual is most often associated with small thefts and fraud and tends to both first engage in crime at an early age and end his or her criminality early in life. The athletic body type person is most likely to be engaged in violent crime and usually has fairly stable patterns of criminal behavior throughout life. Pyknic body type individuals are somewhat more likely to be involved in theft or fraud, although they may also be found among violent criminals fairly frequently. What distinguishes these individuals, however, is that they tend to start their criminal behavior later in life than the asthenic or athletic body types. Later in his career, Kretschmer responded to some of the critics of his work by adding a fourth category of body types to his somatotype typology: the dysplastic (mixed) body type. A dysplastic individual, who possessed a combination of characteristics of the other three body types, also engaged in a variety of types of crimes. The inclusion of this fourth category essentially rounded out the theory; now truly anyone could be placed into a category. If an individual could not be easily fit into one of the three original categories, they must have traits of more than one category, so therefore they fit into the new group.

William Sheldon, a physician, brought the basic ideas and general directions of the somatotyping school of thought originated by Kretschmer to American thinking about crime in the 1940s. Sheldon's (1940, 1942, 1949) work reflects many of the core ideas originated by Kretschmer, but he is credited with both refining the ideas and using a much more rigorous scientific approach to validate and support his ideas. Sheldon also proposed three basic body types—endomorphs, ectomorphs, and mesomorphs—each associated with certain types of behavior. However, one of the important ways that Sheldon's work advances that of Kretschmer is that Sheldon acknowledged that all people have some degree of characteristics of each body type. With this in mind he proposed a way of evaluating body types and rating the degree to which any individual possesses the ideal type traits of each category. Based on a seven-point rating scale, every individual can be assigned a three-number score, reflecting his or her degree of each ideal type's characteristics. The ideal type endomorph is a shorter, smaller, but heavier individual with small bones and is generally soft/smooth. The pure form of the ectomorph body is a thinner person who is often relatively tall, lean, and "fragile" and tends to have a small face. The ideal type mesomorph body is a more athletic person with more-developed muscles and an overall larger body frame and limbs.

Each of the ideal forms of body types, Sheldon (1942) argued, can be associated with a type of personality or temperament. The variety of temperaments are therefore associated with different likelihood of criminal engagement. People who score high on the endomorph body type tend to be outgoing, comfortable, and a bit "soft." Those who score high on ectomorph body type are much more introverted, tend to avoid crowds and others, and often have allergies, illnesses, and other "functional problems." The mesomorph is typically an active, assertive, and perhaps aggressive type of person. Each of these types of personalities and behavioral sets can be relatively easily translated into types of crimes that are most expected for each body type. Obviously the more assertive or aggressive mesomorph would be most likely to be involved in violence, and the ectomorph who prefers to avoid others is most likely to be involved in property crimes or crimes of theft, those that do not require interacting with or confronting others.

The most likely body type for involvement in crime is the mesomorph. This idea was the foundation for continued study in this area in the 1950s by the husband-and-wife team of Sheldon and Eleanor Glueck (1950, 1956). Their interests focused on the delinquency of mesomorph boys, and after comparing 500 chronically delinquent boys with a group of 500 nondelinquents, they concluded that twice as many delinquents were of a mesomorph body type than nondelinquents. However, in keeping with the thinking that biological and physical factors only predispose rather than determine behaviors, the Gluecks also showed that involvement in delinquency was also related to social factors, including weak family ties and involvement. This acknowledgment of the role of nonphysical factors fits well with the historical era; as is discussed in other chapters, the mid-twentieth century was a time when criminological theories emphasizing social and cultural factors were most prominent. The Gluecks essentially "softened" the role of physical body types in the explanation of crime, although they did see it as an important factor.

GENETIC THEORIES

Another way of thinking about why people commit crimes is to work from the idea that not only are some individuals "bad" people that have something wrong with them, but instead there might be entire "bad" families that are likely to continue to produce criminal offspring. This is the idea of a group of people who, because of their shared genetic lineage, are predisposed to share a trait of criminality. Many people believe that some of us are just born into situations and families that are criminal and either we have no real chance not to be criminal or the family we are born into just makes it more likely that we will be criminal.

Genetic theories are different, yet still build on the general ideas that were put forth by people like Lombroso. Just as physiognomy and phrenology had faded from importance earlier, Lombroso's views lost their importance, although not completely. In fact, a couple of decades after Goring disproved Lombroso, others stepped forward with somewhat similar arguments, suggesting that biological determinism might still be able to explain many criminals' actions.

Theories that emphasize an individual's **genetic predisposition** say that criminal behavior is inherited and runs in families. The premise in these explanations centers on the belief that there is something genetic in the cause of crime, and criminality is passed along some lines of families just like other inherited traits such as appearance, diseases, or genetic mutations. While these theories do not claim to explain all criminals or all crime, they do argue that a significant amount of crime can be explained by looking to families where crime "runs in the family."

Crime as an inherited trait has been a commonly argued part of several theories, with some suggesting that it is a deterministic inheritance (i.e., those who inherit the trait definitely will be criminal) and others suggesting that inheritance simply predisposes one to a greater likelihood of being criminal.

The idea of biology being a deterministic influence was most strongly advocated by the anthropologist **E. A. Hooten** in the 1930s and 1940s. Hooten's (1939) ideas were based on a massive study of 14,000 prisoners and a comparison group of more than 3,000 noncriminals. In comparing individuals in the two groups, he concluded that there were numerous physical differences between criminals and noncriminals, and in almost every way he compared the two groups the criminals were "inferior." This included physical measurements and assessments as well as mental/intellectual abilities.

Hooten argued in favor of addressing the crime problem in society by targeting the genetically predisposed for either segregation or elimination from society. As he stated in his book *The American Criminal* (1939), "Criminals are organically inferior. Crime is the resultant of the impact of environment upon low grade human organisms. It follows that the elimination of crime can be effected only by the extirpation of the physically, mentally, and morally unfit; or by their complete segregation" (p. 309). His position is clear; criminals cannot be changed, they do not deserve to live in society, and sterilization of known criminals is an acceptable practice. As we might expect, Hooten's work was controversial and drew a large amount of criticism. He does deserve credit though for being clear about his beliefs and proposing a solution to the problem of crime.

Both Richard Dugdale (1877/1895) and Henry Goddard (1912) offered a less deterministic view, although they still emphasized the idea of criminality being something that we inherit. The work of these two men, both coming earlier than that of Hooten, focused on examining family trees to identify lines of inheritance of criminality and concentrations of crime among family members. This theory suggests that criminality is a trait that is inherited, but the inheritance is only of a propensity for criminality, not a definite behavior. Dugdale began his work when as a staff member of the Prison Association of New York he discovered six members of the Jukes family in prison. Intrigued by this fact, he began researching the Jukes family tree and discovered that among the approximately 1,000 descendants he could trace back to one woman, Ada Jukes, nearly 50 percent were criminals. Similarly, Henry Goddard (1912) tracked the family tree of a Revolutionary soldier, Martin Kallikak. The interesting aspect of the Kallikak family study begins with the immediate branching of the tree from Martin Kallikak into a family line born of a legitimate son and one from an illegitimate son. The tracking of both major branches of the family tree showed that there were many more criminals in the family branches stemming from the illegitimate son than from the legitimate son. Goddard attributed this to the fact that the mother of Martin Kallikak's illegitimate son was obviously "not of high quality" (as evidenced by the fact that she had an illegitimate son). The moral aspect of Goddard's interpretation of these data is clear, as is the different way that "crime" and "high-quality" character have been defined at various times in history.

Although there are clearly problems with both Dugdale's and Goddard's work—such as failing to consider social aspects of the families' situations—this type of theorizing had a major influence on American criminal laws and policies. Because it was assumed that criminality ran in families, this meant that the offspring of criminals (and especially criminals who had other criminal family members) could be expected to be criminals themselves. Therefore, it only made sense to many policymakers to remove the possibility of these likely criminals being born. As a result, a number of states implemented laws allowing forced sterilization of habitual criminals as part of their criminal sentences. When these laws were challenged in the courts, the U.S. Supreme Court upheld them as constitutional in 1927. In perhaps one of the most frequently quoted Supreme Court decisions of all time, *Buck v. Bell*, 274 U.S. 200 (1926), Justice Oliver Wendell Holmes, Jr., wrote, "it is better for all the world, if instead of waiting to execute the degenerate offspring for crime, or to let them starve for their imbecility, society can prevent those who are manifestly unfit from continuing their kind....Three generations of imbeciles are enough." Again, the message and position are quite clear. However, research continues to show that crime runs in families. In 2008, van de Rakt, Nieuwbeerta, and Dirk de Graaf showed that when looking at criminality of fathers and their children over a 40-year period, there is a strong connection between a father's criminal record and that of his children. Not only are children of criminal fathers more likely to be criminal themselves, but fathers who were persistently involved in crime tend to have children who are involved in more serious forms of delinquency/crime, and for longer periods of time. Although there certainly could be a number of nonbiological factors involved to explain this relationship, the fact that the study involved more than 8,000 children and tracked their behavior for up to 40 years suggests that genetic factors must play at least some role in this relationship.

Other theorists and researchers have also looked at the idea of crime as an inherited trait, although not focusing so strongly on the idea that crime runs in families. In looking to see whether some genetic crime factor can be passed between generations, or whether genetics or environment plays a larger role in determining whether someone engages in crime, some researchers have studied the behavior of twins and others have examined whether adopted children have more similarity to their biological or adoptive families. The questions asked by these studies very clearly focus on whether something is passed between parents and children that is associated with greater or lesser likelihood of being criminal.

One of the best ways to study whether a behavior, such as criminality, may be related to genetics is to examine the behavior of twins. The basic approach to this type of science is to track the behavior of sets of twins (or other multiple births, but they are much more rare) and see if and how their behaviors are similar and different. Especially when research can include identical twins (who have identical genetic makeup), it can be a very powerful way to study the causes of behavior. In studies of this variety, researchers look for concordance rates of behavior. A concordance rate is the frequency with which twins have the same behaviors. So, if a study of sets of twins shows a concordance rate of 100 percent when one twin is criminal and the second is also criminal, and 100 percent when one twin is not a criminal and neither is the other, then we would have very strong evidence suggesting that genetics is related to becoming a criminal. While it is unrealistic to expect concordance rates of 100 percent for any type of behavior, it is interesting to note that numerous researchers have shown a higher concordance rate for identical twins than fraternal twins (who do not have identical genetic makeup). This by itself is fairly strong evidence suggesting that genetics significantly influences behavior.

The study of twins and criminality was especially popular in the United States, as well as Europe and Japan, starting in the 1930s. Most of this line of research tapered off, however, in the 1960s. Some large-scale, longitudinal studies continue to be done today, although most are focused on issues other than criminality (health issues, psychological functioning, and so on). The ideal way to study twins is to compare behaviors for identical twins raised in separate families. One of the problems with this approach, however, is that not very many families that have twins choose to give one away. In the early 1900s, this may have happened in families that had more children than they could afford to support, but today it is very difficult to find twins who were separated at birth. Therefore, most modern studies of twins look at comparisons of concordance rates for identical twins and fraternal twins.

One of the largest studies of twins was done with more than 6,000 sets of twins born between 1881 and 1910 in Denmark (Christiansen, 1977).

Identical twins showed a concordance rate three times as high as fraternal twins (36 percent vs. 12 percent). Similar findings were reported for a 1985 study in Ohio (Rowe, 1995). In this study, the findings went a bit further and showed that not only criminality is highly correlated among twins but so too are emotions and actions such as anger and impulsiveness. And in a review of all of the available studies of twins done over nearly a half-century, Wilson and Herrnstein (1985) reported that across the studies identical twins showed a concordance rate of 69 percent compared to only 33 percent for fraternal twins. These studies, taken as a whole, strongly support the importance of genetics in determining behavior, especially criminal behavior.

Twin studies, though, do have some problems. The usual criticism of these studies is that it may be impossible to separate out the influence of genetics and social environment. When twins are raised in the same household, they are exposed to the same sets of social influences. And, as many people know, identical twins are more likely to be treated "identically" than fraternal twins (especially when the fraternal twins are different sexes). We have all seen twins who are dressed alike, given very similar names, and treated more or less as copies of one another. This approach to child rearing is assumed to be more common with identical twins than fraternal twins. The problem this raises for research on the possible genetic link to crime is that if in fact identical twins are more likely to be treated the same than are fraternal twins, it may not be possible to conclude that similarities in criminality are due to genetics.

One way to try to overcome this problem is to study children who are not raised by their biological parents. Studies of adopted children enable researchers to compare the influence of genetics with that of one's social environment. The basic approach of such studies is to compare an adopted child's criminality with that of the biological parents (who provided his or her genetic structure) and that of the adoptive parents (who provided his or her social environment).

The most important of the adoption studies is based on data collected on more than 4,000 Danish boys (Mednick, Gabrieli, & Hutchings, 1984). This research has shown that genetics does seem to play a role in criminality, although the researchers argue that this is only a predisposition to crime, not a true deterministic influence. This study has shown that adopted boys who had both biological and adoptive parents who were criminal were more likely (24.5 percent) than those boys who had only criminal adoptive parents (14.7 percent) and only criminal biological parents (20 percent) to be criminal themselves. It is important to keep in mind, though, that even at the level of having both sets of parents being criminally involved, only one in four of the boys were identified as criminal. And one in eight (13.5 percent) of boys with neither a biological nor adoptive parent that was a criminal ended up as criminal himself. Similar results have also been found among more than 1,700 adopted children in a Swedish study (Bohman, Cloninger, Sigwardsson, & von Knorring, 1982) and adopted children in Iowa born between 1925 and 1956 to female criminals (Crowe, 1972, 1974).

Clearly, then, while genetics appears to be influential, it is not the only, or even perhaps the most powerful, influence on criminality. The conclusion that our genetics plays a role in our behavior may be frightening to some of us. To think that our behavior is not something we can completely control can be scary and disheartening. For others of us, however, it may come as a bit of a relief to realize that different people in fact do have different chances, opportunities, or challenges with which they are born. However, if our behavior is not really completely under our control, questions are sure to arise about what is best and appropriate for responding to the crimes of people who do not have full control. As a policy question it may be important to ask what should be done with people whom we can identify as likely to be or become criminal. Did Hooten and Justice Holmes have the right idea? Would it be best to "eliminate" or sterilize people we believe have a genetic predisposition to crime? What if we could show particular genetics meant a person definitely would be criminal? Would it be a good idea to "eliminate" them (and their offspring) from society?

One additional way of looking at a pure genetic influence on crime is to try to identify the gene that leads to a predisposition for crime. The real push for this research began in the 1960s following the discovery that a small percentage of men (about one-tenth of 1 percent or fewer, or one in every 1,000–2,000) have a genetic anomaly of two Y chromosomes (see Amir & Berman, 1970; Fox, 1971). So, whereas women have an XX pair of sex-determining chromosomes and most men have an X and a Y chromosome, this very small proportion of men have an extra Y chromosome. Research of these men with the **XYY chromosome** pattern found that they tend to be physically larger and taller, have more and stronger masculine traits, and also tend to score lower on intelligence tests. Interestingly one of the most common places where researchers found men with the XYY chromosome pattern was in mental institutions. Because these men were "more masculine," the assumption carried that these men were also more aggressive and prone to violence.

Several researchers (Jacobs, Brunton, & Melville, 1965; Kessler & Moos, 1970; Price, Strong, Whatmore, & McClemont, 1966; also see Amir & Berman, 1970; Fox, 1971) have tested the chromosomal makeup of male criminals, looking to see if those with an XYY chromosome are in fact more likely to be involved in crime. Most of the research in this area supports the argument that these men are more likely (but not always) involved in crime. However, the problem with this theory for explaining crime is that this "abnormality" is very rare. The incidence of an XYY chromosome in men has always been shown to be less than 1 percent (and sometimes less than one-tenth of 1 percent) of all men. Also, the most common finding among these men is that they show a lower level of intelligence. So the extra Y chromosome might just make these men more likely to be caught if they are involved in crime, not necessarily more likely to be violent or criminal in the first place.

If in fact an XYY chromosome pattern truly has something to do with someone becoming a criminal, it is still a long way from explaining most crime. The situation with the XYY chromosome pattern research highlights one of the basic problems with much of the biological theory approaches. While a particular factor or physical trait might be shown to be statistically related to criminal activity, if the trait is rare among the population, we still have not explained most, or even very many, criminals.

CONTEMPORARY GENETIC THEORIES

In the first decade of the twenty-first century, there has been a strong return to prominence of biological theories, especially those emphasizing genetics, as an explanation for crime. Whereas earlier work in this vein simply pointed to correlations between parents' and children's involvement in crime and violence as evidence of a presumed genetic contributor to crime, the recent genetic theories have focused on identifying specific genes that are associated with involvement in delinquency/crime. This line of research was made possible in 2001 by the major scientific breakthrough of the successful mapping of the human genome. Scientists have successfully linked the presence of a variety of specific forms of genes to a wide range of behavioral issues. These correlations have included such diverse things as musical preference (Harris, 1995) and attention deficit/hyperactivity disorder (ADHD) (Plomin, DeFries, McClearn, & Rutter, 1997). If these types of activities and experiences can be linked to genetic structures, it only makes sense that criminality too can be linked to genes.

In one study of 1,100 adolescent males, Guo, Roettger, and Cai (2008) have shown that even when controlling for social and environmental conditions in an adolescent's life, those who have one of three different genetic polymorphisms are statistically more likely to be involved in violent forms of delinquency. The presence of these specific genetic structures, however, is not sufficient in and of themselves to predict who is a delinquent. Rather, it is necessary to also have present family, school, and peer processes and supports. Without these in addition to the genetic structures, the adolescent was not likely to be involved in delinquency.

Another recent study (DeLisi, Beaver, Wright, & Vaughn, 2008) has shown linkages between the genetic polymorphisms DRD2 and DRD4 and variations in adolescents' likelihood of arrest. However, it is important to note that DeLisi and his colleagues were able to show the connection between these genetic structures and arrest only for youth from low-risk family environments. This suggests that social factors (such as those explained later in the text) may be even more important than the genetic factors, although the genetic explanation is certainly important for at least some youth.

Somewhat similarly, Beaver, Wright, DeLisi, and Vaughn (2008) combined the influence of genetic factors with self-control theory (see Chapter 8) and found that variations in genetic structures of youth were responsible for 50–64 percent of the variation in the youth's level of self-control (our inner ability to restrain our behavior). In this respect, while an individual's propensity to engage in crime may be a result of their level of self-control directly, it is important to note that the level of self-control may be a primarily biological/genetic factor.

And, Beaver (2008) has also shown that genetics and prior victimization experience may interact to create a greater likelihood of violent criminal behavior for at least some male adolescents. Beaver (2008) looked at a sample of adolescents who did and did not have a history of sexual abuse victimization. He found that genetics interacts with prior sexual abuse victimization in enhancing the likelihood of violent delinquency for males. However, for adolescent females (for whom there is a well-known significantly higher rate of sexual abuse victimization), there is no effect of genetics interacting with victimization experiences in predicting violent delinquency.

The genetics–crime link has also been shown to be present for criminal victimization, as well as for the commission of crimes. Beaver and colleagues (2007) have demonstrated that some variants of the D2 dopamine receptor gene (DRD2) in white adolescent males are correlated with increased criminal victimization experiences. Specifically, when white adolescent males have peers who are involved in delinquency, the presence of several specific variants of the DRD2 gene is statistically related to increased levels of victimization.

However, it is important to keep in mind that whereas the early researchers focusing on genetics and crime were of the perspective that genetics determined whether one would be a criminal or not, the research in the twenty-first century has altered this view and, today, argues that genes may predispose someone to criminal ways, but that environment is important as well. It takes the combination of particular genetic structures and the individual being exposed to particular environmental issues (usually types of peers, parents, or other persons) for the individual to become criminal. The importance of genetic influences is seen in that research that looks at social/environmental factors offers a much stronger statistical explanation for crime when genetics are included (McCartan, 2007). So, while environmental factors may have importance for explaining the occurrence of crime, genetic factors also need to be taken into account, although as McCartan (2007, p. 228) concludes, "today genetic influence is viewed as having a relatively small effect on behavior. Genetic influence can be equated to a nudge (and sometimes a strong nudge) towards certain behaviors rather than an inevitable outcome. Thus, the results support the environment as playing a critical role on behavior even with the inclusion of genetic factors."

RECENT BIOLOGICAL THEORIES

Some more recent theories for explaining why and how crime happens have also looked at biological factors. And, as most biological theories before have argued, the most recent theories also suggest that biological factors may make a person more likely to be involved in crime, but these factors do not mean that a person definitely will be criminal. The more recent versions of biological theories have moved away from suggesting that something about our physical bodies or our genetics predisposes us to crime. Instead, the biological theories of the late twentieth century and early twenty-first century have focused more directly on either the biological and physiological results of things we put into our bodies (such as food or drugs) or on how malfunctioning parts of our brains may be associated with crime.

One of the more commonsense approaches that has been developed to explain crime is a focus on **hormones** and their effects on behavior. These views have looked both at men and women separately and suggest that the levels of sex hormones (testosterone and estrogen) in our bodies influence our emotions and levels of aggression. Research on men has focused on the idea that high levels of testosterone produce high levels of aggression. And some theories about women's criminality have suggested that premenstrual syndrome (PMS) and varying estrogen levels are behind criminal behavior.

The research on men's testosterone levels begins with the idea that men commit most crime. And when we think about the men who do commit crime, especially violent crimes, we often think of a certain type of man. Very masculine, large, and aggressive men are often associated with crime. These men are often found to have higher levels of testosterone in their bodies, so it seems logical to assume that when a man has more testosterone, he would likely be predisposed to violence (i.e., crime). Decades of research have shown that boys in general are more aggressive than girls, even at very young ages. Numerous researchers (Booth & Osgood, 1993; Olweus, 1987; Rada, Laws, & Kellner, 1976; Rubin, 1987; Rushton, 1995) have shown that boys and men with higher testosterone levels are also more likely to be involved in violence and crime.

This line of thinking is often offered as an explanation for the high levels of crime committed by athletes. Recent years have shown a higher-than-expected amount of crime (especially violent crime) committed by high school, college, and professional male athletes. At least once a month a news story appears about either an individual athlete or a group of athletes (such as the Duke University men's lacrosse team) who are alleged to be involved in assaults, domestic violence, robberies, or sexual assaults. Athletes typically have high levels of testosterone, which facilitate not only muscular development but also competitiveness and aggression. Therefore, the link seems somewhat obvious: A man with high testosterone levels is likely to behave in ways that are criminal. These ideas have also received a great deal of attention as a result of a number of highly publicized incidents in recent years, whereby men (especially bodybuilders and other athletes) who take anabolic steroids have engaged in criminal and violent behavior (Pope & Katz, 1990). When men take anabolic steroids, they boost their production of testosterone and in turn facilitate their muscular development and competitiveness (as they increase their levels of testosterone). One common consequence (some would say "side effect") of taking steroids is that the individual often becomes very aggressive and sometimes violent (" 'roid rage"). Such instances are commonly interpreted as yet further evidence supporting the theory that high levels of testosterone are related to criminal behavior. Interestingly, others (Dabbs & Hargrove, 1997) have also shown that testosterone levels are related to violent behavior among women as well as men. So, while at first glance it may appear that this is somewhat of a sexist theory, in fact, any "blame" needs to be laid on the hormone (testosterone), and not the persons with whom the hormone is typically associated.

The research on testosterone levels and aggression/violence/crime needs to be viewed with caution, however. A number of social influences may affect both testosterone levels and behavior. In fact, one recent review of the research in this area suggests that testosterone levels may be the result of hostility and not the cause of or contributor to aggression (Aromaki, Lindman, & Eriksson, 1999). Viewed in this way, we start to get into a proverbial "chicken and egg" question.

In regard to women's hormone levels and criminal behavior, some research has looked at whether PMS (in which women's hormones change in volume and intensity) may be related to criminality. Some researchers have reported that either a majority of women's criminal offenses are committed during their premenstrual periods (Cooke, 1945; Morton, Addison, Addison, Hunt, & Sullivan, 1953) or women with PMS are significantly more likely than other women to engage in verbally or physically aggressive acts (Bond, Critchlow, & Wingrove, 2003). At the risk of again seeming a bit sexist, consider how your own experience fits with this. Does it seem logical that women with PMS would be responsible for most crimes committed by women? And, would the real cause of such crimes be the hormones and their effect on a woman or the way society (and especially men) reacts to women with PMS?

Critics of the hormone-level theorizing, however, suggest that the cause-and-effect order may actually be misinterpreted. According to sòme (Horney, 1978; Katz & Chambliss, 1991), the fact that hormone levels vary among violent criminals may actually be the result of aggression/violence/crime, not the cause of or a contributor to it. Whether we believe that hormones are related to crime or not, the important point is that it is in many ways a logical proposition, and both theorists and criminal justice officials often do see hormones as a factor in why some people are criminally involved.

Another approach to looking at biological factors and their relation to crime draws a bit more on social influence and suggests that our diet may play a role in determining our behavior. Most often this line of research has focused on the idea that eating foods that produce either high or low amounts of sugar in our bloodstream affects how we act. Low blood sugar levels (hypoglycemia) often produce irritability, nervousness, and depression (much like PMS), and these feelings can lead to aggression and crime. On the other end of the spectrum, when we have a very high level of sugar in our systems we are susceptible to hyperactivity and sometimes learning disabilities. As any of us know who have ever interacted with a child who eats a pile of candy, sugar gives us energy and can make us hyperactive. Think of times like Halloween or Easter when children get lots of candy; most parents try to limit the amount of candy their children eat, so as to try to control the child's behavior. Think about a time when you have been under pressure to cram for an exam or to get a paper done. Many of us stock up on candy, soda, or other high-sugar (or high-caffeine) foods/drinks, so that we can stay alert and awake. If you have done this, try to remember what you felt like when you finished eating a couple of donuts or a candy bar or two and washed it all down with some sugar/caffeine drinks. We often end up not only being wide awake but also feeling jumpy and irritable when something goes wrong. These same types of reactions are likely to lead us to strike out at someone or something that we feel interrupts our efforts or does something to annoy us. This is a perfect situation for aggression (i.e., crime) to happen.

One of the more controversial areas of research linking biological factors and crime/violence centers on the role of nutrition. As we saw in the opening story of this chapter, there are some definite connections between nutrition and behavior, including violent and criminal behavior. Although somewhat controversial, this line of thinking and research is actually one of the most rapidly developing biological explanations for crime. One of the first studies to examine this came from the Italian researcher Liggio (1969), who studied the diets of both delinquent and nondelinquent adolescents and found a correlation between their diets and their status as delinquents. Specifically, delinquents were found to eat more pasta, bread, and potatoes—foods that are high in starch, which when eaten is transformed into sugar. As a result, adolescents who ate more of these foods had shorter attention spans, reduced learning abilities, and a greater likelihood of being delinquent.

It is not only the nutrition of the individual that is important; the nutrition of an expectant mother is influential on the behavior of her child, too. A recent series of studies by Joseph Hibblen, including one that tracked over 14,000 women and children, has shown that women who eat diets rich in fatty acids are likely to have children who later test higher on IQ tests, have better fine-motor skills, and are least likely to be involved in antisocial behaviors. Pregnant women who consumer fewer fatty acids in their diets have children with greater likelihood of mental illness, including depression and aggression. Not only is the diet of a pregnant woman important for her health, the health of her baby, and the baby's later behavior, but also how a new mother feeds her infant is important for the child's later behavior. Data from more than 102,000 parents and guardians of children who participated in the 2003 National Survey of Children's Health have shown that infants who were breastfed are significantly less likely to have a diagnosis of behavioral/conduct problems and also less likely to receive mental health care (Knutson, 2008). Not only did the fact of whether or not a baby was breastfed influence the child's subsequent behavior, but the longer that a mother breastfed, the lower the likelihood of behavioral problems.

More recently other research (Liu, Raine, Venables, & Mednick, 2004) has shown that malnourished three-year-olds are significantly more likely to be aggressive, hyperactive, and involved in delinquent behavior as they approach and reach adulthood. It has also been shown that nutritionally deprived pregnant women are 2.5 times as likely as other women to have male children with antipersonality disorders (Neugebauer, Hoek, & Susser, 1999). Furthermore, individuals with vitamin and mineral deficiencies are more likely to display aggressive and violent behavior (Breakey, 1997; Grantham-McGregor & Ani, 2001; Werbach, 1992). Perhaps the core of the nutrition and violence/crime link is the fact that malnutrition has also been shown to be linked to lower levels of intelligence (Grantham-McGregor & Ani, 2001; Lozoff, Jimenez, Hagen, Mollen, & Wolf, 2000). What all of this suggests, then, is that perhaps the old adage that "you are what you eat" does have some truth to it: If you eat lots of sugars and starches and do not eat healthy/nutritious foods, you may well end up an aggressive, distracted, less intelligent, and criminal person.

Another approach to this focus on biology says that individuals whose brains and central nervous system (CNS) functioning are "different" process information differently, see the world and others in their world differently, and are likely to react to their environment differently than those of us who have "normal" brain and CNS functions. The research in this area tends to work backward from known criminals and shows that among (especially violent) criminals, there are higher-than-expected rates of individuals with organic brain diseases and excessive amounts of "abnormal" electrical activity in their CNS.

A number of studies have found varying levels of support for these types of explanations. For instance, Satterfield, Satterfield, and Schell (1987) reported that children who were hyperactive when they reached adolescence were six times as likely to be arrested as children not diagnosed as hyperactive. Others (Moffitt & Silva, 1988) have shown that children with attention/deficit disorder (ADD) may also be more likely to be involved in crime. More recently a set of researchers tracked samples of 6- to 18-year-olds, both diagnosed with ADHD and without such a diagnosis, for 10 years to see if and how ADHD might be related to behaviors later in life (Biederman et al., 2006). The results of this study showed that even though 93 percent of the ADHD sample received counseling and/or medication, the diagnosed sample was much more likely to engage in both antisocial (including criminality) and addictive behaviors. Additionally, Johnson and Kercher (2007) have also shown that among college students with a diagnosis of ADHD, there is less ability to effectively cope with strain and therefore a greater potential for involvement in criminal acts.

Other researchers have suggested that "abnormal" brain development, from before birth and through the first several years of life, may predispose a person to violence and crime. For instance, Adrian Raine and colleagues (1994; Raine, Brenna, & Mednick, 1997; Raine, Bushsbaum, & LaCasse, 1997) reported that birth complications and subsequent rejection of the infant by the mother predisposed individuals to violence in adulthood. Other forms of prenatal complications and maternal behaviors may also be linked to increased levels of violence and crime. One large-scale longitudinal study from Finland examined whether a pregnant woman's smoking had negative consequences for her child. In fact, women who smoked during pregnancy (even if they stopped during their first trimester) had a significantly greater chance of having a child who would grow up to be a delinquent/criminal than nonsmoking mothers (Rantakallio, Laara, Ishohanni, & Moilanen, 1992). The development of criminal behavior in these offspring, according to the researchers, is not necessarily a biological consequence, as social influences may also be involved. Diana Fishbein (1994) has suggested that brain disorders may be related to violence and drug abuse in similar ways.

One of the strongest links between brain development and later criminality centers on the issue of prenatal exposure to alcohol. For several decades we have known that fetuses exposed to alcohol are at risk for a number of birth defects—most notably fetal alcohol syndrome. Exposure to alcohol while in the womb can have other effects, some of which may not be as noticeable. For instance, in 2009, Elizabeth Disney and her colleagues studied 1,252 17-year-olds, focusing on the adolescents' behavior as well as their mothers' use of alcohol during pregnancy. They found that even low levels of alcohol exposure prenatally were linked with the development of conduct disorders for the adolescents. Pregnant women who drank as little as three alcoholic drinks per week during pregnancy were significantly more likely to have children with conduct disorders. This study also showed that for mothers who were alcoholic prior to becoming pregnant had especially high rates of children with conduct disorder. Alcoholic mothers who continued to drink had a 44 percent greater likelihood of a child with conduct disorder, and even those alcoholic mothers who were sober during their pregnancy had a 20 percent greater likelihood of a child with conduct disorder.

Other lines of research beginning to develop have recently shown that slight variations of genes can raise serotonin levels in the brain, which in turn may reduce an individual's ability to control any aggressive impulses. Also, "abnormalities" of the brain—such as epilepsy, traumatic brain injuries, childhood encephalitis, or meningitis—are also being linked to severe levels of violence, including sexually related murders (Briken, Habermann, Berner, & Hill, 2005).

Also addressing the idea of brain development and crime, Raine et al. (1997) have also shown that murderers who plead guilty by reason of insanity have "indications of a network of abnormal cortical and subcortical brain processes that may predispose to violence" (p. 495). This type of research has been made possible by the development of brain imaging technology, which allows researchers to both see and map out the areas of brain activity associated with different types of activities. This line of research (Fishbein, 1990; Goyer et al., 1994; Raine et al., 1997; Volkow & Tancredi, 1987) has suggested that both the temporal cortex and frontal brain regions are involved in violence. Others (Kruesi, Casanova, Mannheim, & Johnson-bilder, 2004) have shown that adolescents with conduct disorder (which is a strong predictor of later criminal involvement) have smaller frontal and prefontal lobes of their brains.

However, it is important to remember that although some types of biological/physiological factor may be found to be more common among known delinquents/criminals, it may not be possible to separate out the effects of the biological factors from social influences. Just because a particular biological issue is present or active for an individual does not necessarily mean the individual is destined to be criminal. After all, hyperactive people and those with ADD may simply call more attention to themselves (and their criminal activities) and be more likely to be caught/identified. Or, as others have argued, the diagnoses of ADD or hyperactivity (as well as many learning disabilities) may simply be a labeling process that is applied to disruptive (i.e., criminal or "precriminal") children and adolescents. Just because a certain factor is seen more frequently among known criminals does not necessarily mean that the factor is a cause of crime, it could simply be something that is correlated with criminality, and perhaps both issues are "caused" by some third issue. Or, a biological issue may allow for an individual to more easily move into criminal behavior, if and when the setting and other influences are right. Remember, it is very important to distinguish between things that are simply correlated and those that have a cause-and-effect relationship.

CONCLUSION

Biological explanations for crime and criminals have been around in one form or another for at least several centuries. In fact, theories that focused on biological or physical traits of criminals were the original impetus for attempts to use science to explain and understand behavior. This is logical though; it was not until at least the eighteenth century that individuals and societies began to focus on and understand social influences on behavior, nor was there significant understanding of psychology. What was obvious and available for consideration was the body and people's behaviors. So when we wanted to better understand how and why certain people acted in certain ways, we looked at what was available for inspection: the body.

The earliest biological theories differ from our more recently developed ideas in two important ways. First, the content of these theories was on the size, shape, and distinguishing features of the body. These characteristics were assumed to represent something about what was happening inside the body, and our external characteristics were taken as symbols for our internal workings. Second, our early biological theories differed from almost all more recently developed theories (both those with and without a biological focus) in that these early explanations for crime worked on the premise that certain features in an individual meant that the person definitely would be criminal. This deterministic view arose out of fairly simple logic and thinking, and today we recognize that there are so many different characteristics of people, environments, and other influences that one quality of a person cannot and will not control his or her behavior. Today's theories that include biological components place these factors in a social context and emphasize that physical/biological factors may make it more or less likely that someone will act in particular ways. We can see this shift in thinking about whether biological issues are deterministic or not very clearly in the contrast between early and twenty-first-century theories that focus on genetics. Genetic influences today are seen as important for explaining behavior, but only when interacting with particular types of supportive environments and social contacts.

Biologically centered theories suggest that deciding the appropriate and best ways to deal with criminals will depend on whether it is possible to correct or cure the biological factors that contribute to the individual's criminal ways. Early deterministic theories clearly argued that it was in the best interest of society to remove criminals, because they could not be changed. This often meant permanently removing criminals by killing them. However, more humane approaches have also been used over the years, in which we may not end a criminal's life but severely curtail his or her social life. Incapacitating criminals by removing them from society and relocating them to secure hospitals or correctional facilities is widely believed to be the best way to accomplish this. If we see criminals' biological composition as unfailingly causing them to be criminal, we cannot hope to change their behavior. All we can do in such a situation is protect others from the criminal.

SUMMARY

Biological theories are among the oldest explanations offered for why some people commit crimes and others do not. A number of biological factors have been the focus of explanations of crime throughout history. The earliest explanations suggested that criminals were underdeveloped forms of human beings, and that their lack of proper physical development reflected their also being underdeveloped mentally and socially. Other biological theories have suggested that crime is an inherited trait that can be seen either in the family lineage of criminals or in their genetic construction. Other biological theorists have argued that our actual bodies—the size, shape, and form of them—indicate criminal tendencies, and that different types of bodies suggest different types of criminal behaviors. More recently, biological theories have focused on the idea of crime as the result of some socially influenced biological factors such as hormone levels or diet.

The early deterministic theories are largely a thing of the past. For the last century or so we have seen biological/physiological factors theorized not as causing crime but rather as predisposing individuals to criminal ways. People with particular traits may be more likely than others, especially in certain types of situations, to be criminal. From this view, it may be possible to provide some type of treatment, corrective action, or restrictions on other influences that can prevent the individual from falling into criminal ways. Treatment programs, both during and separate from incarceration, would be appropriate ways to address crime. Most common would be some type of drug therapy in which the individual criminal is provided with "medicine" to either reduce/eliminate or control the biological aspect that may trigger crime. We might also use drugs to limit the ability of the person to act out and have his or her behaviors harm others. Either way, the belief is that something can be done to control or eliminate crime from the individual's behavioral repertoire.

Explaining criminal behavior through reference to biological traits was once the primary way for understanding why crime occurred. By the early twenty-first century, though, such approaches have moved to the margins of criminological theory, largely being replaced by theories that focus on social or psychological issues. This is not to say that biological theories have lost their influence completely, for some theorists and research continue to find connections between socially influenced biological factors and many types of behavior, including crime (see Fishbein, 1990). However, suggesting that our behaviors, whether criminal or otherwise, are a direct and clear result of our body's shape, size, appearance, chromosomal makeup, inherited traits, or internal chemical composition is difficult to support. There may be some value to seeing biological factors that can be triggered by social influences, in some situations, at some times, for some people. But beyond this, biological theories are among our weaker and less-supported theories for explaining crime.

KEY TERMS

atavism   the condition of being less developed than "normal" people; a "genetic throwback" to an earlier physical and social form of person

Cesare Lombroso   the father of positivism; he believed that criminals were underdeveloped forms of humans and exhibited a wide range of atavistic stigmata, indicating their less-developed state

Charles Goring   a researcher who largely disproved Lombroso's ideas, although his research showed some degree of physical differences between criminals and noncriminals

E. A. Hooten   an anthropologist whose book *The American Criminal* reported on numerous physical and mental "inferiorities" among criminals evolutionary psychology a recent, interdisciplinary theoretical development that says crime is the result of both programming that is passed through generations and social and cultural factors

Ernst Kretschmer   a theorist who introduced the idea of different body types being associated with different forms of crime; proposed three basic body types: asthenic, athletic, and pyknic

genetic predisposition   the idea that some people have genes that make them more likely to have a certain trait or behavior (such as criminality) than others

hormones   the chemicals in the human body that are most responsible for sex characteristics and, according to some theories, different types of behavior

phrenology   an idea from the 1790s and early 1800s that as different parts of the brain developed to a different degree, this could be seen through bumps on the head; the belief that bumps on certain parts of the head indicated criminality

positivism   the belief that it is possible to identify causes of a phenomena using scientific methods

somatotyping   the theory and practice of measuring and assessing body types and associating different forms of physical bodies with different types of criminal behavior

William Sheldon   a theorist who refined and revised the idea of different body types being associated with crime; proposed three body types: endomorphs, ectomorphs, and mesomorphs

XYY chromosome   a genetic abnormality found among less than 1 percent of men; argued by some to be a cause of a high level of aggression and, hence, criminality

DISCUSSION QUESTIONS

1. How have the factors on which biological theories focus changed over time?

2. What are the strengths and weaknesses of trying to explain crime from a biological perspective?

3. What are the common threads/ideas that run through the biological theories, from those originally proposed in the eighteenth century through those still discussed today?

REFERENCES

Amir, M., & Berman, Y. (1970). Chromosomal deviation and crime. *Federal Probation, 34*(2), 55–63.

Aromaki, A. S., Lindman, R. E., & Eriksson, C. J. P. (1999). Testosterone, aggressiveness and anti-social personality. *Aggressive Behavior, 25*(2), 113–123.

Beaver, K. M. (2008). The interaction between genetic risk and childhood sexual abuse in the prediction of adolescent violent behavior. *Sexual Abuse: A Journal of Research and Treatment, 20*, 426–443.

Beaver, K. M., Wright, J. P., DeLisi, M., Daigle, L. E., Swatt, M. L., & Gibson, C. L. (2007). Evidence of a gene X environment interaction in the creation of victimization. *International Journal of Offender Therapy and Comparative Criminology, 51*, 620–645.

Beaver, K. M., Wright, J. P., DeLisi, M., & Vaughn, M. G. (2008). Genetic influences on the stability of low self-control: Results from a longitudinal sample of twins. *Journal of Criminal Justice, 36*, 478–485.

Biederman, J., Monuteaux, M., Mick, E., Spencer, T., Wilens, T., Silva, J., et al. (2006). Young adult outcome of attention deficit hyperactivity disorder: A controlled 10-year follow-up study. *Psychological Medicine, 36*, 167–179.

Bohman, M., Cloninger, C. R., Sigwardsson, S., & von Knorring, A. L. (1982). Predisposition to petty criminality in Swedish adoptees: Genetic and environmental heterogeneity. *Archives of General Psychiatry, 39*, 1233–1241.

Bond, A. J., Critchlow, D., & Wingrove, J. (2003). Conflict resolution in women is related to trait aggression and menstrual cycle phase. *Aggressive Behavior, 29*, 228–233.

Booth, A., & Osgood, D. W. (1993). The influence of testosterone on deviance in adulthood: Assessing and explaining the relationship. *Criminology, 31*, 93–117.

Breakey, J. (1997). The role of diet and behaviour in childhood. *Journal of Pediatric and Child Health, 33*, 190–194.

Briken, P., Habermann, N., Berner, W., & Hill, A. (2005). The influence of brain abnormalities on psychosocial development, criminal history and paraphililas in sexual murderers. *Journal of Forensic Sciences, 50*(5), 1–5.

Christiansen, K. O. (1977). A preliminary study of criminality among twins. In S. A. Mednick & K. O. Christiansen (Eds.), *Biological basis of criminal behavior.* New York: Gardner Press.

Cooke, C. R. (1945). Presidential address: The differential psychology of the American woman. *American Journal of Obstetrics and Gynecology, 49*, 457–472.

Crowe, R. R. (1972). The adopted offspring of women criminal offenders. *Archives of General Psychiatry, 27*, 600–603.

Crowe, R. R. (1974). An adoption study of antisocial personality. *Archives of General Psychiatry, 31*, 785–791.

Dabbs, J. M., Jr., & Hargrove, M. F. (1997). Age, testosterone, and behavior among female prison inmates. *Psychosomatic Medicine, 59*(5), 477–480.

DeLisi, M., Beaver, K. M., Wright, J. P., & Vaughn, M. G. (2008). The etiology of criminal onset: The enduring salience of nature and nurture. *Journal of Criminal Justice, 36*, 217–223.

Disney, E. R., Iacono, W., McGuie, M., Tully, E., & Legrand, L. (2009). Strengthening the case: Prenatal alcohol exposure is associated with increased risk for conduct disorder. *Pediatrics, 122*, e1225–e1230.

Dugdale, R. L. (1895). *The Jukes: A study in crime, pauperism, disease and heredity* (3rd ed.). New York: Putnam. (Original work published 1877)

Fishbein, D. H. (1990). Biological perspectives in criminology. *Criminology, 28*(1), 27–72.

Fishbein, D. H. (1994). Neuropsychological function, drug abuse, and violence: A conceptual framework. *Criminal Justice and Behavior, 27*(2), 139–159.

Fox, R. G. (1971). The XYY offender: A modern myth? *Journal of Criminal Law, Criminology and Police Science, 62*(1), 59–73.

Glueck, S., & Glueck, E. (1950). *Unraveling juvenile delinquency*. Cambridge, MA: Harvard University Press.

Glueck, S., & Glueck, E. (1956). *Physique and delinquency*. New York: Harper & Brothers.

Goddard, H. H. (1912). *The Kallikak family: A study in the heredity of feeblemindedness*. London: Macmillan.

Goring, C. (1972). *The English convict: A statistical study, 1913*. Montclair, NJ: Patterson-Smith. (Original work published 1913)

Goyer, P. F., Andreason, P. J., Semple, W. E., Clayton, A. H., King, A. C., Compton-Toth, B. A., et al. (1994). Positron-emission tomography and personality disorders. *Neuropsychopharmacology, 10*, 21–28.

Grantham-McGregor, S., & Ani, C. (2001). A review of studies on the effect of iron deficiency on cognitive development in children. *Journal of Nutrition, 131*(Suppl. 2), 649S–666S.

Guo, G., Roettger, M. E. & Cai, T. (2008). The integration of genetic propensities into social-control models of delinquency and violence among male youth. *American Sociological Review, 73*, 543–568.

Harris, J. R. (1995). Where is the child's environment? A group socialization theory of development. *Psychological Review, 102*, 458–489.

Hooten, E. A. (1939). *The American criminal: An anthropological study*. Cambridge, MA: Harvard University Press.

Horney, J. 1978. Menstrual cycles and criminal responsibility. *Law and Human Nature, 2*, 25–36.

Jacobs, P. A., Brunton, M., & Melville, M. M. (1965). Aggressive behavior, mental subnormality and XYY male. *Nature, 208*, 1351–1352.

Johnson, M. C., & Kercher, G. A. (2007). ADHD, strain, and criminal behavior: A test of general strain theory. *Deviant Behavior, 28*, 131–152.

Katz, J., & Chambliss, W. J. (1991). Biology and crime. In J. F. Sheley (Ed.), *Criminology: A contemporary handbook*. Belmont, CA: Wadsworth.

Kessler, S., & Moos, R. H. (1970). The XYY karyotype and criminality: A review. *Journal of Psychiatric Research, 7*, 164.

Knoblich, G., & King, R. (1992). Biological correlates of criminal behavior. In J. McCord (Ed.), *Facts, frameworks, and forecasts: Advances in criminological theory* (Vol. 3). New Brunswick, NJ: Transaction.

Knutson, K. (2008). *Breastfeeding associated with decreased childhood behavioral problems*. Paper presented at the annual meetings of the American Public Health Association, San Diego.

Kretschmer, E. (1925). *Physique and character*. New York: Harcourt, Brace. (Original work published 1921)

Kruesi, M., Casanova, M., Mannheim, G., & Johnson-bilder, A. (2004). Reduced temporal lobe volume in early onset conduct disorder. *Psychiatry Research: Neuroimaging, 132*, 1–11.

Liggio, F. (1969). Interference in the performance of mental activities due to the wrong diet which lacks the protein factor of animal origin and nervous disorders which are complementary and reversible. *Acta Neurologica, 24*, 548–556.

Liu, J., Raine, A., Venables, P. H., & Mednick, S. A. (2004). Malnutrition at age 3 years and externalizing behavior problems at ages 8, 11 and 17 years. *American Journal of Psychiatry, 161*, 2005–2013.

Lombroso, C. (1876). *L'uomo delinquente*. Milan: Hoepli.

Lozoff, B., Jimenez, E., Hagen, J., Mollen, W., & Wolf, A. W. (2000). Poorer behavioral and developmental outcome more than 10 years after treatment for iron deficiency in infancy. *Pediatrics, 105*, E51.

McCartan, L. M. (2007). Inevitable, influential, or unnecessary? Exploring the utility of genetic explanation for delinquent behavior. *Journal of Criminal Justice, 35*, 219–233.

Mednick, S. A., Gabrieli, W. F., & Hutchings, B. (1984). Genetic influences in criminal convictions: Evidence from an adoption cohort. *Science, 224*, 891–894.

Moffitt, T., & Silva, P. (1988). Self-reported delinquency, neuropsychological deficit, and history of attention deficit disorder. *Journal of Abnormal Psychology, 16*, 553.

Morton, L., Addison, H., Addison, R., Hunt, L., & Sullivan, J. (1953). A clinical study of premenstrual tension. *American Journal of Obstetrics and Gynecology*, 65, 1182–1191.

Neugebauer, R., Hoek, H. W., & Susser, E. (1999). Prenatal exposure to wartime famine and development of antisocial personality disorder in early adulthood. *Journal of the American Medical Association, 4*, 479–481.

Olweus, D. (1987). Testosterone and adrenaline: Aggressive antisocial behavior in normal adolescent males. In S. A. Mednick, T. Moffitt, & S. Stack (Eds.), *The causes of crime: New biological approaches.* Cambridge, UK: Cambridge University Press.

Plomin, R., DeFries, J. C., McClearn, G. E., & Rutter, M. (1997). *Behavioral genetics* (3rd ed.). New York: W.H. Freeman.

Pope, H. G., & Katz, D. L. (1990). Homicide and near-homicide by anabolic steroid abusers. *Journal of Clinical Psychiatry, 51*, 28–31.

Price, W. H., Strong, J. A., Whatmore, P. B., & McClemont, W. R. (1966). Criminal patients with XYY sex-chromosome complement. *The Lancet, 1*, 565–566.

Rada, R. T., Laws, D. R., & Kellner, R. (1976). Plasma testosterone levels in the rapist. *Psychosomatic Medicine, 38*, 257–268.

Rafter, N. H. (1992). Criminal anthropology in the United States. *Criminology, 30*(4), 525–545.

Raine, A., Brenna, P., & Mednick, S. A. (1997). Interaction between birth complications and early maternal rejection predisposing individuals to adult violence. *American Journal of Psychiatry, 154*, 1265–1271.

Raine, A., Buchsbaum, M. S., & LaCasse, L. (1997). Brain abnormalities in murderers indicated by positron emission tomography. *Biological Psychiatry, 42*, 495–508.

Raine, A., Buchsbaum, M. S., Stanley, J., Lottenberg, S., Abel, L., & Stoddard, S. (1994). Selection reductions in prefrontal glucose metabolism in murderers. *Biological Psychiatry, 36*, 365–373.

Rantakallio, P., Laara, E., Ishohanni, M., & Moilanen, I. (1992). Maternal smoking during pregnancy and delinquency of the offspring: An association without causation? *International Journal of Epidemiology, 21*(6), 1106–1113.

Rowe, D.C. (1995). *The Limits of Family Influence: Genes, Experience, and Behavior.* New York: Guilford Press.

Rubin, R. T. (1987). The neuroendocrinology and neurochemistry of antisocial behavior. In S. A. Mednick, T. Moffitt, & S. Stack (Eds.), *The causes of crime: New biological approaches.* Cambridge, UK: Cambridge University Press.

Rushton, J. P. (1995). *Race, evolution and behavior: A life history perspective.* New Brunswick, NJ: Transaction.

Satterfield, J. H., Satterfield, B. T., & Schell, A. M. (1987). Therapeutic interventions to prevent delinquency in hyperactive boys. *Journal of the American Academy of Child and Adolescent Psychiatry, 26*, 56–64.

Sheldon, W. (1940). *The varieties of human physique.* New York: Harper.

Sheldon, W. (1942). *The varieties of human temperament.* New York: Harper.

Sheldon, W. (1949). *Varieties of delinquent youth.* New York: Harper.

Volkow, N. D., & Tancredi, L. (1987). Neural substrates of violent behavior: A preliminary study with positron emission tomography. *British Journal of Psychiatry, 151*, 668–673.

Werbach, M. R. (1992). Nutritional influences on aggressive behavior. *Journal of Orthomolecular Medicine, 7*, 45–51.

Wilson, J.Q. & Herrnstein, R. (1985). *Crime and Human Nature.* New York: Simon and Schuster.

CHAPTER 4

PSYCHOLOGICAL THEORIES OF CRIME

At the time this text was going to print, the United States was in the midst of the 2009 economic crisis. Across the nation, unemployment was approaching or topping 10 percent, home foreclosures were at record levels, banks were failing and closing, and numerous industries were in dire financial straits. Although crime rates did not seem to be going up dramatically, people feared an expected spike in crime rates and were taking steps to try to protect themselves. Perhaps the most obvious move toward self-protection was the rapid growth in the number of people purchasing guns and applying for permits to carry concealed weapons. During the first half of 2009, the number of applications for permits to carry concealed weapons equaled or exceeded the number of such applications for the entire year of 2008 in many states (Adams, 2009). In order to be granted such a permit, however, individuals have to pass a criminal background check, pay a fee, be fingerprinted, and meet some basic criteria. A near-universal criterion in state laws that *disqualifies* an individual for such a permit is being "mentally defective." As the law in Colorado specifically states, an individual can be denied a permit to carry a concealed weapon if they have "been adjudicated mentally defective, which includes having been adjudicated incompetent to manage their own affairs, or has been commited to a mental institution." Individuals in the state of Indiana are required to report on the application whether they "have ever been treated for psychiatric health care or an emotional or mental illness." In simple terms, someone who has been determined to be mentally ill or intellectually impaired can be (and often is) deemed unable to carry a gun.

As the above discussion of requirements to obtain a permit to carry a gun clearly shows, concerns about psychological issues are closely tied to concerns in our society about criminality and violence. The assumption behind many of our laws and policies is that individuals with mental "deficiencies"—whether these be impaired intellect, mental illness, or emotional disturbances—are likely to be criminal and/or violent. Our laws, then, are designed to enhance community safety through actions such as denying such individuals the legal right to own and carry a gun.

Thinking about crime resulting from a psychological or mental issue is a commonsense approach, and one that at least on the surface appears to be very logical. After all, if an individual is not intelligent enough to understand what is happening in their community and among their family and acquaintances, or if the individual has a mental illness that prevents them from able to perceive and understand their own and other's actions correctly, it would only seem to make sense that some of the ways that such individuals react to their environment would include actions that are harmful to others and/or against the law. There are also a number of facts about known criminals that would seem to support the claims of some theorists who point to psychological deficiencies as the root cause of crime. First, for many years we have known that prison inmates have lower-than-average educational achievement and measured intelligence levels (Harlow, 2003). Second, we also have long known that there are significantly higher rates of mental illness among convicted criminals than among the general population (James & Glaze, 2006). Both of these facts are supportive of the claims that crime is caused by something "wrong" in the way an offender's mind works.

It is not only seemingly logical to think of crime as coming from mental problems, but such an explanation for crime is also comforting to many of us. If crime is the result of being "different" mentally, or having a mental illness, the rest of us can feel better about ourselves and see "criminals" as different from "us." This view also allows people to (perhaps incorrectly) believe that they can spot the "crazy people," and therefore avoid letting ourselves become vulnerable to them. Thinking about criminals as mentally ill (or having personality disorders or being less intelligent or having some other problem with their cognitive abilities) is an easy way to view criminals, especially for those of us who do not consider ourselves criminals.

Psychological explanations for crime are some of our most popular views and are regularly reinforced through media presentations about crime and criminals. Hundreds, if not thousands, of movies and television shows every year portray crime and criminals, with many of them showing offenders as deranged, psychotic, mentally ill, thinking in ways that do not fit with "normal" people, or just not as intellectually capable as law-abiding citizens. Just think about some of the television shows and movies you may have seen in the recent past. How often is the "bad guy" either implied or definitively shown to be suffering from some mental problem or abnormality of the brain? The deranged mental institution patient who breaks out and kills is a long-time staple of the horror movie industry. And, even though people may know that such media presentations are fictional, these images still have a significant influence on how they think about crime and criminals.

At the core of most psychological theories of crime is the belief that people who commit crimes are different, especially in the ways they (do and do not) think. This core idea is brought to life in specific theories that focus on how an individual's thought processes operate, how offenders perceive and react to their world, how they process, interpret, and use information, and whether there are identifiable problems in the way the individual's personality is organized and played out in social settings. More specifically, common approaches in the psychological perspective suggest that a criminal's personality is the result of poor or flawed socialization, or that the criminal is not able to (fully and accurately) understand the harms that come from crime, or that criminals are simply less intelligent than the rest of us (and therefore they cannot understand either that crime is wrong or that their behavior is inappropriate/criminal). Psychologically oriented theories attribute the problems and errors in criminals' thinking on (1) socialization experiences, (2) some traumatic event in the individual's past that caused him or her to process information and make decisions differently than the rest of us, or (3) some organic (e.g., physical) problem with the brain. A few psychologically based theories, however, are less concerned with the source of our ways of thinking and more interested in how criminal thinking is supported and maintained.

Whereas in the last chapter we saw that biological explanations for crime have been around in one form or another for well over 200 years, the psychological view of crime is a more recently developed perspective. It has only been in the last 100 or so years that a focus on the mind, thinking processes, and mental illness has been prominent in criminology. The main reason for this is that such an approach to crime was not possible until the field of psychology itself began to develop as a science, which was largely a development of the twentieth century.

One of the important things to keep in mind about psychological explanations for crime is that this perspective (much like the biological theories discussed in the previous chapter) provides the opportunity to see criminality as something that can be prevented, and that individuals who are criminal can be offered some form of treatment to "fix" the problems that lead them to crime. The science of psychology is concerned with both understanding how people think and perceive the world as well as offering forms of treatment and therapy to correct problems in individuals' thinking. Basically, according to psychological theories of why crime occurs, if in an individual we can identify a cause of crime that does not have a permanent or physiological basis, we should be able to engage experts to work with the individual to overcome problems in thinking or ways of processing and understanding information, and thereby prevent them from engaging in crime. This is the idea at the core of the psychological perspective of **rehabilitation.** Because psychological theories of crime assume that it is possible to identify problems in thinking or mental abilities that lead one to commit crime, these theories also assume that it is possible to provide some form of treatment to the individual that will allow them to control, manage, or overcome (e.g., be "cured" of) their mental problems. For criminal justice practice, then, those who adhere to a psychological explanation for crime tend to favor treatment of criminals, not punishment nor the elimination of offenders from society (like we saw in the discussion of biological theories).

Although certainly still influential and important, the time of greatest prominence for psychological approaches to crime—when society was most interested in trying to rehabilitate criminal offenders—was during the mid- to late-twentieth century. It was primarily from the 1950s to 1970s when the criminal justice system, especially prisons, emphasized rehabilitation and treatment. In the years after, this policy and practices in the criminal justice system moved away from a focus on treatment and instead emphasized punishment simply for the sake of punishment or incarceration as a way to incapacitate those considered to be a danger to the rest of us. The success of efforts to rehabilitate criminals is obviously contingent on the accuracy of theories regarding what types of mental problems are associated with crime, and the abilities of experts both doing diagnoses and providing treatments to accurately address an individual offender's problems. One of the primary reasons that the focus on rehabilitation lost prominence in the last two decades of the twentieth century is that the successes of rehabilitation efforts have been seriously questioned (Martinson, 1974). For some theorists and practitioners, the idea is that rehabilitation programs were less than optimally successful because psychological issues are not the cause of crime, while others have argued that the failures of rehabilitation have more to do with inaccurate diagnoses than poor theorizing. Regardless of the reason, today we continue to move further and further away from thinking about criminals as individuals with illnesses or deficiencies that can be corrected (despite the fact that we continue to find that known criminals on the whole have low levels of intelligence and high rates of mental illness). These theories, however, continue to make logical sense and to appeal to our commonsense understandings of social events.

In order to fully understand our current thinking about the role of mental illness and mental deficiencies in crime, it is important to trace the development of this line of thinking. This chapter will present and discuss some of the major and most influential psychological theories regarding crime, including psychoanalytic theory, criminal personalities and personality disorders, mental illness, mental deficiency (low intelligence), and life course perspectives for explaining crime and criminals.

PSYCHOANALYTIC THEORY

A **psychoanalytic perspective** on crime offers explanations based on the ideas of Freudian psychology and its theory of personality. The essential idea as it relates to why people commit crimes is that the three parts of the personality (id, ego, and superego) conflict with one another as a result of some early life trauma or deprivation. Alternatively, one part of the personality dominates the other two so strongly that various types of deviant behavior (including crime) are likely to occur. It is important to keep in mind, though, that Sigmund Freud actually wrote very little about how his theory could be used to explain crime. Instead, later followers of his ideas, most notably August Aichorn (1935), applied his concepts and perspective to the study of crime (discussed shortly).

One way that psychoanalytic theory stands apart from most other theories is in its assumption that people are basically antisocial from the start. Most theories seek to explain why some people commit crime, which is thought of as the exception and the "different" sort of behavior. However, criminological theory based on Freudian psychology suggests that we should expect people to be involved in crime, because people are not generally caring and concerned about others. Only a few other theories (as you will see in the remaining chapters) take this approach, including the ideas of some early biological theorists that we read about in the previous chapter.

Freudian psychology proposes that the personality is composed of three primary parts. The id is the part of the personality that represents the set of instincts and drives that need (or demand) immediate gratification. The id is the unsocialized part of the personality and is focused on seeking pleasure and fulfilling wants and needs for the individual. The superego represents opposite forces and serves as the social authority or conscience of the person. The superego is the part of the personality that seeks to have the person "fit in" with society and others and seeks acceptance and positive views of the person by others. The ego is the mediating force between the id and superego. The ego attempts to balance the drives of the id and superego and in a well-adjusted person provides balance and continuity for meeting personal needs and achieving social acceptance. The ego is the conscious part of the mind, and the id and superego represent the unconscious mind.

In order for a person to be well adjusted, socially productive, and functional, it is necessary for the id to be socialized and the superego to be kept in check. Crime, in the psychoanalytic perspective, is the result of one of three basic types of situations:

1. People are not appropriately socialized, and the id controls the personality and the individual's activities. The id drives these people to do as they please and be concerned only with their own desires. As a result, social rules and norms for behavior (including laws) may be ignored, go unnoticed, or simply be disregarded in pursuit of their own wants and needs.
2. People are overly socialized, with the superego dominating the personality and establishing behavior patterns. When this happens, the id is

so tightly held in check that it is all but silenced and repressed. If the id of these individuals leads them into actions and situations early in life for which they later feel guilty, the superego may lead them into situations and behaviors that will draw attention to them and lead them to be caught by authorities. This may be done so that the person is subsequently punished, because it is needed and deserved, which also alleviates the individual's feelings of guilt. This process is the primary cause of crime, according to Freud.

3. People who effectively (or overeffectively) repress their guilt over early misdeeds may eventually experience a breaking through of the repressed guilt and id, which will lead to an "explosion" of acting-out behavior. In essence, the id is so extremely held down that the pressure on it eventually gets so great that it pushes through and overtakes the superego (and ego) and runs wild. We can think of this as analogous to a balloon (with the air inside being the id) being pushed down more and more (the force outside being the superego). Eventually the id is under so much pressure that it breaks through both the pressure of the superego and the controlling force of the balloon (the ego) and explodes. The explosion is the socially unacceptable behavior (the crime).

Beginning in the 1930s, theorists began to offer significant revisions and applications of Freud's ideas and explanations for crime. These new interpretations and applications of basic Freudian psychology are generally referred to as neo-Freudian theory. The best known of the neo-Freudians for applying the psychoanalytic perspective to the explanation of crime is August Aichorn (1935). At the center of Aichorn's argument is that three factors must be in place in order for crime to emerge from the individual. First, the individual (via the id) needs to have a strong desire for immediate gratification. Second, the id must be in control and outweigh the influence of the superego and ego, making the primary drive of the individual self-gratification, not a concern with relationships the individual has with others. Third, the individual must have a lack of guilt regarding his or her actions. This third factor is a direct departure from Freud's principal view on crime, in which attempts to draw punishment to oneself to alleviate and satisfy guilt were central to most criminal actions.

Most neo-Freudian theorists have argued that criminals experience some type of damage to their ego early in life, as a result of which the id is strengthened and becomes overly dominant. When such a situation occurs, the individual's behavior is likely to become "out of control" and easily and often exceed the bounds of social norms or laws. In this way, the neo-Freudian approach is very similar to the ideas of theorists who identify the cause of crime as a personality disorder. These perspectives will be discussed in the next section.

PERSONALITY THEORIES

One commonly heard view about criminals is that "they just seem to think differently than other people." A view such as this is the foundation of the theories that focus on what some call a criminal personality, as well as theories that say particular types of disorders are the root cause of criminal behavior. When we talk about a criminal's **personality,** we are referring to a conceptually broad term that describes the totality of an individual's behavioral and emotional characteristics. Psychologists have defined personality in a wide range of specific ways, and different aspects of the concept are emphasized in various psychological theories. For our purposes, it is sufficient to recognize that criminological theories emphasize different aspects of personality as the reason for crime. Yet what all of the personality theories have in common is that they all focus on the idea that something about the process and contents of people's thinking patterns leads to crime. Some personality theorists point to a particular disorder or problem in the thought process of criminals as the reason for the individual's criminality. For other theorists, the overall way in which the individual processes and uses information is the cause of crime.

Among the more influential personality approaches to explaining crime is the idea of a **criminal personality** (Yochelson & Samenow, 1976). Yochelson and Samenow did psychiatric clinical work during the 1960s and 1970s with offenders in a psychiatric hospital, and through their work they identified common traits and ways of thinking that when taken together they called the criminal personality. While focused on the idea of personality, just as the psychoanalytic theorists did (and, in fact, both Yochelson and Samenow were trained in Freudian psychoanalysis), the work of Yochelson and Samenow directly refuted the neo-Freudians' claims that the causes of crime are deep-seated, inner aspects of the personality/mind. Rather, Yochelson and Samenow's approach largely relies on the assumption that criminal ways of thinking are something with which an individual is born, not something that develops due to social influences. A second core assumption of this approach is that the criminal personality is not a deterministic approach to crime, but instead serves to predispose individuals to criminal behavior. Criminal ways of thinking begin early in life, and such thought patterns lead individuals to make choices about their behavior—often decisions to commit crime.

The criminal personality theory provides a focus on the thought patterns that Yochelson and Samenow claimed were common among offenders. These thought patterns are called errors of criminal thinking; 52 different traits or processes are included in the overall view of the criminal personality. Generally speaking, criminal thinking tends to be concrete rather than abstract. As Yochelson and Samenow originally proposed their ideas, they claimed that all 52 errors of criminal thinking could be found in all offenders;

however, as you might imagine, research proved it very difficult (actually impossible) to apply all 52 criminal thinking errors to all criminal offenders. Included among these errors of criminal thinking are impulsivity, self-centeredness, chronic lying, perceiving property of others as available for anyone to take, lacking interest in education/school, being sexually active early in life and having a "great deal of sexual thinking," extreme optimism about the future and the risks of dangerous situations, getting great amounts of enjoyment from reckless and illegal activities, manipulativeness, being very energetic, having intense fear of pain and injury, feeling superior to others, having a very high self-image, and becoming extremely angry very quickly. These last four traits often combine when the individual feels that his or her self-image is being attacked or threatened; when such individuals feel threatened (whether that perception is accurate or not), they are likely to quickly become extremely angry and lash out at what they perceive is threatening them.

A somewhat similar approach is presented in the works of White and Walters, who present what is known as the **lifestyle perspective** (1989; Walters, 2002). However, instead of focusing narrowly on the idea of personality, these theorists emphasize what they term *lifestyle criminality*. Crime, in this theory, arises from how individuals live their lives, including the social environment they are in, the choices they make about their behaviors, and the thinking patterns they use to make choices in their everyday lives. Stated succinctly, "Lifestyle theory holds that crime is a consequences of the *conditions* to which a person is exposed, the *choices* he or she makes in life, and the *cognitions* he or she invokes in support of an evolving criminal pattern" (Walters, 2002, ix, emphasis in original).

In the view of these theorists, lifestyle is centered on thought processes, specifically the beliefs the individual holds and uses to interpret and make sense of his or her environment and situations. These belief systems are generated by a collection of four critical and interrelated factors: irresponsibility, self-indulgence, interpersonal intrusiveness, and patterns of social rule breaking. Irresponsibility is the general unwillingness of individuals to see themselves as accountable for their behavior. Instead, they see their behavior as the result of other factors, especially social factors that are beyond their control or influence. Self-indulgence is the tendency of criminals to put their own desires and wants ahead of any concerns about others or considerations of how their actions may negatively affect others. Interpersonal intrusiveness refers to how criminal individuals pursue their self-indulgent goals, ignoring and acting without regard to the rights of others. Finally, because of their disregard for others, dedication to pursuing their own desires, and being unwilling to see that their behaviors are the result of their own choices, criminal behavior is often the result.

Important in understanding how these cognitive factors influence decisions about behavior is the position that reality—the way the world is known to exist and how we experience it—is a socially constructed phenomenon. Individuals all experience the world somewhat differently, and we strive to maintain our belief systems about how our world is put together. We do this through our considerations of schematic representations, or tools for interpreting and making sense of things: attributions, outcome expectancies, efficiency expectancies, goals, values, and thinking styles.

It is also important to consider that "measurements" of personality, or evaluations to determine an individual's "type" of personality or the characteristics of one's personality, are based on tests developed and used by psychologists. Perhaps the most common of these is the Minnesota Multiphasic Personality Inventory (MMPI). This test, commonly used in clinical settings, court cases, correctional classification decisions, and many other types of settings, was originally developed in the late 1930s and then completely revised in 1989. The test is actually a compilation of a number of scales that measure various personal components using true/false questions. The patterns of responses to items on each scale are used to determine the presence and strength of various components of an individual's personality. Included in the MMPI scales are hypochondriasis (falsely believing that one is experiencing a medical condition), depression, paranoia, masculinity/femininity, schizophrenia, and social introversion. The scoring and interpretation (which requires a specially trained psychologist) of the results of an individual's MMPI is often used for making decisions about the diagnosis and treatment of mental illnesses and personality disorders. While tests such as the MMPI are obviously very useful in these types of situations, not all theories and assumptions about the role of personality in crime rely on such scientific approaches to measurement and assessment. Instead, many personality-based theories of crime draw on assumptions and commonsense understandings of people's thought processes, behavior, beliefs, and approaches to life.

The similarities between the White and Walters approach and that of Yochelson and Samenow (1976) are in the central role that the offender's thought processes and ways of thinking plays in explaining crime. Very similar to what Yochelson and Samenow argued, although discussed using different terms, lifestyle criminality is about faulty thinking. This way of thinking in turn leads to decisions about behavior that may well be criminal.

The lifestyle criminality view suggests that criminal events are initiated by the individual's making choices about behavior based on irresponsibility, self-indulgence, and a desire to have power and control over others. The choice to commit a criminal act is supported and reinforced by the individual's being able to attribute his or her behavior to some external factors, not to making a decision. In explaining how a psychology of disresponsibility encourages and supports the criminal actions of individuals, White and Walters explain that a criminal individual "uses the criminologic excuses and myths we have so conveniently provided for him to justify a lifelong pattern of victimizing others" (1989, pp. 259–260). These excuses and myths are the "various psychological hypotheses, complex nonanswers, and inaccurate 'common sense' explanations" (White & Walters, 1989, p. 260) that they claim dominated criminological theory and thinking in the late twentieth century.

The reliance on excuses and justifying one's behavior with reference to existing (but supposedly erroneous) theories serves as a coping strategy for the criminal offender. This is a conscious process, not an unconscious one. Criminals simply live lifestyles that center on disavowing themselves of responsibility for their actions, and the resources for doing this are provided by society. But in the end, "crime is not caused by heredity, drugs and alcohol, psychological trauma, lack of job skills, or social class/status. Rather, crime is caused by criminals, pure and simple" (White & Walters, 1989, p. 260). Lifestyle criminality theory says that individual criminals decide to commit crime, and because of their ways of thinking about themselves, their environments, and what society has suggested about "causes" of crime, these people can be expected to continue committing crimes.

MENTAL ILLNESS

Thinking of criminals as having a **mental illness** is another commonsense, and for most of us logical, way to understand why some people commit crimes and others do not. Mental illnesses, although sometimes difficult to actually diagnose and treat, are usually thought of as misdirected and error-ridden ways of thinking and perceiving the world. There are many different forms of mental illnesses, ranging from relatively minor and occasional disturbances in our emotions and thought processes to severe forms, known generally as psychoses.

We know that many convicted criminal offenders have some type of mental illness. Estimates range from one in five to three in five prison inmates having some form of mental illness. Interestingly, a much smaller number of prison inmates are reported as receiving mental health care or services (Beck & Maruschak, 2001). Eighty-nine percent of state prisons provide mental health services to inmates, with 13 percent of all inmates receiving some form of counseling/therapy and 10 percent being prescribed psychotropic drugs. The two most common mental illnesses associated with criminality are schizophrenia and antisocial personality.

Schizophrenia

Schizophrenia comes in several different forms, varying in degree of severity. Generally speaking, people with schizophrenia are withdrawn and apathetic in their behavior and affect (emotional display). Common symptoms include being unable to remain focused on ideas or behaviors, having delusions, hallucinating (including the stereotypical portrayal of schizophrenics as "hearing voices"), and being unable to follow through with a logical progression or relation of ideas. Schizophrenia is among the most serious and debilitating form of mental illnesses. Sadly, there is no known cause or cure for schizophrenia (American Psychiatric Association, 1994).

The common way most people think of those with schizophrenia is that they are "out of touch with reality." Because their perception of reality significantly differs from that of "normal" people, those with schizophrenia often have (possibly severe) difficulties functioning in the social world. They do not interpret the environment, other people, or others' actions in the ways that most people do. Consequently, they behave in ways that do not fit with the smooth flow of social settings, and their behaviors often are unpredictable and violate social norms and laws.

Schizophrenia has been linked with a variety of crimes, including both violent and property offenses. However, only a small portion of convicted violent offenders are diagnosed as schizophrenic, and only a very small percentage of people with schizophrenia are arrested for violent crimes. Researchers (Philips, Wolf, & Coons, 1988) report that no more than 2 percent of all people with schizophrenia are arrested for violent crimes, and at most 2 percent of annual violent crime arrests are of people with schizophrenia. Other, more recent, research though suggests that schizophrenia may be a major factor in criminal behavior. A study of 1,056 Swedish mental patients followed up for 10 years after diagnosis shows that across the variety of mental illness patients, those diagnosed as schizophrenic had the highest rate of criminal behavior, with violent offenses being especially prevalent (Belfrage, 1998).

Antisocial Personality

Antisocial personality disorder, also commonly referred to as either *psychopathy* or *sociopathy* (although these are distinct diagnoses), is a state in which individuals experience a significant lack of development of moral order or ethics. A sociopath/psychopath is an individual often referred to as without a conscience. In simple terms, these individuals are self-centered and do not display feelings of guilt or remorse for any of their actions. While common assumptions may hold that psychopaths are rare in society, it has also been shown that there is a relatively stable 1–3 percent of the adult population that are diagnosable as psychopaths/sociopaths (see Walsh & Wu, 2008). However, in prison populations, the rate is typically estimated to be several times higher. This suggests that individuals with antisocial personalities are very likely to be involved in crime (and also very likely to be caught).

Individuals who do not experience feelings of empathy, guilt, or remorse have few checks on their behavior. The primary distinguishing factor of the psychopath is that they have heavily muted emotions, which allows them to focus exclusively on pursuing their own self-centered goals (Walsh & Wu, 2008). Sociopaths, in contrast, are considered to be products of adverse environments, which affect their autonomic nervous system and neurological development. These changes to their physiological functioning are what is central to their distinction from psychopaths. As the name for this disorder implies, "sociopaths" are products of social environments.

The term *antisocial personality* is actually a legal/clinical label that is used to encompass both psychopaths and sociopaths. The disorder of antisocial personality is defined by the American Psychiatric Association (1994, code 301.7) in the *Diagnostic and Statistical Manual of Mental Disorders* (*DSM*) as follows:

> There is a pervasive pattern of disregard for and violation of the rights of others occurring since age 18 years, as indicated by three (or more) of the following:

> Failure to conform to social norms with respect to lawful behaviors as indicated by repeatedly performing acts that are grounds for arrest.

> Deceitfulness, as indicated by repeated lying, use of aliases, or conning others for personal profit or pleasure, impulsivity, or failure to plan ahead.

> Irritability and aggressiveness, as indicated by repeated physical fights or assaults reckless disregard for safety of self or others.

> Consistent irresponsibility, as indicated by repeated failure to sustain consistent work behavior or honor financial obligations.

> Lack of remorse, as indicated by being indifferent to or rationalizing having hurt, mistreated, or stolen from another.

As this definition makes clear, individuals diagnosed as such are likely to do things that "normal" personality individuals would never consider actually doing. To understand how this is likely to occur, also consider the following list of characteristics that have been associated with the antisocial personality (Cleckey, 1964):

1. The psychopath is charming and of good intelligence.
2. He is not delusional or irrational.
3. There is an absence of nervousness or psychoneurotic manifestations.
4. The psychopath is unreliable.
5. He is insecure, and he is a liar who can be trusted no more in his accounts of the past than in his promises of the future.
6. He is lacking in either shame or remorse.

7. His antisocial behavior is inadequately motivated. He will commit all kinds of misdeeds for astonishingly small stakes, and sometimes for no reason at all.
8. His judgment is poor, and he never learns from experience. He will repeat over and over again patterns of self-defeating behavior.
9. He is pathologically egocentric, and has no real capacity for love, although he often simulates affection or parental devotion.
10. His emotions are shallow.
11. The psychopath lacks insight to a degree usually found only in the most serious mental disorders.
12. He does not respond to consideration, kindness, or trust.
13. Drunk or sober, but especially drunk, he is guilty of fantastic and uninviting behavior.
14. Psychopaths often threaten suicide but almost never carry it out.
15. The psychopath's sex life is impersonal, trivial, and poorly integrated.
16. The psychopath shows a consistent inability to make or follow any sort of life plan.

Additionally, and directly linked to the high rate and frequency of criminality of the psychopath, four characteristics are common in this population. First, these individuals tend to have a lower arousal level, meaning they get biologically less aroused than "normal" individuals when they encounter what others would perceive as frightening, threatening, or alert-raising stimuli. Second, psychopaths have less ability to learn and benefit from conditioning. Third, psychopaths are also highly impulsive, and fourth, they tend to display low levels of anxiety. Each of these factors is associated with involvement in crime, because these conditions suggest that an individual is not likely to be deterred by threats of punishment or sanction, is not anxious about the possibility of being detected/caught, tends to act on impulse, and is not alarmed by situations that would typically be alarming. Psychopaths often perceive a need for physical stimulation or excitement, because many things are not experienced as exciting for them. This, coupled with a lack of remorse or feelings of guilt, impulsivity, and poor judgment, is likely to lead them to situations in which they commit crimes.

Antisocial personality is linked to an increased likelihood of being involved in violence (Coid, Yang, & Roberts, 2006), especially among repeat offenders (Weizmann-Henelius, Viemero, & Eronen, 2004). The importance of psychopathic characteristics for the commission of crimes, although not all forms, has been shown in a recent study of adolescent females (Vaughn, Newhill, Delisi, Beaver, & Howard, 2008). In this study, the authors looked at whether or not individual girls had characteristics of psychopathy and their involvement in violence, theft, and drug abuse. There were clear links between narcissism (an excessive interest in one's own comfort, important, abilities, and appearance) and a "carefree nonplanfulness" and involvement in violence and theft. However, drug abuse was not linked with psychopathic characteristics. When we think about the characteristics of psychopaths listed above, these relationships make sense. Impulsivity, an inability to learn from experience, and low levels of anxiety about their behavior would seem to logically be linked to being violent and stealing things that one would want. However, the idea that psychopaths also experience a need for physical stimulation or excitement would correspond well with their lower likelihood of abusing drugs. Drug abuse is usually about moderating experiences and emotions, which is not something that psychopaths necessarily need or want to achieve.

The lack of emotional reactions and recognition and the link to criminal involvement among psychopaths has been suggested as most importantly being hinged on a lesser consciousness of the feeling of shame (Holmqvist, 2008). Specifically, when individuals have higher scores on measures of psychopathy, there is a correspondingly lower consciousness of shame for their actions and less degree of empathy exhibited for victims. The consequence is that while pursuing their own interests almost exclusively, these individuals fail to feel bad about their actions and either are unaware of or disregard the consequences of their actions for others.

Interestingly, there are other qualities that are common among psychopaths but appear to be only indirectly tied to criminal behavior. One recent study has reported that psychopaths with higher levels of IQ are those who engage in the most severe forms of violence (Johansson & Kerr, 2005). The most interesting point here is that this finding is directly contrary to what is usually seen among criminals; typically criminality and violence is associated with lower levels of IQ. However, it is important to keep in mind that psychopaths, as highly self-interested individuals, are typically seeking to gain things that they want, and may have to plan their behavior, or at least be able to quickly and efficiently devise a plan for getting to their goals. This idea is also supported by research (De Barros & De Padua Serafim, 2008) that suggests that individuals with antisocial personality may be more likely than other mentally ill criminal offenders to be involved in property crimes, because of the need for property crimes to often require a great degree of planning than violent offenses. Second, psychopaths are also more likely than the general population to be left handed (approximately 90 percent of the population is right handed) (Mayer & Kosson, 2000). This anomaly among psychopaths is believed by some researchers to be due to a lack of symmetry of the brain, but this has not been definitively proven. So, what does this mean? Perhaps it would be useful to think about whether you have any really smart, left-handed friends who do not get frightened or threatened easily and often seem to act on impulse. Do they also tend to be more involved in crime or other antisocial types of activities? If so, there would appear to be a good chance that your friend is at least somewhat psychopathic.

Interest in the link between antisocial personality and criminality has experienced a revival in the last couple of decades. Most of this research has been conducted in other countries, most notably in the Scandinavian countries (Hodgins, Mednick, Brennan, Schulsinger, & Engberg, 1996; Modestin & Ammann, 1996; Tiihonen, Isohanni, Rasanen, Koiranen, & Moring, 1997). This line of thinking is being revived due to the findings of these researchers that there is a statistically significant link between schizophrenia/antisocial personality and violence/crime.

One important area where a focus on antisocial personality disorder has been applied is that of domestic violence (or intimate partner violence). Men who engage in domestic violence have higher rates of antisocial personality disorder than men in the general population (Peek-Asa, Zwerling, & Young, 2005). Fals-Stewart, Leonard, and Birchler (2005) studied the relationship between antisocial personality disorder and domestic violence but added controls for men's alcohol consumption. They show that while the long-known relationship of alcohol consumption and intimate partner abuse is a powerful explanation for men's violence, this relationship does not appear to apply to men with antisocial personality disorder. For men with antisocial personality disorder, there is no connection between drinking and minor forms of violence—these men are violent without the contributing effects of alcohol. However, when looking only at severe forms of violence against intimate partners, alcohol does play a more important role for men with antisocial personality than for those without antisocial personality (Fals-Stewart et al., 2005). Others have shown that women who engage in domestic violence have high rates of antisocial personality (as well as high rates of previous victimization, depression, panic disorder, and substance use) (Stuart, Moore, & Gordon, 2006).

It is important to note here, though, that not all people with one or some of these characteristics are necessarily criminals. We can all think of people we know who do not get very excited by most things that excite others (have a low level of arousal), do not seem to learn very well from experience (are not very susceptible to conditioning), or are either very impulsive or have generally low levels of anxiety. Do not assume that just because a friend has one, or even all, of these characteristics, he or she is a sociopath. Many "normal" people have some or all of these characteristics. The point is not that all people with these characteristics are sociopaths, but that most sociopaths have these characteristics.

Sociopaths/psychopaths are unique among the criminals addressed by psychological theories in that they tend not to be affected by treatment (American Psychiatric Association, 1994). This condition is often thought of as a biological condition, and for this reason it is difficult (if not impossible) to change. However, there simply is no confirmed cause of this disorder, and in fact, DSM-IV states, "The cause of this disorder is unknown, but biological or genetic factors may play a role." Note that this is not definitive, only speculative.

All of this also means that in some ways a focus on psychopathy/sociopathy is a biologically grounded theory; in fact, some textbooks discuss this perspective in a chapter on biological theories. This is not the only psychological perspective that has direct ties to biological perspectives, however. In fact, there are a number of ways in which biology and psychology either overlap or influence one another. While we have strong evidence that mental illness is connected to criminal behavior, we also are discovering that mental illness is more common among persons with certain biological characteristics. For example, at least one set of researchers have shown that babies born with very low birth weight are as much as four times more likely to have mental health problems by the time they are adolescents (Botting, Powls, Cooke, & Marlow, 1997). In this way, the biological factor of low birth weight is a factor in increased likelihood of future criminal behavior, but this is an indirect effect through the intervening issue of mental illness.

Mental illness, and the problems that arise from mental illnesses, also may be affected by biological factors as well as a number of environmental and contextual factors. There is an old wives tale that says that "things get weird," including the occurrence of more crime, based on the phases of the moon. Usually this means that when there is a full moon, we can expect odd things to occur. While this appears to be little more than a myth, there actually is research that shows that variations in barometric air pressure are associated with the number of people who experience psychiatric symptoms (and, therefore, engage in more criminal behavior). A team of psychiatrists studied the daily barometric air pressure, humidity, and wind speeds and correlated these with psychiatric emergency room visits and violent acts in the community (Schory, Piecznski, Nair, & El-Mallakh, 2003). They found that when the barometer drops, there is a significant increase in both emergency room visits for psychiatric problems and violence in the community. This is explained by the idea that as the barometric pressure drops, there are changes in the blood flow to the brain. So, while it might not be the case that the full moon brings out the strangeness in people, it might be that the "heavy air" brings out violence.

Not all psychological theories are tied to biological factors; other theories are more clearly and unequivocally psychological in focus and content. As we will see in the next section, some psychological theories focus exclusively on what is in one's mind and how the mind operates.

Affective Disorders

In addition to documentation of the relationship between schizophrenia and antisocial personality with crime and aggression, there is also a growing body of research that suggests that other forms of mental illness, including affective disorders (most notably depression) may be linked with crime and delinquency. Work being done with juvenile delinquents has shown that there is a higher-than-expected (based on general population statistics) rate of depression and mania among such youth. One study (Knox, King, Hanna, Logan & Ghaziuddin, 2000) focused on a sample of 13- to 17-year-olds who were seen in a clinical setting for a diagnosis of depression. Among these teens the researchers found that 70 percent had a history of frequent verbal aggression at home, 24 percent reported frequent physical aggression against family members, and 14 percent had been arrested due to their aggressive actions. There were no significant differences between the aggression levels and frequency for males and females. But, what is very interesting about this study is that when asking the parents of these depressed teenagers to describe or estimate the aggressive actions displayed by their children, the parents significantly underestimated how aggressive their children were and how often their children were aggressive. Other researchers have also reported similar findings.

Additional research also shows that juvenile delinquents are more likely than nondelinquents to suffer from substance use and affective disorders (Pliszka, Sherman, Barrow, & Irick, 2000). Looking at the issue from the other direction, another study reports that more than twice as many depressed juveniles display angry, aggressive outbursts (48 percent vs. 21 percent) than nondepressed teens (Fava et al., 1996). Others (Modestin, Hug, & Ammann, 1997) have shown that a history of hospitalization for depression is a significant and powerful indicator of criminality.

MENTAL DEFICIENCIES

One of the longest-standing and perhaps most popular beliefs about crime is that criminals are simply not as smart as other people. In many ways this is a very commonsense belief, and one that has been popular with theorists, criminal justice authorities, and the general public for many years. Researchers who investigate the idea that **mental deficiency** is the cause of crime tend to show a relationship between measured intelligence levels and being a known criminal offender. One large-scale study reviewing research from four nations (Australia, Dubai, New Zealand, and the United States) reported that intellectual disabilities were found at rates at least equal to or exceeding the level of impaired intelligence for prison inmates (Fazel, Xenitidis, & Powell, 2008).

The first significant and influential research suggesting that intelligence and crime are related appeared almost a century ago (Goddard, 1914). Simply looking at the IQ scores of prison inmates led to the conclusion that between one-quarter and one-half of inmates were unable to "manage their affairs" due to lack of mental ability. However, controversies arose almost immediately, with other researchers suggesting that low intelligence is common among many populations, not just prisoners. Although we might be able to interpret intelligence in several ways, examination of IQ scores for enlisted soldiers during World War I showed that they had lower levels of measured intelligence than prisoners. The most popular conclusion reached from this was that there were problems with the measurement instruments and procedures, not that these populations were necessarily seriously lacking in mental abilities.

In the 1960s and 1970s, numerous researchers (Hirschi & Hindelang, 1977; Reiss & Rhodes, 1961; Sorensen & Mednick, 1977; West & Farrington, 1977) reported results showing that juvenile delinquents and adult criminals had lower IQ scores than noncriminals. Researchers and theorists have argued that intelligence is more influential and important in criminality than other factors including social class, parental education levels, and, for some researchers, race. However, the strength and size of this relationship depends on how one chooses to do the research. As Hirschi and Hindelang (1977) showed, when IQ scores are related to official crime records, there is a fairly strong relationship. But when low IQ and self-report data on criminality (which tends to show more crime) are linked, the relationship is signifi cantly smaller and weaker. The research done in the years since Hirschi and Hindelang's conclusions, however, has been mixed, with a significant body of research supporting a link between IQ and crime and a significant body of work showing just the opposite. Some believe that low IQ means that a person has a diminished ability to conduct moral reasoning (Wilson & Hernstein, 1985), which in turn establishes the context for criminal activities.

Those who adhere to the idea that crime is a result of low IQ often cite the idea that intelligence has a strong genetic link. Horn (1983) examined IQ levels of adopted children and showed that they had more similarity to the IQ scores of the children's biological rather than adoptive families (other research has, however, suggested that IQ is not "primarily" biological). Based on these findings it can be argued that intelligence is at least to some degree inherited, and if minority groups tend to have lower IQ scores, this would suggest that they might be (as a group) mentally inferior to white people. And since minority groups in the United States have higher rates of delinquency and criminality, this "natural" factor is seen by some as a logical explanation.

The movement to view crime (among other "weaknesses" or deficien cies) as a result of low intelligence was a central component to a philosophi cal and political movement in the United States that was prominent during the late 1800s and the first two decades of the twentieth century called the **eugenics** movement. The push of the eugenics movement was to stop the hereditary lines of inferior people by forcibly sterilizing individuals deter mined to be genetically (as indicated by low-intelligence levels) inferior. As numerous scholars have historically detailed (see Haller, 1963; Rafter, 1997), this movement claimed to be for the public good, but was largely a political movement to control society's poor and "different" people. Not only did the eugenics movement push for forced sterilization of many criminals but also argued for strict quotas on immigration of people from other nations. The idea was that in order to "keep America strong," the government had to limit the number of inferior people. This meant that poor, undereducated, and criminally involved groups of people should be numerically limited. As we might expect, there were strong racial undertones to this movement, as those who made decisions about who and what behavior constituted inferiority were wealthier, more educated white people (primarily men too).

For several decades, various state statutes allowed judges to sentence some categories of offenders to be forcibly sterilized. While these practices were largely abandoned by the middle of the twentieth century, in some jurisdictions and for some types of offenses, such practices have periodically reemerged in the late twentieth and early twenty-first century.

Although the eugenics movement claimed to show statistical evidence that criminality—via low-intelligence levels—was passed on through heredity, these thoughts and practices have always had a racist tone. One of the reasons for the decline in influence of the eugenics movement is the fact that there has not been a consistent view on how intelligence may or may not play a role in explaining crime rates across racial groups. Controversies have raged for many decades about how IQ may or may not be related to race. One of the milestones in this debate occurred in 1967 during a speech by the Nobel Prize–winning physicist William Shockley, who suggested to the National Academy of Sciences that differences in IQ between blacks and whites could explain differences in poverty and crime rates. It is true that nonwhite (especially black) people have higher rates of arrest, conviction, and incarceration in our society. We also know that on the tests that are commonly used to measure intelligence, whites tend to score (as a group) about 15 points higher than blacks. However, this pattern needs to be viewed with caution. Some critics believe that intelligence tests are culturally biased (Greenfield, 1997; Mercer, 1972; Sternberg, 1986). This means that the difference in test scores may have more to do with the actual content of these tests, and not reflect true differences in intelligence.

Robert Gordon (1987) tied these issues together and argued (and supported his claims with research data and results) that the higher rates of delinquency and criminality among black boys and men could best be explained by differences in intelligence levels. Even when controlling for issues such as urban/rural location, income, educational level, and occupation, intelligence levels were the most powerful explanations for high rates of crime among black males. And it is not only whites and blacks for whom intelligence is important in explaining crime rates. Gordon went on to argue that the low rates of delinquency/crime for Japanese, Chinese, and Jews could be explained by their IQ scores, which are slightly higher than those of whites. The reason for the controversial reception of such research and thinking is clear: Gordon was seen as suggesting that black males were simply not as intelligent (as a group) as their white counterparts.

The controversy about the idea that minorities are more likely to be involved in crime due to a lower level of intelligence was revived and enhanced in the mid-1990s with the publication of **Richard Hernstein and Charles Murray's** controversial book *The Bell Curve* (1994). In this book, Hernstein and Murray went into great detail in examining the research linking intelligence measures and criminality. Based on their review of the research at the time, they argue that the IQ–crime link is among the "most powerful" predictors of criminality. They then link this idea to research showing that minorities (especially African Americans) are more involved in crime (at least according to official statistics) and have lower average IQ scores. This argument was interpreted by many as powerful and convincing evidence for the "natural" involvement and high rates of criminality among African Americans. However, this was also seen as a highly racist and inflammatory interpretation of research by many others. The critics of this perspective argue that Hernstein and Murray overlook many of the other social contributors to both measured IQ and criminality, and their interpretation is seen as justifying very repressive and unfair responses to crime.

There are a number of problems with mental deficiency theories. First is the often-shown fact that intelligence tests are culturally biased. Gordon's (1987) research is a good example of research findings that can probably be explained (at least in part) by the fact that minority individuals are at a disadvantage on intelligence tests due to cultural biases. Another problem with mental deficiency theories is that while it may be true that known criminal offenders show lower IQ scores, this could easily be attributed to a number of factors other than a greater propensity of less-intelligent people to commit crimes. First, we could attribute this "fact" to what we know about intelligence levels being correlated with poor school performance, and in turn low levels of commitment to pursuing education and abiding by the expectations that school puts on behavior.

We also need to keep in mind that what we think we see as intelligence may really be a consequence of individuals missing particular pieces or types of knowledge. People who have difficulties learning some types of materials—those with learning disabilities—may appear to be "less smart" to some of us, although their innate abilities are really not any different. Interestingly, although the research does not suggest a difference in measured intelligence level, at least one study has shown that there is a correlation between sex offending and learning disabilities (Langevin & Curnoe, 2008). Additionally, there is research evidence to suggest that low levels of intelligence interact with psychopathy (as discussed above) in producing sex offenders. Beggs and Grace's (2008) study of child molesters showed that while low levels of intelligence by itself was not a predictor of child molestation, low measured intelligence levels and high scores on a psychopathy scale were related to a four-time greater likelihood of being convicted of sexual offending. And, learning disabilities are not necessarily innate factors: biological factors may play important roles in learning disabilities. Children who grow up in environments with high levels of pesticides have been shown to have higher levels of learning disabilities, eye–hand coordination, and short-term memory (Guillette, Aquilar, Soto, & Garcia, 1998). Similarly, not only are cognitive functioning levels linked to criminality, delinquency, alcohol/drug abuse and poor language skills, but so too are low levels of cognitive functions connected to a deficiency of iron in the body (Bruner, Joffe, Duggan, Casella, & Brandt, 1996). The latter connection is especially strong in adolescent girls and young women, as significant amounts of iron are lost from the body in menstrual blood. Here again, we see the overlap of biological and psychological theories.

However, these are not the only difficulties with applying mental deficiency theories to the explanation of crime. It might also be possible to attribute a large number of known offenders' having low intelligence test scores to these offenders' simply being more likely than "smarter" criminals to get caught. Remember, a research that shows a particular trait as common among known offenders or prison inmates does not look at all criminals, but only a rather small subset of offenders.

LIFE COURSE THEORIES

Not all psychologically oriented theories for explaining crime focus exclusively on processes and events internal to the individual. Although early psychological theories located the cause of crime wholly in the mind of the individual (through mental structures, intelligence, or mental illnesses), more recent, and most would argue more influential, psychologically oriented theories have expanded to look at how the thinking and decision making of individuals (e.g., their psychological processes) are influenced by factors external to the mind and body. Recognizing that individuals' type and degree of involvement in crime changes over time and that the external influences to which individuals are exposed to likely change over time, theorists have come to focus on both changes, identifying and accounting for them in their explanations. Life course theories emphasize that there are different issues at the core of why persons do, and then often later do not, engage in criminal behavior. And, many of the life course theories emphasize aspects of our social world that influence individuals' behaviors (especially their involvement in crime). These outside influences are important for how they affect the thinking and decisions of individuals—psychological issues.

One of the greatest contributions of life course theory is that it provides ways—through an emphasis on variations in criminal activity across age, in the development of a "criminal career" and through looking at trajectories across time for individuals and groups—for explaining if, how, and why involvement in crime varies throughout an individual's life. This means that life course theory has brought to front and center the variable of age in explaining crime, with an emphasis on if, how, and why various experiences at different ages may help to explain crime. There are several significant strands of thinking that are subsumed under the general label of life course theories. In this section, we discuss the theoretical perspectives offered by five theorist groups: Catalano and Hawkins, Sampson and Laub, Moffitt, LeBlanc, and Thornberry and Krohn. Each of these theorist teams has suggested important advances in applying life course theory to the explanation of crime, with all of them beginning from a common ground. At the core, life course criminology is concerned with three primary issues—the development of offending behavior, identification of risk factors unique to individuals of varying ages, and the effects of experienced events on how one's offending behavior does or does not develop. Where life course theory advances prior perspectives is in the central attention devoted to risk factors and experienced life events. Previous scholars and theorists have discussed the idea of a "criminal career," with attention to if and how an individual's offending behavior evolved over time, but paid little attention to the issues that may or may not guide or steer the development of behavior.

The first important variation on life course theory (although not the first to actually be proposed) is that of Richard Catalano and J. David Hawkins (1996). They refer to their perspective as the social development model and emphasize the degree to which individuals are bonded to society through socialization agents. Individuals make rational decisions weighing the costs and benefits of their actions, with their decisions influenced by how well they are bonded to society. Central to the development of criminal behavior is whether the individual has more of prosocial or antisocial bonding to society. Prosocial bonds are built through involvement and the skills that lead to positive, prosocial behavior and rewards. Antisocial bonding arises from opportunities (which are acted on) for negative types of behavior. All persons are assumed to be exposed to both prosocial and antisocial opportunities and experiences, and whichever bonding is stronger for the individuals is the one that is likely to guide their lives and behaviors.

Central to the risk factors (as opposed to protective factors, which promote resilience to crime) are poverty, impulsiveness, poor child-rearing experiences, and criminal parents and delinquent peers. Early life experiences (through the elementary school years) are primarily guided by the influence of family members, and from the period of roughly middle school through adulthood the individual is most strongly influenced by peers. Criminal offending may begin early in life if one's family is supportive of antisocial behaviors, or it could begin in adolescence if despite positive influences of family the individual becomes enmeshed with peers who are supportive of criminal ways. The ways the individual thinks and processes the potential costs and benefits of criminal actions are psychological issues that arise from those to whom one is exposed and how strongly one becomes bonded to those influences.

A second version of life course criminology is seen in the work of Robert Sampson and John Laub (1993, 1995). This version of life course theory makes primary later-in-life events, and emphasizes that criminal offending is more or less driven by self-interest. However, especially during later adolescence and adulthood, the individual may be exposed to positive influences that hold them back from (e.g., desisting from) engaging in crime. In this view, there are stable individual differences in some underlying propensity for criminal ways and also relatively stable informal social controls at work. It is these informal social controls (such as investment in one's family life and job/career) that are the important factors for explaining decisions to do (or not do) criminal activities. In the Sampson and Laub view, our development as criminals or noncriminals is heavily influenced by our bonds to aspects of life that would be harmed or lessened if we embarked on criminal ways.

Our third version of life course theory is that originally proposed by Terrie Moffitt, a psychologist. In this view, Moffitt argues that there are two basic varieties of young offenders: those who engage in crime/deviance only while they are young (adolescents) and those who begin their criminality during adolescence and remain involved in criminal activities. The reasons for engaging in crime are direct outgrowths of neuropsychology and developmental psychology. The central tenet of Moffitt's (1993) theory is that those individuals who first engage in criminal behavior during childhood/adolescence and either continue with such behaviors throughout life (life course persistent offenders) can be differentiated psychologically from those who begin criminal behavior early but then refrain from such activities as they move into adulthood (adolescence-limited offenders). Moffitt suggests that it is encouraging that the majority of young offenders are in fact adolescence-limited offenders; those who are criminal throughout their lives are in the minority. If you think about your own activities and those of your friends, this perspective has a great deal of face validity. We can all think of teenagers who engaged in a range of illegal and just simply "wrong" behaviors, but later graduated out of these types of activities when they entered into adulthood.

In the Moffitt-inspired view, the factors associated with initiating criminal behavior include hyperactivity, low verbal ability, and impulsiveness. Also, it is important to consider the biological issues of psychological abnormalities that arise from maternal drug abuse, poor prenatal nutrition, or exposure (either pre- or postnatal) to toxic substances that can influence neurological development. Development of psychological structures (and consequently our thinking and behavior) is presented as influenced by early childhood experiences, including our receipt of affection, stimulation, and nutrition. One of the areas where offenders' lack of or slow neurodevelopment is most clearly and strongly seen is in the area of verbal skills. When an individual lacks verbal skills, there is strong association with learning difficulties, problem solving, self-expression, memory, and difficulties in forming and maintaining social relationships. All of these are issues that we fairly easily see would be likely to be related to difficulties in social situations and subsequent delinquent or criminal behavior. These types of problems are especially likely for children and adolescents. Again, think back to your time in elementary or middle school. Can you remember any of your classmates who just seemed "slow" and had trouble making friends? Did they fit some of these characteristics? Were they left out of your friendship groups? Did they try to find ways to either get accepted or get back at others? Did any of these kids end up being involved in delinquency or other types of "bad behavior"?

For the adolescence-limited offenders, peer influence and pressure is often an important factor in their delinquency and deviance. Moffitt argues that this is really not the case for the life course persistent offenders, as they are somewhat "outsiders" to begin with, so they really do not have as much susceptibility to peer pressure. Life course persistent offenders also continue to experience the difficulties associated with their slower or lower levels of psychological development, and these issues remain more influential over their behavior than their peers. The issues of peer pressure, and who amongst our peers is likely to have what type and how much influence on our criminal ways are all issues we will address later in this book. For now, think of these issues as ones that we can understand from our experience and common sense, and remember that according to some theories (such as Moffitt's version of life course theory) peer pressure is not always a significant issue. Instead, we may have to include how our neurological/psychological systems develop and are (or are not) influenced by physiological and social factors. And, just because someone's psychological state may lead them into criminal ways, they are not necessarily going to be criminal forever. Our behavior (usually) evolves and changes over time, just as our psychology evolves and changes over time (and situations).

The fourth version of life course theory is that proposed by Marc LeBlanc (1997). This is a view including bonding to society as well as personality development, modeling of prosocial and antisocial behavior by others, and internal and social constraints. The instigation of criminal ways according to LeBlanc is a product of both individual factors that influence personality development and social environment issues (such as economics and community influence) which set the stage for various types of bonds to society to be established. This perspective suggests that criminal behavior is initiated when bonds to society are weak, when the individual is exposed to more antisocial models of behavior and when the individual perceives and experiences few (if any) intervening constraints on behavior from outside socialization/control agents. It is possible for those who begin criminal activities to be diverted from such actions if they are exposed to significant new influences and become closely connected to others modeling noncriminal, prosocial activities. When the life course is composed of continuity in antisocial influences, the decisions of the individual to engage in criminal activities are also most likely to be continuous over time.

Terence Thornberry and Marvin Krohn (2001) focus their explanation for crime on how other aspects of life (such as attachment of parents and commitment to school/work) develop and change (or not) over time. In this regard, Thornberry and Krohn's version of life course theory emphasizes that the causes of criminal activity vary across different stages of life, as the individual both encounters new and different opportunities and reflects on his or her past behaviors as successful or not. Thornberry and Krohn contend that an additional difference in this perspective from other life course approaches is that not only do other life events influence one's level of involvement in crime, but the individual's changing level of involvement in crime influences (e.g., strengthen or weaken) connections to other aspects of life.

Thornberry and Krohn argue that early-onset delinquents differ from later-onset delinquents/criminals only in degree, not in any fundamental way. Early-onset offenders are likely to see the greatest degree of continuity in their criminal ways, as these behaviors have influences on the opportunities and potential prosocial and antisocial influences to which the individual is exposed. Those individuals who initiate criminal ways later in life are more malleable and susceptible to change because they do not have strong antisocial influences built up by their own actions throughout life.

Looking at the life course theory perspective in a global way, this explanation for crime is based on (and reinforces) the following 10 "facts" about crime (Farrington, 2003):

1. The prevalence of criminal offending peaks in the last teen years, primarily between ages 15 and 19.
2. The peak age for the onset of criminal offending is between the ages of 8 and 14.
3. When individuals initiate their criminal activities at an early age, this is predictive of a coinsistent and continuous criminal career.
4. The patterns of criminal offending (and just about all forms of antisocial behavior) show continuity from childhood to the teenage years and to adulthood.
5. Only a relatively small proportion of the society commits a large proportion of all crimes (those referring to as "chronic offenders").
6. Criminal offending careers tend not to include a high degree of specialization in only one form of criminal activity.
7. Involvement in criminal activity is symptomatic of involvement in a wide range of antisocial behaviors (noncriminal deviance).
8. Criminal activities committed through the late teen years tend to be committed with others, while criminal activities of adulthood are more likely to be completed alone.

9. The explanations offered by younger (e.g., adolescent and teen) offenders are widely variable, while the explanations offered by adult offenders typically emphasize utilitarian motives.

10. The onset of different types of criminal offenses typically vary with age; "lesser" offenses tend to appear earlier, with a building of severity. As new forms of criminal activities are initiated, they are added to the individual's repertoire of crimes, not replacements for those crimes already being committed. When specialization in offending occurs, it tends to appear only during the adult years.

CONCLUSION

Psychological theories for explaining crime and criminals are popular with many people because they both seem to make a great deal of sense intrinsically and clearly argue that criminals are distinct and different from the rest of us. Criminals not only act differently from "good people" but also think differently, have an illness, are just not as smart as the rest of us, or have been exposed to things in life that steer them into crime—things that the rest of us have not internalized in the same ways.

There are two major problems with psychological theories. First, many of the ideas and concepts that are used by these theories are things that are difficult—if not impossible—to validate scientifically. Much of our thinking about "personality" and what is (or is not) present in the minds of people, whether they be criminals or not, is based on beliefs and hypotheses (theories). Whereas other types of theories such as biological theories or the social theories we will look at later in the book can have their factors and influences validated (e.g., we can find whether a genetic difference is or is not present), we simply cannot know whether most of the psychological factors the theories in this chapter point to are "real" and present in individuals. This means that a major problem with psychological theories is that they frequently are just not that effective at explaining why crime happens. This does not mean that crime is not caused by psychological processes and patterns, but most of our current psychological theories do not enable us to very effectively explain crime.

Despite the problems inherent in psychological theories, identifying the cause of crime as a psychological difference is something that many of us find comforting and one that makes sense to us. We know that crime is wrong and socially unacceptable behavior. Therefore, to say that people who commit crime either have some type of brain defect or mental illness helps us to feel better about ourselves. To say that criminals have something "wrong" with them that leads them to interpret their environments, other people, themselves, and even reality in different—and "wrong"—ways clearly and cleanly distinguishes the good people from the bad people.

Psychological theories also offer a great deal of promise to criminal justice officials, treatment providers, and the general public for hopes of ending crime. If we can identify what it is in a person's thinking or mental abilities that leads him or her to break the law, we are well on the way to taking steps to both try to correct that cause of crime and to protect ourselves from these people. Psychology as a science offers much hope both for helping people effectively and efficiently cope with their problems and for curing, correcting, or rehabilitating those whose behavior is socially unacceptable. It is in these ways that both biological and psychological theories share a number of commonalities. Both sets of theories work from the premise that there is an identifiable problem in a criminal's body or mind. Where the problem is, how it affects behavior, and why the problem exists will vary across different theories and theorists, but the reason for the problem in thinking and behavior is not the primary concern. Instead, the promise offered by these types of theories is that something can be done to remove, control, or cure the problem in thinking and perception, and this in turn will likely lead to law-abiding behavior.

Psychological theories, especially those such as life course criminality that include the idea that criminal offenders make choices about their actions, emphasize that crime can be controlled. The best way to control crime is through some type of treatment program that focuses on addressing the problems in thinking, reasoning, and interpretation of the individual or curing/controlling their criminally oriented thought patterns. These theories, however, do not say that punishment and official criminal justice system processing is without merit. When individuals make choices about their behavior, they need to be held accountable for those decisions. Accountability, however, should be combined with treatment, not seen as separate and distinct.

Proponents of psychological theories of crime, then, tend to be optimistic about the possibility for addressing society's crime problem. Although we may not currently have highly effective treatments—although some would argue that drugs, counseling, education, and behavior modification in fact are effective treatments—we know what issues need to be addressed. If we at least know what needs to be fixed, removed, or changed, we can experiment with various treatments until we find out what does work. This is among the more optimistic views of crime in our society.

SUMMARY

Psychological theories for explaining crime focus on the content, processes, and outputs (e.g., decisions) of people's minds and thinking and are occasionally linked to biological/physiological issues. The thought processes, parts of the personality, presence and form of mental illnesses, levels of intelligence, ways that our neurological/psychological systems develop, and how differing exposure to social influences differentially impact our thinking and decisions are the main foci of psychological theories. Psychological theories have been very popular over the years, largely because they appeal to us in a commonsense sort of way and allow us to see criminals both as "different" from us and as people who can be helped through some sort of treatment. Psychological theories that are most prominent today (life course theory perspectives) also draw on social influences of behavior, yet maintain their emphasis that crime is the result of thinking and decisions.

KEY TERMS

antisocial personality   a form of mental illness in which individuals have no sense of empathy, are highly impulsive, seek immediate gratification, and often harm or take from others in criminal ways; sometimes referred to as sociopathy or psychopathy

criminal personality   the idea of Yochelson and Samenow that some people experience errors of thinking that lead them to have an outlook on the social world that accepts and endorses criminal behavior

eugenics   a movement of the early twentieth century that sought to impose sterilization of criminals and quotas on immigration for "inferior" people in an attempt to rid society of weak, less-intelligent, and criminal groups of people

lifestyle perspective   an idea proposed by White and Walters that the thought processes and beliefs of individuals are guided by the factors of irresponsibility, self-indulgence, interpersonal intrusiveness, and patterns of social rule breaking, which lead the individual to make choices in social settings that produce criminal behavior

mental deficiency   a mental state in which a person is lacking (usually) in intelligence compared to normal or most people; used to explain crime by saying

that those with less intelligence are more likely to violate social rules/laws

mental illness   a diagnosable disturbance to the emotional or perceptual abilities of an individual that leads the person to experience interactions and social environments differently from healthy people

personality   a conceptually broad term that refers to the totality of an individual's behavioral and emotional characteristics

psychoanalytic perspective   an idea first proposed by Sigmund Freud; based on the idea that three parts of the personality—id, ego, and superego—compete and conflict and the result is our mental state and behaviors

rehabilitation   processes and activities that seek to change a criminal into a non-criminal

Richard Hernstein and Charles Murray   authors of *The Bell Curve*, a mid-1990s book that argued that minorities' greater involvement in crime could be explained by the "natural" differences in measured intelligence

schizophrenia   a mental illness that leads the person to perceive reality differently, to be socially withdrawn, and to react to social stimuli in inappropriate ways, including violently/criminally

DISCUSSION QUESTIONS

1. Which personality theory seems the most plausible for explaining crime? Why?

2. What is it about mental illness that would lead such people to be involved in crime?

3. How is a link between low levels of intelligence and criminal involvement explained? Why would a less intelligent person be more likely to be a criminal?

4. How are the various life course theory perspectives similar and different from one another? What are the core ideas of life course theory perspectives?

5. What are the policy implications of relying on psychological theories for explaining crime?

REFERENCES

Adams, H. J. (2009, July 6). Gun permits surge since Obama election. *Louisville Courier Journal*, pp. A1.

Aichorn, A. (1935). *Wayward youth*. New York: Viking Press.

American Psychiatric Association. (1994). *Diagnostic and statistical manual of mental disorders* (4th ed.). Washington, DC: Author.

Beck, A. J., & Maruschak, L. M. (2001). *Mental health treatment in state prisons, 2000*. Washington, DC: Bureau of Justice Statistics.

Beggs, S. M., & Grace, R. C. (2008). Psychopathy, intelligence, and recidivism in child molesters: Evidence of an interaction effects. *Criminal Justice and Behavior, 35*, 683–695.

Belfrage, H. (1998). A ten-year follow-up of criminality in Stockholm mental patients: New evidence for a relation between mental disorder and crime. *British Journal of Criminology, 38*(1), 145–155.

Botting, N., Powls, A., Cooke, R. W., & Marlow, N. (1997). Attention deficit hyperactivity and other psychiatric outcomes in very low birth weight children at 12 years. *Journal of Child Psychology and Psychiatry, 38*(8), 931–941.

Bruner, A. B., Joffe, A., Duggan, A. K., Casella, F., & Brandt, J. (1996). Randomised

study of cognitive effects of iron supplementation in non-anaemic iron-deficient adolescent Girls. *The Lancet, 347*(9033), 992–996.

Catalano, R. F., & Hawkins, J. D. (1996). The social development model: A theory of antisocial behavior. In J. D. Hawkins (Ed.), *Delinquency and crime: Current theories*. Cambridge: Cambridge University Press.

Cleckey, H. (1964). *The mask of sanity* (4th ed.). St. Louis, MO: Mosby.

Coid, J., Yang, M., & Roberts, A. (2006). Violence and psychiatric morbidity in a national household population – A report from the British household survey. *American Journal of Epidemiology, 164*, 1199–1208.

De Barros, D. M., & De Padua Serafim, A. (2008). Association between personality disorder and violent behavior pattern. *Forensic Science International, 179*(1), 19–22.

Fals-Stewart, W., Leonard, K. E., & Birchler, G. R. (2005). The occurrence of male-to-female intimate partner violence on days of men's drinking: The moderating effects of antisocial personality disorder. *Journal of Consulting and Clinical Psychology, 73*, 239–248.

Farrington, D. P. (2003). Developmental and life-course criminology: Key theoretical and empirical issues – the 2002 Sutherland award address. *Criminology, 41,* 221–255.

Fava, M., Davison, K., Alpert, J. E., Neirenberg, A. A., Worthington, J., O'Sullivan, R., et al. (1996). Hostility changes following anti-depressant treatment: Relationship to stress and negative thinking. *Journal of Psychiatric Research, 30*(6), 459–467.

Fazel, S., Xenitidis, K., & Powell, J. (2008). The prevalence of intellectual disabilities among 12,000 prisoners – A systematic review. *International Journal of Law and Psychiatry, 31,* 369–373.

Goddard, H. H. (1914). *The Kallikak family: A study in the heredity of feeblemindedness.* New York: Macmillan.

Gordon, R. (1987). SES versus IQ in the race-IQ-delinquency model. *International Journal of Sociology and Social Policy, 7,* 30–96.

Greenfield, P. M. (1997). You can't take it with you: Why ability assessments don't cross cultures. *American Psychologist, 52,* 1115–1124.

Guillette, M. M. M., Aquilar, M. G., Soto, A. D., & Garcia, I. E. (1998). An anthropological approach to the evaluation of preschool children exposed to pesticides in Mexico. *Environmental Health Perspectives, 106*(6), 347–353.

Haller, M. (1963). *Eugenics: Hereditarian attitudes in American thought.* New Brunswick, NJ: Rutgers University Press.

Harlow, C. W. (2003). *Education and correctional populations.* Washington, DC: Bureau of Justice Statistics.

Hernstein, R. J., & Murray, C. (1994). *The bell curve.* New York: Free Press.

Hirschi, T., & Hindelang, M. (1977). Intelligence and delinquency: A revisionist review. *American Sociological Review, 42,* 571–586.

Hodgins, S., Mednick, S. A., Brennan, P. A., Schulsinger, F., & Engberg, M. (1996). Mental disorder and crime: Evidence from a Danish birth cohort. *Archives of General Psychiatry, 53,* 489–496.

Holmqvist, R. (2008). Psychopathy and affect consciousness in young criminal offenders. *Journal of Interpersonal Violence, 23,* 209–224.

Horn, J. M. (1983). The Texas adoption project: Adopted children and their intellectual resemblance to biological and adoptive parents. *Child Development, 54,* 268–275.

James, D. J., & Glaze, L. E. (2006). *Mental health problems of prison and jail inmates.* Washington, DC: Bureau of Justice Statistics.

Johansson, P., & Kerr, M. (2005). Psychopathy and intelligence: A second look. *Journal of Personality Disorders, 19*(4), 357–369.

Knox, M., King, C., Hanna, G. L., Logan, D., & Ghasiuddin, N. (2000). Aggressive behavior in clinically depressed adolescents. *Journal of the American Academy of Child and Adolescent Psychiatry, 39*(5), 611–618.

Langevin, R., & Curnoe, S. (2008). Are the mentally retarded and learning disordered overrepresented among sex offenders and paraphillics? *International Journal of Offender Therapy and Comparative Criminology, 52,* 401–415.

LeBlanc, M. (1997). A generic control theory of the criminal phenomenon: The structural and dynamic statements of an integrative multilayered control theory. In T. P. Thornberry (Ed.), *Development mental theories of crime and delinquency* (Advances in Criminological Theory, vol. 7). New Brunswick, NJ: Transaction.

Martinson, R. (1974). What works? Questions and answers about prison reform. *Public Interest, 10,* 22–54.

Mayer, A. R., & Kosson, D. S. (2000). Handedness and psychopathy. *Neuropsychiatry, Neuropsychology, and Behavioral Neurology, 13*(4), 233–238.

Mercer, J. (1972, September). IQ: The lethal label. *Psychology Today,* 44–47.

Modestin, J., & Ammann, R. (1996). Mental disorder and criminality: Male schizophrenia. *Schizophrenia Bulletin, 22,* 69–82.

Modestin, J., Hug, A., & Ammann, R. (1997). Criminal behavior in males with affective disorders. *Journal of Affective Disorders, 42,* 29–38.

Moffitt, T. E. (1993). Adolescence-limited and life-course-persistent antisocial behavior: A developmental taxonomy. *Psychological Review, 100*(4), 674–701.

Peek-Asa, C., Zwerling, C., & Young, T. (2005). A population-based study of reporting patterns and characteristics of men who abuse their female partners. *Injury Prevention, 11*, 180–185.

Philips, M. R., Wolf, A. S., & Coons, D. J. (1988). Psychiatry and the criminal justice system: Testing the myths. *American Journal of Psychiatry, 145*, 605–610.

Pliszka, S. R., Sherman, J. O., Barrow, M. V., & Irick, S. (2000). Affective disorder in juvenile offenders: A preliminary study. *American Journal of Psychiatry, 157*(1), 130–132.

Rafter, N. H. (1997). *Creating born criminals.* Urbana: University of Illinois Press.

Reiss, A., & Rhodes, A. L. (1961). The distribution of delinquency in the social class structure. *American Sociological Review, 26*, 720–732.

Sampson, R. J., & Laub, J. H. (1993). *Crime in the making: Pathways and turning points in life.* Cambridge, MA: Harvard University Press.

Sampson, R. J., & Laub, J. H. (1995). Understanding variability in lives through time: Contributions of life-course criminology. *Studies on Crime and Crime Prevention, 4*, 143–158.

Schory, T. J., Piecznski, N., Nair, S., & El-Mallakh, R. S. (2003). Barometric pressure, emergency psychiatric visits, and violent acts. *Canadian Journal of Psychiatry, 48*, 624–627.

Sorensen, L. K., & Mednick, S. A. (1977). A prospective study of predictors of criminal: Intelligence. In S. A. Mednick & K. O. Christiansen (Eds.), *Biosocial basis of criminal behavior.* New York: Gardner Press.

Sternberg, R. J. (1986). *Intelligence applied: Understanding and increasing your intellectual skills.* New York: Harcourt Brace Jovanovich.

Stuart, G. L, Moore, T. M., & Gordon, K. C. (2006). Psychopathology in women arrested for domestic violence. *Journal of Interpersonal Violence, 21*, 376–389.

Thornberry, T. P., & Krohn, M. D. (2001). The development of delinquency: An interactional perspective. In S. O. White (Ed.), *Handbook of youth and justice.* New York: Plenum.

Tiihonen, J., Isohanni, M., Rasanen, P., Koiranen, M., & Moring, J. (1997). Specific major mental disorders and criminality: Twenty-six year prospective study of the 1966 Northern Finland birth cohort. *American Journal of Psychiatry, 154*, 840.

Vaughn, M. G., Newhill, C. E., Delisi, M., Beaver, K. M., & Howard, M. W. (2008). An investigation of psychopathic features among delinquent girls: Violence, theft, and drug abuse. *Youth Violence and Juvenile Justice, 6*, 240–255.

Walsh, A., & Wu, H.-H. (2008). Differentiating antisocial personality disorder, psychopathy, and sociopathy: Evolutionary, genetic, neurological, and sociological considerations. *Criminal Justice Studies, 21*, 135–152.

Walters, G. D. (2002). *Criminal belief systems: An integrated-interactive theory of lifestyles.* Westport, CT: Praeger/Greenwood.

Weizmann-Henelius, G., Viemero, V., & Eronen, M. (2004). Psychological risk markers in violent female behavior. *International Journal of Forensic Mental Health, 3*, 185–196.

West, D. J., & Farrington, D. P. (1977). *The delinquent way of life.* London: Heinemann.

White, T. W., & Walters, G. D. (1989). Life style criminality and the psychology of disresponsibility. *International Journal of Offender Therapy and Comparative Criminality, 33*, 257–263.

Wilson, J. Q., & Hernstein, R. J. (1985). *Crime and human nature.* New York: Simon & Schuster.

Yochelson, S., & Samenow, S. E. (1976). *The criminal personality: Vol. 1. Profile for change.* New York: Jason Aronson.

■ ■ ■ ■ ■

CHAPTER 5

THE SOCIAL ECOLOGY
OF CRIME

Herschel Scriven was a youth minister at the Greater Mount Ephraim Church in Rochester, New York. According to police reports, he had just attended a stage showing of "The Lion King" and had dropped off a child at the child's home when he put his car into reverse to leave. At that moment, three African American men, ranging from 19 to 21 years old, were robbing someone when Scriven's car suddenly backed up between them and their victim. Antwon Owens, one of the robbers, then shot the minister in the head. As a result of the gunshot wound, Scriven died four days later.

This story reports a single tragedy; however, Scriven's murder is also part of a larger pattern. For instance, this particular homicide was one of approximately 50 that happen each year in Rochester. Rochester in fact has the highest homicide rate in the state of New York. One would think that Rochester is a dangerous place, but, interestingly, the city's metropolitan region is filled with many areas where violence is almost unheard of. The Rochester Institute of Technology has a Center for Public Safety Initiatives, and one of the tasks for this center is to map the crimes that occur in the city for the Rochester Police Department. These maps show that the violence, and quite a lot of crime, is mostly concentrated in several pockets surrounding the downtown area. Is there something about these relatively few parts of Rochester that promote so much crime?

Most theories of crime cannot answer this question except to say, perhaps, that luck placed people with criminal tendencies in these areas. Such theories are more concerned with individuals and why some commit crime and others do not. These theories focus on causes of crime like neuropsychological deficits, a person's peer group, mental defects, or ineffective deterrence. Over the years, researchers have found interesting patterns that suggest that this approach does not give us the full story about what is responsible for crime. The consideration of *place* as a cause of crime, rather than people, is the central focus of this chapter. The idea that place might have something to do with crime is—believe it or not—something we have known for a long, long time. In the 1830s, two Belgians, Andre-Michel Guerry and Adolphe Quetelet, used some of the first national arrest statistics ever collected and discovered that some regions of France had more problems with crime than other areas (Bierne, 1993). Guerry and Quetelet were also the first to relate regional crime rates to a variety of social factors such as area poverty and education levels. They found, for instance, that areas with less poverty had more property crime (committed, disproportionately, by the poor and unemployed living there), suggesting that the greater wealth in these regions offered more inducements to offend. Moreover, these regional variations appeared to be stable over long periods of time: Areas with the highest arrest rates always tended to have them, and arrested offenders everywhere (in the 1830s as well as today) tended to be young, male, and poor, although the level of involvement in crime by these individuals varied considerably based on area.

All this tells us something about the characteristics of high-crime areas, but we need theory to sort out what facts are actually important and which ones are deceptive. In this chapter, we will look at two leading explanations for how the characteristics of *places* or *situations* might influence levels of criminal activity. While the two theories presented here are different from each other in significant respects, their common thread is the de-emphasis of the individual or group and an emphasis on the setting. Although criminologists have been aware that certain contexts seem to have unusually high levels of criminal activity since Guerry and Quetelet's work, not until the twentieth century did sociologists begin to give much attention to places as possible breeding grounds for crime. This chapter focuses on two major perspectives for looking at places and situations: social disorganization theory and routine activities theory.

SOCIAL DISORGANIZATION THEORY
Basic Features of Social Disorganization Theory

Social disorganization theory contains several assumptions that distinguish it from many of the other perspectives that we describe in this text. First, this theory is a "macro theory." That is, social disorganization theory attempts to explain why some *communities* have higher *crime rates* than others, rather than why some *individual people* commit crime and others do not. The theories described in the chapters on control theory, biological theories, and psychological theories explain crime among individual people and are sometimes referred to as "micro theories." Second, the theory assumes that social organization—schools, churches, businesses, police, informal networks of friends and neighbors, and government—when functioning normally enables a community to deal with problems of crime. In other words, the theory assumes that effective neighborhood crime control is not really a matter of individual choice, in which an individual decides to clean up an area (because the theory assumes that individuals all want less crime), but instead that a collective effort on the part of the community is necessary. Third, crime in an area is not primarily due to "defective" people with biological or psychological abnormalities, but happens in communities of otherwise normal people who live where larger social institutions have failed. Social disorganization theory, then, is a theory that links an area's high crime rates to the inability of the community to organize in order to act collectively. Moreover, the theory attempts to explain why institutions within a community are unsuccessful.

As individuals, we often have a hard time thinking about how things operate at the macro (community or societal) level, so we digress for a moment to explain this important point. Our personal perspective and experience is entirely focused on the individual (or "micro") level, so it seems much easier and more natural for us to look at individuals and pick out what is wrong or different about them that leads them into criminal activity than it is to argue that the community one lives in may have some responsibility for supporting high levels of crime. To say that a place or situation matters when it comes to crime causation would be to suggest that you or I could become criminals were we in that same context. This is an uncomfortable admission that many people might not be quite prepared to make. But what if our environment can in fact structure our lives in significant ways, meaning that we don't have completely unfettered freedom to make choices? Our location at a certain place might cut off choices we could have made, as well as open the door for other opportunities. For instance, try looking for a job in a community where no jobs are available because an economic downturn led companies to scale back their operations and close offices. In this case, no action the individual can take will successfully result in a job. But we tend not to think in this way. Most of the time we think that individuals are completely responsible for their circumstances—that our failure to find a job is because we are not trying hard enough, or are just uncompetitive, or not skillful enough at interviewing. The broader influences associated with the characteristics of the community in which we live might be very much relevant to crime as to finding a job, whether we're even aware of these influences or not.

The Intellectual Origins of Social Disorganization Theory

Social disorganization theory did not emerge suddenly out of nowhere. It was during the early twentieth century that we first find the ideas that contributed in recognizable ways to modern social disorganization theory. The early social disorganization theorists, it turns out, were originally concerned with the issues of their own times. Specifically they lived in the midst of a huge shift in the population from rural to urban areas, and so they wanted to understand the effects (good or bad) that followed these significant changes.

The City of Chicago was one of the places where rapid population growth was very much evident. Between the incorporation of Chicago in the 1830s and 1910, the population of the city had grown from 4,000 people to more than two million, and this growth was associated with the influx of people caused by growing industry and immigration (Palen, 1981).

It is in this context where two University of Chicago sociologists, Professors Robert Park and Ernest Burgess, began their work. Both were steeped in the principles of human ecology, and so it was natural for them to extend these ideas to what was happening in Chicago. The notion of "social ecology" held that people struggled for survival in a community of mutual dependence. At first, this seems a rather odd way of describing the conditions of human life. Many of us get the idea that people compete with each other for desirable things, but what does "mutual dependence" even mean? In fact, the idea of mutual dependence might be something that we're so used to that we do not really think about how much our quality of life depends on it. But consider, for instance, whether you could survive for long if you were entirely on your own. That is, how would you rate your odds of survival and prosperity in a world where you would have to find your own food, make your own clothing, provide your own shelter, and see to your own defense? Our guess is that the struggle for survival would be difficult indeed. However, we generally can rely on grocers, clothing stores, builders, and the police to help meet many of our needs. And they, in turn, depend on others to support them (including us, as we support them via sales, taxes, and fines). These networks of interdependence are the basis of communities. Communities would be impossible, or unnecessary, if we did not have to rely on others. So, to recap, two principles that will be of particular interest to social disorganization theory are (1) the idea that people compete for resources and (2) that people exist in a world of mutual dependence.

Park and Burgess also explored how human communities can change over the years. Just as some plants can invade a clear field and in turn be succeeded by new species, the same can happen in human neighborhoods. A given neighborhood might, for a time, be dominated by a particular ethnic group but eventually be succeeded by another group. This pattern of invasion, dominance, and succession extends out from the center of the city—that is, the immigrant "invaders" do not start at the outer edge of the city, but they do try to work outward.

Why do the immigrants establish themselves in the middle of the city and work outward? The fact that most of the new immigrants were destitute had something to do with it. Since they lacked the wherewithal to successfully compete for the best places to live, they were obliged to begin their new lives where they could, which was in the least expensive parts of the central city. These areas were inexpensive to live in for a very good reason: They were in terrible condition and had an abundance of decay and disorder.

Thus, the poorest parts of a city had "social disorganization." Burgess in fact developed a five-zone model of an urban area, with each zone radiating outward from the least desirable city core area and generally becoming more affluent farther out. We will present this model in greater detail in a moment. Burgess believed that crime and other social problems, such as disease, would be highest in the areas where the newest (and poorest) residents in the city lived.

The Location of Crime

Clifford Shaw and Henry McKay (1942), two researchers at the Institute for Social Research located in Chicago, were the ones who developed the connection between social disorganization and crime. Shaw and McKay looked at how crime was spread across Chicago during the 1930s and 1940s. They took a map of Chicago and stuck pins wherever crimes occurred as well as at the home addresses of the juvenile delinquents, in order to see if crime and criminals seemed to cluster in the city core and become less dense the closer one got to the city edge. If place did not matter, then the pins would be scattered all over the map with no real pattern to their location. They found instead something interesting: Crime indeed tended to be concentrated in the slum areas, which were located toward the center of the city, and the concentration of the pins representing crimes grew less the farther away one went from Chicago's center. Place mattered.

Moreover, the pattern appeared to be persistent over time. In other words, the central city zones always had more crime than city zones farther out. But why? Most people would conclude that the high-crime areas are merely teeming with criminal people. Back in the early twentieth century, in fact, it was common for people to view the then unpopular ethnic groups, such as the Irish, the Sicilians, and the Poles, as criminal. Think of the movie *Gangs of New York,* for instance, which depicted the violence and disorder in lower Manhattan's Five Points between newly arrived Irish immigrants during the 1860s. But what might you conclude about these groups if you were to learn, as Shaw and McKay did, that crime appeared to be concentrated in certain areas no matter who lived there? When the slums teemed with Irish, there was high crime; but the Irish eventually moved out and were succeeded by another ethnic group, and the crime seemed to stay put and not follow the Irish out. In other words, the Irish seemed to abandon their reputed criminal tendencies as soon as they left the slums. Shaw and McKay thus provided further evidence that place, and not necessarily "defective" people or cultures, seemed to contribute to the crime problem.

The question then turned to why place mattered. Shaw and McKay looked at how the parts of Chicago differed from each other, using the "concentric zone model" of Burgess that we mentioned earlier. This model broke Chicago into five distinct zones radiating outward from the city's center:

Zone I: (inner city): central business district

Zone II: transitional zone (where the high crime is)

Zone III: working-class zone

Zone IV: residential zone

Zone V: (suburbs): commuter zone

We will describe each of the zones, but will focus primarily on Zone II (the transitional zone) because crime is most likely to occur here. At least during the years in which Shaw and McKay were doing their research, the central business district (Zone I) was located in central Chicago and contained numerous railroads, slaughterhouses, large factories, and stockyards for hogs and cattle. Given the noise, smell, and general unpleasant scenery associated with such industry, one might reasonably suppose that few people would voluntarily choose to live in this area, so the central business district is almost exclusively industrial.

While industry is concentrated in the central business district, any further industrial expansion would necessarily come at the expense of the surrounding residential area. This meant that many neighborhoods located close by the central business district were changing from residential use to business use— houses were demolished to make way for factories and other places of business. For that reason, this area—Zone II—is called the **transitional zone.** The homes still standing in the transitional zone tended to be older and in poor condition, as landowners intended to sell their properties to businesses and thus saw little advantage in doing any renovation. After all, what sense would there be in repairing a house when the expense of the repairs would exceed the gain realized from selling the property? If you live in an apartment or rental unit where the landlord never bothers to maintain the place, you probably have a good idea of the appearance of homes and apartments in the transitional zone. If decaying and obsolescent buildings is not bad enough, people living in the transitional zone also have to put up with being close to the unpleasing features of the slowly—but inexorably—encroaching central business district. As any real estate agent will tell you, the value of property depends significantly on location, and proximity to what these agents euphemistically call "incurable defects" (such as railroad tracks, factories, and airports) ruins market value. Houses in Zone II are thus extremely cheap, but we would hesitate to call them a bargain. For a recent example, think of the huge mansions in the City of Detroit selling for $100 (no joke!). The reason for the great price is that no one wants to buy! No one is going to pay a premium to live 20 feet from abandoned, fire-scorched buildings and busy railroad tracks. What person blessed with enough means would want to put up with that? Those who can afford higher rents and mortgages thus move away to neighborhoods where the scenery is a bit more pleasant, while those who cannot afford to move must make do with living near industry and slaughterhouses. Such neighborhoods therefore house the poorest residents of the city, as well as newly arrived immigrants. One may also reasonably expect that residents will move out of the area the moment their financial situation allows. Thus, platitudes from our political leaders about it "taking a village" notwithstanding, the people living in the zone of transition have little tangible incentive to make much of a personal investment in their community. But we will say more on this in just a moment.

Traveling farther out from the transitional zone, one encounters the **working-class zone,** where second-generation immigrants live as well as members of the working class. Since industry is not yet moving into the area, homeowners—to the best of their ability, given their limited financial means—are more likely to live in the area for a longer length of time and thus have incentive to create relatively permanent infrastructure for working with other residents. You can see this infrastructure working in that property looks cared for, the schools look in reasonable shape and are well attended, and people take part in civic functions. This trend in community organization continues as one travels out from the city's center. One next encounters the **residential zone,** consisting of middle-class families and better residences. Finally, the affluent **commuter zone** exists on the outskirts of the city, where urban blight, noise, and traffic are minimal.

Social Disorganization and Its Causes

The buildings and scenery in Zone II are not pleasant to look at, but chronic signs of disorder in transitional communities suggest deeper problems. Abandoned cars might line the streets. You might also see unsupervised youth idling in vacant lots, which are also overgrown with weeds and filled with trash to boot. The buildings themselves might be beyond merely old and drab, but decayed to the point where they are falling apart or are no more than burnt-out ruins—and yet nobody ever seems to do anything about it. Even with railroad tracks close by and encroachment from industry, it does not necessarily follow that residents in the transitional zone are personally incapable of keeping their streets clean and of performing basic maintenance. Why is disorder, as well as crime, associated with Zone II?

Shaw and McKay concluded, as had Burgess and other Chicago sociologists, that **social disorganization** is endemic within Zone II. That is, the community is unable to function as its residents would desire (or, to use the jargon of disorganization theory, the area in transition is unable to "realize its values") by having clean streets, no crime, attractive housing, low disease, and so forth. This is an important point in social disorganization theory: No one in the community wants to live where there is lots of disease, filth, stench, and hoodlums, but some communities are unable to do anything to prevent these problems from occurring. The point you must understand is that a basic desire for order and a pleasant life on the part of individual residents is not enough to make such things actually happen. After all, if wishes and hope were all anybody needed, then everybody would have a pony.

More useful than wishes or hope is organization; however, the areas with the worst crime problems tend not to have any. Why do the residents fail to work together? We will get to social disorganization theory's answer to this question in a moment, but we can say right now that conditions in Zone II are such that organized activity by residents is difficult to create, let alone sustain. At first this is difficult to understand. After all, we just said that residents do not want crime. This would suggest that persuading people to organize *should* thus be an easy task. Except that residents in Zone II in fact do not organize, even when reminded by well-meaning political leaders and experts that they probably should. This is not because denizens are stupid, ignorant, or lack common sense. Rather, it is because we fail to look at the situation from the perspective of the people actually living in Zone II. In fact, the conditions in Zone II are such that residents generally (although not universally) believe that it is more to their advantage to *not* cooperate with others. Put another way, expending personal effort in collective activity on behalf of the community goes *against* what many residents see as common sense. This lack of cooperation, of mutual dependence, is the essence of social disorganization.

But since the theory assumes that residents want order, how can we turn around and say that not enough residents see any advantage toward working to achieve order? Shaw and McKay have focused on three factors that create the natural conditions for social disorganization: (1) residential instability, (2) racial or ethnic heterogeneity, and (3) poverty. Each of these sources of disorganization undermines the ability of residents to work in concert and prevent crime from occurring.

Residential Instability. Disorganization theory posits that communities with a lot of population turnover—in which many residents move from their homes during a given time period—tend to have higher crime. Remember that the zone of transition is a place in terrible physical condition. Effective formal and informal community organizations require a relatively stable population, but this isn't possible when the population is always looking to move. For instance, think about how moving affects your own relationships. Would you spend a lot of effort getting to know someone who is going to move away? Would you get to know people in the area, or invest time and energy in community projects, if you know you're going to leave? In most cases, people will reason—and it is hard to fault them for this—that it is not in their interest to form close ties with or sacrifice on the behalf of people they will only know for a short while.

Racial/Ethnic Heterogeneity. Shaw and McKay found that communities where many different cultures and races lived in close proximity tended to have higher crime rates. At first glance, this finding seems puzzling. We normally think of diversity as a good thing, but the people of different backgrounds must share something in common and have meaningful interaction with one another. What happened instead in disorganized communities was that the different races and cultures tended to isolate themselves and avoid interacting with other groups. Sometimes this was because the language barrier was insurmountable. Other times the groups saw each other as simply too alien to comfortably interact with. Regardless, communication decreases under such conditions, which means that the community as a whole is less effective at being able to organize and control neighborhood crime.

Poverty. Communities with high poverty tend to lack the resources needed for effective community organization. Concentrated poverty in the community, for instance, seriously weakens the local tax base, which supports such community institutions as schools and recreational facilities. Additionally, the difficult circumstances of poverty mean that a significant portion of residents are focused on survival—asking them to spend time and energy organizing to help the community (which they likely want to leave as soon as possible) is to advise them to spend time in activity that is counterproductive to addressing their most pressing problems. Good luck with that! Thus, poverty is not in itself a cause of crime, but it promotes disorganization and prevents the community from being able to effectively deal with local problems.

These three features of Zone II thus create conditions where there are not enough residents who see any advantage to working with others on behalf of the neighborhood. And so crime can flourish because residents cannot mount a coordinated defense against it. An organized community, in contrast makes supervision and detection of deviance more effective, making the area less hospitable for crime. While families might be able to supervise and control their children on their own, the organized nature of the community means that the parents are nevertheless not alone in their task. One of the authors, when he was much younger, was with a friend who had locked himself out of his house. They tried to enter the house through a window, and were quickly confronted by a neighbor who wanted to know what the two kids were doing. Adults in an organized community are thus willing to do something about suspicious activity. Beyond direct supervision, the community is also better able to work collectively to socialize youth away from crime.

Where such organizations either do not exist or have failed, however, residents can rely only on themselves. How else can one manage if the neighbors do not speak to each other, or if hardly anyone goes to the local church? Consequently, the community is socially disorganized, and one sees high crime, teenage pregnancy, and disease because the residents cannot work together to tackle these problems before they become entrenched. Once crime becomes embedded in a disorganized community, Shaw and McKay theorized, persistent neighborhood "criminal traditions" and values would appear to compete with conventional values among the youth living in the area. In short, crime becomes a tolerated, if not normal, part of life in disorganized communities.

Superb illustrations of these subcultures exist. The University of Pennsylvania sociologist Elijah Anderson (1999) described how criminal subcultures emerged in disorganized areas characterized also by racial discrimination. Anderson did field research in Philadelphia—that is, rather than collecting data with a survey, he literally left his office and hit the streets, systematically observing a disintegrated community and the lives of the people living there. In so doing, Anderson discovered what he called "the code of the street," which is a system of rules that many people living in these areas abide by. Because disorganization means that normal avenues of dispute resolution (like courts and police) are not available or have retreated from the area, individuals are obliged to look after themselves. Without responsible institutions capable of enforcing order, and lacking the sort of leverage needed for peaceful negotiation, residents must use the threat of violence as the leverage. This plainly means that to survive in a disorganized community with dignity and health intact, one has to adopt a tough, violent persona and be ready to fight. Thus, we have the origins of the street code subculture. We can experience street code sentiments quite often just by listening to some rap music (Kubrin, 2005). More recently, Jacobs and Wright (2006) presented a similar picture in St. Louis. Research has also found that contrary to the expectations of inner-city youth that being aggressive makes them safer, street code attitudes actually made them significantly more likely to be a victim of violence (Stewart, Schreck, & Simons, 2006). This may make sense. After all, if you insult people verbally and threaten them, they are likely to react badly (see also, Felson, 1992).

The Development of Social Disorganization Theory.   After Shaw and McKay's work, social disorganization theory languished for many years. There were a couple of reasons for this. First, new theories emerged that became more popular. These theories, operating from a very different worldview from that of disorganization theory, are often critical of disorganization theory for the value judgment that the term "disorganization" implies. That is, to suggest that a community is "disorganized" might be inappropriate if poor and lower-class neighborhoods are simply "differently organized." William Whyte (1943), a contemporary of Shaw and McKay, was one of the scholars with such a view. Chapter 6 discusses some of these subcultural theories in which, for instance, members of the lower class simply have different values and needs, and therefore organize their lives in a way that best makes sense to them. Crime, then, is merely a by-product of the culture, just like the apparent social organization—crime and community characteristics may correlate with each other, but one does not cause or influence the other. Edwin Sutherland (1947) termed this phenomenon *differential social organization* rather than *social disorganization*. It was in part due to the work of these important sociologists that social disorganization theory fell out of favor for several decades.

All this might sound like petty academic squabbling, but the consequence of this disagreement for policy purposes is quite significant. If an area is only differently organized (indeed, functioning exactly as it is supposed to be, according to the values of the area), then it is unclear whether anyone has the moral prerogative to change it. Changing it, after all, would be an ethnocentric act—we would simply be changing the organization of a perfectly functioning community to suit our own tastes. Indeed, the residents of the community would not be able to understand our interference and would likely view it with suspicion or contempt. And one would predict that residents would do whatever they could to resist or short-circuit any changes.

A second reason that social disorganization theory became unfashionable was a result of the data limitations that mid-twentieth century disorganization theorists faced. Early research in social disorganization theory tended to focus on "structural" or neighborhood-level correlates of disorganization: poverty, racial heterogeneity, and residential instability. These researchers would typically identify a community and use such data as the U.S. Census to measure the median income (to ascertain level of poverty), the racial composition, and residential mobility. While crime appeared to be connected to these structural factors, the disorganization itself—the weakness of community networks—was not measured in these studies (see Kornhauser, 1978; Pratt, 2001). This limitation is quite important. Many theories begin with the idea that poverty leads to crime (e.g., strain theories; see Chapter 7), so how then do we know that the crime problem isn't due so much to lack of community networks but actually to strain or anomie? If strain is responsible for the crime in an area, then giving residents better job skills might alleviate it. If it is disorganization that is responsible for all the crime, then simply giving people job skills would be a waste of time because (1) good jobs aren't present anyway, and (2) it does nothing to strengthen community institutions. (Since the person who can parlay the skills into a good job is likely to move out, one could even go so far as to say that providing job skills hastens the disintegration of a community.) Therefore, to prevent well-intended policies from having potentially catastrophic effects, crime researchers must have more detailed data measuring precisely what disorganization theory says causes crime.

For many decades, such detailed data did not exist, and so this was one of the reasons that social disorganization theory faded in importance. All disorganization theorists could show in support of their claims was essentially maps with dots on them. Yes, these dots tended to cluster in what the theorists called "the zone of transition," but such findings could support disorganization theory or many other theories too. Disorganization researchers also could present data describing how strongly poverty, racial heterogeneity, and mobility were correlated with crime across neighborhoods. But they could not show that these associations took place for the reasons they claimed. Put another way, data limitations meant that social disorganization theory was at a dead end.

After a decent interval, a number of scholars contributed toward the revitalization of social disorganization theory. In 1974, two sociologists, John Kasarda and Morris Janowitz, proposed the idea of communities consisting of informal ties of association between people, such as friendships and family (as opposed to ties of a more formal nature, such as with one's police department). Disorganized communities tended to lack these ties, whereas organized communities tended to have strong bonds of affiliation between people. Ruth Kornhauser (1978) went further, attacking the critics of social disorganization theory and arguing how informal bonds facilitated social control. If you know your neighbors well, for example, you know who belongs in the area and who doesn't. And if you observe the neighbors' kids behaving suspiciously, you are in a better position to report it to the parents as well as have an interest in doing so. Robert Bursik (1988) also responded to earlier critics of social disorganization theory. By 1989, with the work of Robert Sampson and Byron Groves, social disorganization theory had returned as a force in criminology. Sampson and Groves' study was the first to actually test the "intervening mechanisms" linking poverty, mobility, and racial heterogeneity with crime—the informal relationships or ties that existed between residents in an area. And they found that informal neighborhood ties indeed accounted for much of the effects of the three traditional indicators of disorganization, as the theory predicted. Numerous tests followed, along with suggestions for modifying social disorganization theory (e.g., Bellair, 1997, 2000; Kubrin, 2005; Sampson & Wilson, 1990; Warner & Rountree, 1997). Bursik and Grasmick (1993), making an important contribution to disorganization theory, identified three key types of neighborhood-level social control: (1) private, consisting of the density and strength of relationships between family and friends in an area; (2) parochial, which refers to the relationships between residents and semiformal organizations like churches and schools; and (3) public, where residents have relationships with institutions outside the neighborhood, such as government. An organized community, and one with the ability to exert effective social control, would be strong in all three areas. A lesson here is that scientific theories that have merit can and do fall out of favor for reasons having little to do with the evidence. But, as happened with social disorganization theory, otherwise sound theories can reemerge and shape the research agenda of a field for several decades.

The most recent work has continued to refine our understanding of how community organization interacts with crime. The most recent developments have argued that having strong ties is not enough. In fact, the residents have to identify with their neighborhood and be willing to act on its behalf. This notion about residents trusting one another and acting in concert to maintain order in public spaces, such as parks and sidewalks, is what the Harvard University sociologist Robert Sampson and his colleagues (1997) termed *collective efficacy*. One can see **collective efficacy** in action when residents complain to community leaders about problems such as abandoned cars, and also when they organize neighborhood watches and form homeowners' associations. The key is that residents are proactive in protecting the interests of their community. Indeed, residents see their self-interest intertwined with that of the community. But in order for there to be collective efficacy, a community must have **social capital.** Social capital consists of the many informal networks within a community. Everyone you know, for instance, is part of your personal network; communities consist of networks as well. Functioning neighborhood networks might organize trash cleanup days as well as plant flowers along the roads, using the collective power of residents to make the community more attractive. Neighborhood groups, who might vote as a bloc, can wield influence with politicians in order to attract municipal resources to the community, as well as work together to attract jobs that might make the area more attractive to long-term residents. It thus takes viable institutions and residents working together to maintain a community in a way that is free from disorder. Individuals cannot do it alone. When there is a lot of social capital—that is, a lot of effective networks for mobilizing community support and resources (residents know each other and are willing to work together)—then there will be less crime.

Sampson and his colleagues (1997) measured a variety of neighborhood factors from Chicago neighborhoods that they reasoned were indicative of collective efficacy, such as informal social control, social cohesion, and trust. Individual respondents were asked such questions as, "How likely would it be that neighbors would intervene if children were skipping school or spray-painting graffiti on a local building (informal social control)?" and, "How much respondents agreed that neighbors helped each other and that that neighborhood was close-knit (social cohesion)?" These sentiments were then combined to create a measure of neighborhood-level collective efficacy. Sampson and colleagues then examined how well the collective efficacy predicted neighborhood violence. Moreover, communities with high income and higher levels of homeownership (homeownership implies a substantial financial stake in a residence, as opposed to a renter) also had high levels of collective efficacy (Sampson et al., 1997).

Policy Implications

Since social disorganization theory appears to have some support, it is worthwhile to think about what it says ought to be done in order to reduce crime. On one level, disorganization theory suggests straightforward policy.

All one has to do is to promote effective community organizations as well as informal mechanisms of social control. If we can get people to attend homeowners meetings, agree to watch each other's kids, and keep the streets clean, the residents will be better able to exert control and the community will be a less inviting place for crime.

Shaw and McKay developed one of the first large-scale programs to prevent delinquency with their Chicago Area Project. The objective was to use project staff and social workers to help create and maintain community organizations and residents' ability to exert social control in their area. Local organizations included youth athletic leagues, recreation programs, and summer camps. The fostering of informal relationships between residents would also give teenagers the opportunity to interact with law-abiding residents, who could serve as conventional role models. If the project was successful, then the community would be better situated to deal with the symptoms of social disorganization, including crime. Assessments of the Chicago Area Project revealed mixed results, however—some neighborhoods showed decreased levels of crime while others reported higher levels. The Chicago Area Project, as well as later programs such as the Mobilization for Youth, consistently revealed that promoting organization in communities at risk for social disorganization required consistent effort and care, as the organizations cultivated by the projects tended not to be self-sustaining. Once financial support for the programs was withdrawn or cut back, the organizations began to disintegrate. Clearly, the organizations created by these programs were more or less sustained by a sort of artificial life support. The natural conditions were still unfavorable for organization, so the removal of city investment had the same effect on local organizations that disconnecting a diver's air supply would have on the diver. Nevertheless, some communities were able to continue to organize over the long term, with a correspondingly lower level of neighborhood delinquency than similar, but disorganized, neighborhoods (Schlossman, Zellman, Shavelson, Sedlak, & Cobb, 1984).

Why have policies designed to address community problems been so difficult to implement effectively? One large obstacle is residential mobility, in which people, including those who have the talent and inclination to be community leaders, are always looking to leave and as a result never truly integrate within the community. The challenge is to get these people to identify with their communities enough to stay—so why can't we seem to get them to do this? One way to understand the basic problem is to relate it to your own life. Let's say that an urban planner wants to reduce high population turnover at an apartment full of college students. Now pretend you're a college student living there: Would you want to rent that apartment for the rest of your life? Would you do it, especially knowing that college student apartments often are noisy, offer few amenities, and have unresponsive landlords? The urban planner's job is to motivate people to stay and start caring for where they live; but you probably don't see your apartment or dorm as somewhere you would want to spend the rest of your life. The dorm or apartment is simply a temporary abode until you can get something better. This is a problem faced in the policy implications of disorganization theory. If you can think of something the city might do to your apartment complex that would get you to stay even if you were offered a job paying $100,000 per year, then you have taken a big step toward solving the problem of disorganization. This might sound easy, but remember that the improvements cannot price out the poorer residents already living in the complex and neither can the improvements be so appealing that others of your social class descend *en masse* upon the complex and drive up the rent for everybody.

Disorganization theory is fairly clear about the efficacy of incarceration as a source of crime control, however. Since social ties are essential for effective communities, heavy use of incarceration by the criminal justice system essentially churns the community and promotes residential instability. That is, many residents are incarcerated, released back into the community, reincarcerated, and so on, which prevents them from building significant ties to their neighborhood. As with many of the ideas covered in this book, overreliance on *incarceration* would fail to have a beneficial impact on crime and in fact would undermine the very processes that would result in less crime.

ROUTINE ACTIVITIES THEORY

Routine activities theory, like social disorganization theory, was inspired by scholars interested in human ecology. Hawley (1950) observed that human activities followed a definite structure. First, there was a *rhythm* to human life. This means that the things people do occur with regularity. For example, you may notice that "rush hours" (times when heavy demands get placed on transportation) occur predictably. Second, the events of human life follow a consistent *tempo*. That is to say, during a given period particular events will take place a consistent number of times—such as two rush hours each day, once in the morning and once in the afternoon. And third, the events that occur often depend on the co-occurrence of other events (*timing*). For example, have you ever noticed that rush hours are rarely as bad on weekends as on weekdays? Fewer people use transportation in the early mornings and late afternoons of weekends because the use of transportation depends on work being available. Since many people do not work at all on weekends, there is less demand for transportation at those times, and thus no rush hour. Although routine activities theory shares an intellectual heritage with social disorganization theory insofar as both were inspired by human ecology, routine activities theory differs in that it looks for the answers to why crime occurs in the rhythms, tempo, and timing of mundane events rather than the presence of community organization.

The main interest of routine activities theory is in describing crime-inviting situations and explaining how long-term social change can influence the opportunities for crime to occur. The idea that crime requires opportunity did not originate with routine activities theory (see, for instance, Cloward & Ohlin, 1960), but few earlier theories gave much attention to explaining what opportunity really meant. This neglect of opportunity implies that it (whatever it is) is universal, or else of little consequence relative to understanding the criminal offender. Routine activities theory, in contrast, treats opportunity as problematic and the offender as given, and usually focuses on how large-scale social change can be either more or less conducive to crime. Lawrence Cohen and Marcus Felson (1979), two sociologists, provided the initial outline of the theory.

The Necessary Requirements for Crime

Cohen and Felson (1979) reasoned that for a direct predatory crime to occur, three minimum conditions had to be present in both time and space:

- motivated offender
- suitable target (a person or object)
- guardianship

In order to prevent crime, all one needed to do was eliminate one of the conditions. Simple! We discuss these elements next, so that you might see what they refer to as well as their importance.

Motivated Offenders. When it comes to understanding the offender, routine activities theory is a rational choice model (similar to classical deterrence theory and the control perspective) in which all people are assumed to weigh the costs and benefits of alternative courses of action and then proceed to do what brings the most advantage. Consequently, routine activities theory does not attempt to explain why some people commit more crime than others, since it is assumed that any "normal" person would do it when the advantages are great enough and the costs low enough. But it is still instructive to create what research indicates to be a profile of the "representative" offender. Felson described the "typical" **motivated offender** as "a young male with a big mouth who gets into many accidents and makes a mess of everything else" (1998, p. 54). Everything else being equal, situations where such people are likely to be found would have the highest potential for crime. One must also remember that being in situations where the advantages of crime appear to be great means that the odds are higher that even the most moral person might be tempted to commit a crime. But if nobody in the area wants to commit a crime, then crime cannot occur.

Suitable Targets. For a crime to happen it is not enough to simply have a likely offender in the area—there must also be something tempting nearby. People of a vicious temperament can appear to be saints if they are continuously in situations where there are no opportunities for crime that are worth their time. In order to better understand criminal temptation, and what makes a **suitable target,** it is best to look at it from a prospective offender's point of view rather than from our own. Your professors, for instance, might be tempted to steal statistical software and library cards, but we suspect that most students would pass on an opportunity to steal those. Marcus Felson (1998) elaborated on what makes a target suitable, using the acronym **VIVA** (for value, inertia, visibility, and accessibility). Each of these characteristics can help us understand which targets will tempt nearby criminal offenders.

As suggested a moment ago, a target's value varies from person to person and does not solely depend on objective monetary worth. Think, for example, about two music CDs priced at about $15—one by the Jonas Brothers and the other by Yanni. Now put yourself in the shoes of a middle-school teen. Which CD will be more valuable to you? On average, teenagers would be more likely to consider the Jonas Brothers CD valuable, scorning the Yanni CD (even though both are worth, in absolute monetary terms, about the same). If you're the owner of a music store frequented by teenagers, then it's a good bet that you will lose more Jonas Brothers CDs to theft than Yanni CDs.

Tedeschi and Felson (1994) analyzed value in the context of a fight. What makes someone a worthwhile target for assault (and possible homicide)? After all, people do not usually randomly punch passersby. Instead, a fight is worthwhile when there is a grievance between two people. Tedeschi and Felson (1994) found that fights were more likely to erupt when people wanted to exert control over the behavior of someone else. Additionally, grievances can arise from the need to restore justice. In this case, violence is used to settle a score or get even with a former victimizer. Grievances that might make someone a worthwhile target for violence can arise from the need to save face. This might occur if someone challenged your masculinity/femininity or otherwise insulted you. Without these bases for grievances, there would be no point (or value) in fighting someone.

Inertia, which refers to the size and bulk of a target, is another factor that can make a target suitable. Consider two pieces of merchandise: a handheld digital camera and an entertainment center. Let's evaluate these objects from the point of view of someone who considers them equally valuable. (Let's say that both cost about $1,000.) Which one would be more likely to be shoplifted? You'd be right if you guessed the camera, but do you know why? Digital cameras tend to be small and easily concealed, unlike an entertainment center (which would require a forklift and a truck to move, and thus might arouse the suspicion of store staff as well as give the thief a hernia). Not surprisingly, shoplifting tends to be more of a problem at stores selling expensive light electronic goods, and less of a problem at even the priciest furniture stores (Felson, 1998). Lighter and less bulky goods would be more suitable as a target. In the case of a possible personal crime, inertia might refer to the physical size and apparent strength of the prospective victim relative to the attacker. Would-be victims with high inertia will be less suitable as targets for attack.

The suitability of a target also depends on the offender's awareness that a target is in the area—that is, the target's *visibility*. In order for a target to be worthwhile to a would-be offender, the offender has to know that it's there. High visibility can be both intentional as well as inadvertent. Stores, simply to stay in business, make a conscious decision to prominently display attractive merchandise and risk tempting shoplifters. Visibility can be accidental, too. If you have parties at your house where lots of people show up, many will have the opportunity to get a good look at the stuff you have. If you annoy other motorists on the road when you crank up your stereo, then you advertise to all that you have a nice set of speakers worth taking. This is the irony of having nice, expensive stuff; we want to flaunt it at least a little bit, but in so doing we alert people that we have something worth stealing.

Finally, the target must be *accessible* to be suitable. Offenders have to be able to easily get to the target and easily get away. One key aspect of routine activities theory is that the typical offender tends to stumble across opportunities for crime over the course of daily routines (the effort it takes to find the target and afterward escape is viewed as a "cost" and is thus a potential deterrent; in this light, routine activities theory assumes that people naturally gravitate toward convenient targets). Attractive targets that are very difficult to get to and get away from will tend to be relatively safe since they are not suitable.

Effective Guardianship.   While motivated offenders and suitable targets help contribute to crime, one final requirement needs to be met before a crime can occur. The target must be poorly guarded. **Effective guardianship** refers to the presence of anyone or anything in the area capable of making the crime more risky. Generally, offenders prefer to be alone with their targets. By adding other people or security cameras to the setting, either of which might increase protection of the target, things very quickly become difficult for the offender. We normally think of the police as the most important guardians against crime. After all, only the most desperate or brazen criminals would elect to commit a crime in front of them. But if on any given day you were to time how long you can actually see a police officer on duty (including when the police officer is not even watching you and has no idea you're in the area), you'll find that you do not have a whole lot of immediate police protection. In routine activities theory, however, effective guardians can include virtually anyone who can serve as a witness to a crime. Think about the opportunity to steal a backpack containing $500 in cash from a classroom. You might be willing to do it if no one was in the vicinity; however, you wouldn't likely do it if the classroom was full of people, and even if they wouldn't lift a finger to prevent you from leaving the room. Do you see? No police officers are involved, but the presence of eyes watching what you are doing nevertheless makes the theft so much riskier and thus you would probably change your mind. So beside yourself, your parents, friends, and relatives can act as guardians of you and your belongings. Guardians do not even have to be armed—all it takes for guardianship to be successful at deterring most crimes is the knowledge that one is being watched. Guardianship is all the more successful when it is inadvertent and part of natural, everyday routine. Felson (1986), for instance, reasoned that everyday social ties between individuals facilitate guardianship. If you love your parents, you will spend more time around them, but this means that you are under more frequent surveillance. That is, you probably would not smoke marijuana or have sex when your parents are right there, but neither would anyone assault you or steal your belongings with your parents watching.

In sum, for a crime to have the potential of occurring, there must be the convergence, in time and space, of the three necessary conditions for crime just described: a motivated offender, a suitable target, and ineffective guardianship. The key factors responsible for this convergence are the everyday routines of individuals—where do they work or go to school, where do they go for entertainment, how do they get home? As the term "routine" implies, the behavior of offenders is not often distinguishable from that of nonoffenders. That is, there is often nothing particularly special, illegal, or even suspicious about the normal routines of offenders before a crime happens. Offenders will not travel miles out of their way and spend hours seeking suitable targets. Instead, they stumble across opportunities for crime because their daily routines place them in situations where they are near worthwhile and poorly protected targets.

The Role of Social Changes

Cohen and Felson (1979) focused their classic article on linking crime rates with large-scale historical social changes. Some social changes might have relevance for facilitating or impeding situations in which offenders are near poorly defended and worthwhile targets. To think about the influence of these changes in everyday social routines on levels of crime, let us first start with an example. Years ago, people tended to spend a lot more time around the house. Women were expected to maintain the home and raise the children, which was no easy task given that laborsaving devices such as dishwashers and washing machines were still evolving. The children of that day—as our parents and grandparents proudly tell us—had to spend much of their time helping with time-consuming chores. Washing the clothes, feeding the chickens, milking the cows—all of these activities took time away from other activities away from the home. But times changed as gender roles evolved and timesaving appliances proliferated in our lives. Rather than the all-day affair that clothes washing used to be, all one has to do now is throw them in the washer, wait a bit, and throw them in the dryer. Freed from labor at home, children have much more free time to spend outside the home than ever before. The times changed for women as well, as over the past several decades a large proportion of women entered the full-time workforce. Women, in effect, were no longer shackled to their kitchens and nurseries.

In many respects, these changes are good. Now think about these social changes from the point of view of a would-be burglar. Years ago, because the household was so high-maintenance, a typical burglar would have to hazard breaking into an *occupied* residence in order to steal the contents. You can probably already see the lack of appeal of this scenario for most burglars—guardianship is naturally quite high if a residence has occupants. Indeed, having people in the house heightens risk and seldom offers any benefit. For example, people in the house may resist entry, could serve as witnesses, and might even attempt to kill anyone who invades their home. On the other hand, an empty home is ideal. With no one there, the only challenge is to get in and get out unobserved by neighbors and passersby. So with women entering the workforce and children freed from chores at home, the job of the burglar became easier and less risky. Not surprisingly, half of all burglaries these days occur during daylight hours (Gottfredson & Hirschi, 1990).

Recall earlier that Guerry and Quetelet found that the more prosperous regions of France reported higher property crime. At first, this seems odd—prosperity leading to crime? Cohen and Felson (1979), observing crime trends between 1947 and 1970, found a similar pattern in the United States between economic prosperity and property crime and reached the same conclusion as the two Belgians. Offenders were not stealing food or life's essentials. Instead, prosperity increased the availability of items to steal. Between the late 1940s and 1970, there was an increase in the availability of durable (and expensive) electronic goods and automobiles, all of which could be moved relatively easily and quickly sold for cash. In other words, prosperity seems to bring greater temptation in the form of wider availability of suitable targets. One might reason from this that changes in crime rates indeed have less to do with the pool of motivated offenders than with the opportunities available to commit crime.

Policy Implications

The policy implications of routine activities theory are, in the abstract, straightforward: Simply prevent the combination of motivated offenders and suitable targets during moments of ineffective guardianship. Regarding what to do about motivated offenders, Ronald Clarke argued that it is pointless to try to change people. Most theories discussed in this book clearly take the opposite approach, but there may be something to recommend against changing people. Consider the following example. If you have a boyfriend or girlfriend (or significant other), it is likely that he or she has an annoying or embarrassing habit like chewing fingernails, belching loudly, or picking his or her nose. Many people try to "improve" their romantic partners and get them to stop being so annoying by nagging and scolding them. In the experience of the authors, at any rate, most people fail at this miserably, and in many cases the attempts at "rehabilitation" are irritating enough to lead to a breakup. Perhaps eliminating opportunity might be simpler.

Routine activities theory thus argues in favor of manipulating the situation in order to keep motivated offenders from becoming tempted (such as by limiting the time they spend around suitable targets), by making the crime too inconvenient to execute, or by increasing the deterrence inherent in a situation (such as by augmenting guardianship). Felson (1998), for instance, recommended that schools could reduce disturbances on campus by cutting back the landscaping and otherwise designing the campus and its buildings to facilitate surveillance. Moreover, he reported that places that served liquor were able to reduce the amount of injurious and fatal assaults by serving drinks in plastic cups rather than beer bottles (i.e., by reducing the accessibility of potential weapons that might cause injury). It is not easy to kill someone by throwing a plastic cup at her head.

Some ideas consistent with routine activities theory actually predate the work of Cohen and Felson. Oscar Newman (1972), for instance, explored the idea of "defensible space" in public housing, such as designing the facilities with natural surveillance in mind. Ronald Clarke (1992) championed increasing the effort and risk of crime via physical barriers to crime (such as a tougher door), alarms, and security guards. One can also ensure that the rewards of crime make the effort not worth the attempt. Convenience stores often clearly display a sign reporting that they have only a few dollars in cash available, for example. Assuming offenders are rational and can accurately perceive the risks, rewards, and potential effort, an obviously tough or unrewarding target will likely be passed. Note that none of these strategies involve changing people, but instead entail manipulating the environment so that people are kept away from targets, or by making targets too well guarded, or by making targets too unsuitable.

Empirical Research and Criticisms

How have researchers tested routine activity theory? Remember that Cohen and Felson (1979) described their theory as a "macro theory" designed to link broad social changes with crime rates. Cohen and Felson (1979), in their initial work on the theory, showed, for instance, that furniture was much less likely to be stolen than light electronic goods (per $100 consumed)—a clear indication of target suitability. They linked long-term trends in crime from 1947 to 1974 to changes in part to the fact that light, expensive electronics were less available during the 1940s compared with the 1970s. No one had cell phones and video tape players or computers in 1947. By the 1970s, however, video tape players and computers (while not nearly as easily portable as they are now) were increasingly available and expensive enough to make their theft worthwhile. Other research has explored how macro-level social changes, such as modernization and theft rates, relate to victimization. Neuman and Berger (1988), for instance, found that modernization in different countries was related to theft, though not homicide. Pratt (2001) conducted a meta-analysis of research looking at the correspondence between macro-level changes and crime, finding support for the predictions of routine activities theory (particularly the idea of guardianship).

Research has also studied the individual's mundane activities and their connection with risk of crime and victimization. Wayne Osgood and colleagues (1996) found that the amount of time juveniles spent with their peers while engaged in unstructured leisure activities away from adults was a predictor of their delinquency even after controlling for how delinquent the child normally was. Put differently, even otherwise good kids who ride around just for fun, visit with friends, go to parties, and spend evenings out doing recreational activities will have a higher chance of being delinquent. Bonnie Fisher and colleagues (1998) measured a number of not only individual activities but also contextual risk factors. Mustaine and Tewksbury (1998) focused on highly specific activities, like activities away from home, time spent away from home or with friends (i.e., exposure), illegal behaviors, home security, substance use, and neighborhood characteristics. More recently, Schreck and colleagues (2004) focused on how the structure of one's peer networks influences exposure to motivated offenders, target suitability, and guardianship. They found that teenagers who are central and popular members of dense peer networks were generally safer from victimization. But central and popular members of peer networks where there were a lot of deviants had the opposite effect! Clearly, there is great variation across individuals in the activities they participate in, and some of these activities make them more likely to offend or become victims.

Some regard routine activities theory as a "victim-blaming" theory (see, for instance, Karmen, 2008; Meier & Miethe, 1993). The theory, after all, suggests that victims can facilitate or provoke their own victimization through their daily routines, by making themselves into suitable targets, or by weakening their guardianship. In some respects, this criticism is political rather than scientific. The research does indicate that victims are often, through their behaviors and activities, agents in their own victimization (Meier & Miethe, 1993). That being said, readers should be aware that all theories contain inherent ideology. Nevertheless, while it is one thing to object to a theory because it fails to adequately conform to the facts, it is another matter entirely to reject a theory because one does not like the ideology.

SUMMARY

Theories that focus on the social ecology of crime offer something different from many of the theories of crime that we have discussed so far. Rather than looking at how offenders differ from nonoffenders, these theories instead give attention to how situations or places with high levels of crime differ from those with little crime. Social disorganization theory claims that disorganization undermines ties and institutions within a community, thus making it impossible for residents to work collectively to deal with crime problems in the area. Routine activities theory gives its attention to the immediate situation where crime occurs, namely, situations where motivated offenders are in proximity to poorly guarded suitable targets. Both theories have received support in the empirical literature, and both at present are the focus of extensive attention from criminologists. Another common theme for these theories is that neither proposes the rehabilitation of people to prevent future crime from occurring, but they instead suggest that best results might be obtained by changing the situation or the context.

KEY TERMS

collective efficacy   the ability of a community to maintain order in public spaces

commuter zone   in social disorganization theory, Zone V; the outermost edge of the city that has the least crime; the suburbs

effective guardianship   refers to any person or object capable of protecting a victim from an offender, who might report the crime to authorities, or who might serve as a witness. Guardians make crime less likely to occur in that they complicate the execution of a crime

motivated offender   in routine activities theory, one of the three necessary requirements for crime; motivated offenders, on average, tend to be young males who get into trouble a lot, but this term can include virtually anyone who might be tempted by crime in a given situation

residential zone   in social disorganization theory, Zone IV; exists between the working class zone and the commuter zone and consists of relatively desirable residential property

social capital   informal social networks within communities that enable community tasks to get done

social disorganization   the inability of a community to organize effectively to prevent social problems from occurring, due to poverty, residential mobility, and racial/ethnic heterogeneity

suitable target   in routine activities theory, one of the three necessary requirements for crime; suitable targets can be anything that might tempt a nearby offender

transitional zone   in social disorganization theory, Zone II; contains the least desirable residential properties; consequently, only the poorest individuals live here, and they tend to move away when they can; crime is highest in this zone

VIVA   an acronym referring to value, inertia, visibility, and accessibility; all of these are elements of what might make a target suitable to a motivated offender

working-class zone in social disorganization theory, Zone III; zone contains residential properties that are older and less desirable than those in the residential and commuter zones, but the residents tend to live in this zone for relatively long durations

DISCUSSION QUESTIONS

1. Which kinds of theories do you believe are most important for understanding and solving crime: theories about places or theories about people?

2. Can disorganization theory be extended to rural areas?

3. According to routine activities theory, is it possible for crime to increase even when the number of would-be criminals remains constant? Explain why.

4. In recent years, traffic cameras have proliferated in an effort to more effectively catch speeders. Describe speeding from the point of view of routine activity theory and how cameras might or might not influence driving at unsafe speeds. And then propose theoretically relevant (but cheaper) alternatives that might accomplish the same outcome.

REFERENCES

Anderson, E. (1999). *Code of the street*. New York: W.W. Norton.

Bellair, P. E. (1997). Social interaction and community crime: Explaining the importance of neighbor networks. *Criminology, 35*, 677–703.

Bellair, P. E. (2000). Informal surveillance and street crime: A complex relationship. *Criminology, 38*, 137–167.

Bierne, P. (1993). *Inventing criminology*. Albany: State University of New York Press.

Bursik, R. J. (1988). Social disorganization and theories of crime and delinquency: Problems and prospects. *Criminology, 26*, 519–551.

Bursik, R. J., & Grasmick, H. G. (1993). *Neighborhoods and crime: The dimensions of effective neighborhood control*. New York: Lexington Books.

Clarke, R. (1992). *Situational crime prevention: Successful case studies*. New York: Harrow & Heston.

Cloward, R. A., & Ohlin, L. E. (1960). *Delinquency and opportunity: A theory of delinquent gangs*. Glencoe, IL: Free Press.

Cohen, L. E., & Felson, M. (1979). Social change and crime rate trends: A routine activity approach. *American Sociological Review, 44*, 588–608.

Felson, M. (1986). Linking criminal choices, routine activities, informal control, and criminal outcomes. In D. B. Cornish & R. V. Clarke (Eds.), *The reasoning criminal: Rational choice perspectives on offending*. New York: Springer-Verlag.

Felson, M. (1998). *Crime and everyday life*. Thousand Oaks, CA: Pine Forge Press.

Felson, R. B. (1992). Kick 'em when they're down: Explanations of the relationship between stress and interpersonal aggression and violence. *The Sociological Quarterly, 33*, 1–16.

Fisher, B., Sloan, J., Cullen, F., & Lu, H. (1998). Crime in the ivory tower: The level and sources of student victimization. *Criminology, 36*, 671–710.

Gottfredson, M. R., & Hirschi, T. (1990). *A general theory of crime*. Stanford, CA: Stanford University Press.

Hawley, A. H. (1950). *Human Ecology: A Theory of Community Structure.* New York: Ronald Press.

Jacobs, B., & Wright, R. (2006). *Street justice: Retaliation in the criminal underworld.* New York: Cambridge University Press.

Karmen, A. (2008). *Crime victims: An introduction to victimology.* Belmont, CA: Wadsworth.

Kornhauser, R. R. (1978). *Social sources of delinquency.* Chicago: University of Chicago.

Kubrin, C. (2005). Gangstas, thugs, and hustlas: Identity and the code of the street in rap music. *Social Problems, 52,* 360–378.

Meier, R. F., & Miethe, T. D. (1993). Understanding theories of criminal victimization. *Crime and Justice: A Review of Research, 17,* 459–499.

Mustaine, E. E., & Tewksbury, R. (1998). Predicting risks of larceny theft victimization: A routine activity analysis using refined activity measures. *Criminology, 36,* 829–858.

Neuman, W. L., & Berger, R. J. (1988). Competing perspectives on cross-national crime: An evaluation of theory and evidence. *Sociological Quarterly, 29,* 281–313.

Newman, O. (1972). *Defensible space: Crime prevention through urban design.* New York: Collier.

Osgood, D. W., Wilson, J. K., O'Malley, P. M., Bachman, J. G., & Johnston, L. D. (1996). Routine activities and individual deviant behavior. *American Sociological Review, 61,* 635–655.

Palen, J. (1981). *The urban world.* New York: McGraw-Hill.

Pratt, T. (2001). *Assessing the relative effects of macro-level predictors of crime: A meta-analysis.* Unpublished dissertation, University of Cincinnati.

Sampson, R. J., & Groves, W. B. (1989). Community structure and crime: Testing social disorganization theory. *American Journal of Sociology, 94,* 774–802.

Sampson, R. J., Raudenbusch, S. W., & Earls, F. (1997). Neighborhoods and violent crime: A multilevel study of collective efficacy. *Science, 227,* 918–924.

Sampson, R. J., & Wilson, W. J. (1990). Toward a theory of race, crime, and urban inequality. In J. Hagan & R. Peterson (Eds.), *Crime and inequality.* Stanford, CA: Stanford University Press.

Schlossman, S., Zellman, G., Shavelson, R., Sedlak, M., & Cobb, J. (1984). *Delinquency prevention in South Chicago: A fifty-year assessment of the Chicago Area Project.* Santa Monica, CA: RAND.

Schreck, C. J., J. M. Miller, & B. S. Fisher. (2004). The social context of violent victimization: A study of the delinquent peer effect. *Justice Quarterly, 21,* 23-48.

Shaw, C., & McKay, H. (1942). *Social factors in juvenile delinquency.* Washington, DC: Government Printing Office.

Stewart, E. A., Schreck, C. J., & Simons, R. L. (2006). I ain't gonna let no one disrespect me: Does the code of the street increase or decrease violent victimization among African-American adolescents? *Journal of Research in Crime and Delinquency, 43,* 427–458.

Sutherland, E. H. (1947). *Principles of criminology* (4th ed.). Philadelphia: Lippincott.

Tedeschi, J., & Felson, R. (1994). *Violence, aggression, and coercive action.* Washington, DC: American Psychological Association Books.

Warner, B. D., & Rountree, P. W. (1997). Local social ties in a community and crime model: Questioning the systemic nature of informal social control. *Social Problems, 44,* 520–536.

Whyte, W. F. (1943). *Street corner society: The social structure of the Italian slum.* Chicago: University of Chicago Press.

CHAPTER 6

LEARNING AND CULTURAL TRANSMISSION THEORIES OF CRIME

Like social control theory (see Chapter 8), learning and cultural transmission theories generally assume that criminal behavior is like other forms of human behavior in certain basic respects. First, crime is viewed as a result of social interaction. Social interaction provides both a context and process wherein learning occurs and behavior reflects the nature of what is learned through observation of one's environment, ethnocentric perspective, and the socialization process facilitated by an individual's reference groups, generally, and role models, specifically. Within certain situations, crime is simply normative behavior and, reasonably, is to be expected.

Both criminal and noncriminal behaviors are thought to result from a combination of the socialization process (which, in turn, is heavily influenced by a combination of environmental factors), situational circumstances, and group values. Criminality, then, is not considered innate human character, as contended by determinists such as Lombroso, but rather a product of interaction with others. **Learning theories** (differential association theory and social learning theory) emphasize the process in which criminal behavior is observed, learned, and carried out. Cultural transmission theories are similar to learning theories but focus more on group values (which are shaped and perpetuated from one generation to the next by learning) that encourage and condone crime.

LEARNING THEORIES

Learning theories contend that criminal behavior is learned from others, and this learning process necessarily involves the internalization of values, norms, and behaviors that vary across areas and groups. Accordingly, neither free will nor individual characteristics (such as biological or psychological) associated with crime are emphasized, but rather the social environment's effect on the maturation and socialization processes. Learning theory has a rich legacy in criminology and remains an important strand within contemporary theoretical criminology.

By viewing crime as any other behavior that must be learned, a fundamental assumption of the perspective is that behavior results from observing the habits of others and then modeling or copying that which is successful for meeting needs and desires. People model or imitate what appears to work, which may be conventional (such as educational attainment and legal employment) or unconventional (such as crime) (Bandura, 1962). Social environment becomes crucial because role models from family, peer groups, and the larger community can encourage or dissuade delinquency and crime.

In social learning theory, negative outcomes are related to life experiences, such as childhood exposure to domestic violence, sex abuse, recurring conflict with the juvenile and criminal justice system, school failure, poverty, and poor role models. The learning perspective suggests that violent crime, for example, is a rather natural response resulting from observation of adult role models' use of aggression to solve problems. Some youth not only become familiar with domestic violence through firsthand observation but also come to accept it as normal behavior. Similarly, daily observation of adult hustling, scheming, and stealing may lead to a belief that such behaviors are appropriate means to acquire material goods.

Socially learned behavior typically varies by gender, so much so that criminologists observe the *gendered* nature of both offending and victimization trends. Whereas males use physical force and psychological intimidation to exercise will and access desires, females learn that submissiveness and victimization are the social norms often defining the severity of violence as opposed to its mere occurrence. This chapter examines the two foremost learning theories: differential association theory and social learning theory. This chapter will also review the most recent extension of social learning theory: Akers' social learning–social structure **(SLSS) theory.**

SUTHERLAND'S DIFFERENTIAL ASSOCIATION THEORY

Edwin Sutherland (1883–1950) is often considered the founding father of positivistic criminology. Influenced heavily by the Chicago school and its sociological tradition, he focused on social properties and forces that cause and condition crime and rejected the idea that crime was inherited or otherwise predetermined by biological or psychological factors. While criminologists today readily accept that social structural and environmental factors are essential to understanding crime, Sutherland's ideas were presented during an era when perspectives such as Lombroso's criminal body type (Wolfgang, Figlio, & Sellin, 1972) and Freud's personality theories (Andrews & Bonta, 1998) were dominant.

Sutherland emphasized the role of *socialization* in the development of human behavior and interaction. Socialization refers to a process of human interaction on both one-to-one and group levels wherein behavior is (1) learned from others and (2) reflects society's cultural and subcultural values. Sutherland's theory of **differential association** (1939/1942) emphasizes two primary influences: agents of socialization and content of socialization. Agents of socialization refer to who does the socializing, that is, the teaching. Teaching may be in a formal context through a social institution, such as school, church, or family, but also informally through daily interaction in the community and with peer groups. Social interaction directly shapes the socialization process through the related concepts of observation, role modeling, expectation development, and imitation.

Differential association theory might suggest that crime results from those whose role models are criminals and thus who associate with people whose behavior is different or abnormal. While the role of groups is relevant, Sutherland meant that association is based in large part on definitions of behavior that are favorable or unfavorable to breaking the law. Criminals differ from noncriminals in that they are members of groups whose values are favorable to violation of the law. While groups and the idea of association are important, the primary importance of social groups centers on the social interaction and socialization they facilitate. Sutherland's theory is fairly straightforward, presented in nine formal propositions:

1. *Criminal behavior is learned.* This means that crime is not spontaneous or natural, which is opposite from the position taken by many biological theories, as well as the classical and control perspectives. People are basically like computers rolling off an assembly line; computers do not program themselves but acquire their "knowledge" from some external source. Criminality comes from the environment.

2. *Criminal behavior is learned in interaction with other people in a process of communication.* This proposition specifically targets the social environment (as opposed to the physical environment, for instance) as the source of crime.

3. *The principal part of the learning of criminal behavior occurs within intimate personal groups.* This means that not everyone in your social environment will exert the same influence. Your professor might tell you about how cool it would be to go rob a convenience store, but you would be unlikely to do it. But it might be a different matter if the source of your learning was someone close to you, like family or close friends.

4. *When criminal behavior is learned, the learning includes techniques of committing the crime, which are sometimes very complicated and sometimes very simple, and the specific direction of motives, drives, rationalizations, and*

attitudes. Thus, everything associated with crime is learned—even the very reasons why we think we need to commit crime, as well as our excuses.

5. *The specific direction of motives and drives is learned from definitions of legal codes as favorable and unfavorable.* This proposition points to the idea of "normative conflict," in which, in an absolute sense, there is no right or wrong and "crime" is only such relative to the dominant legal code. Some cultures that are ethnocentrically characterized as "criminal" view the reigning legal code with disfavor.

6. *A person becomes a delinquent because of an excess of definitions favorable to violation of law over definitions unfavorable to violation of law.* This proposition says that the preponderance of our socialization will determine whether we turn to crime.

7. *Differential association may vary in frequency, duration, priority, and intensity.* Put differently, the most frequent, longest-running, earliest, and closest influences will be most efficacious or determinant of learned behavior.

8. *The process of learning criminal behavior by association with criminal and anticriminal patterns incorporates all the mechanisms that are involved in any other learning.* This means that criminals are not mentally deficient, but rather "differently learned." Because crime has to be learned, it follows that criminals have average intelligence. Learning crime is also no different than learning arithmetic or anything else.

9. *Although criminal behavior is an expression of general needs and values, it is not explained by those general needs and values, because noncriminal behavior is an expression of the same needs and values* (Sutherland, 1947, pp. 6–8). Stated differently, the motives attributed to crime, such as a need for money, can be satisfied criminally or noncriminally (e.g., by getting a job). Which path one follows depends on the environment one is raised in, as the need for money does not require that one commit crime.

While each of these propositions was significant to the establishment of a broad criminological knowledge base, propositions 5 and 6 are the cornerstone of Sutherland's differential association theory. Motives and drives can be thought of as ends and means, and they are defined ultimately in either support of or opposition to crime. Intimate group interactions or associations, which vary in frequency, priority (importance), duration (period of time), and level of intensity, affect learning through observation of role models.

These association dimensions make crime more likely when compounded. For example, interacting with people several times a week (frequency) for a longer period of time (duration) has greater influence on attitudes about criminal involvement than occasional and superficial social exchanges. Also, it is generally thought that because motives and corresponding courses of action are learned early in life, attitudes shaped by youth are especially consequential (priority) and largely determine learned behavior into adulthood and throughout life. Differential association theory posits that if a person's primary group interactions provide greater exposure to values and observations that favor rather than discourage crime and delinquency, it is more likely that the individual will also be delinquent.

The nine differential association propositions have shaped numerous leading criminological theories, a testament to Sutherland's "founding father" depiction. Albert Cohen, Donald Cressey, Lloyd Ohlin, George Vold, James Short, and numerous other prominent theorists were either students of Sutherland or otherwise heavily influenced by his work. The scope of their work is a testament to his impact on the field, particularly in instilling a sociological paradigm that continues to lead theoretical and applied criminology today. Social learning has remained a driving influence in criminological thought (discussed at length shortly), as has the social context (such as culture) in which learning transpires. Because Sutherland's theory draws on and integrates a range of dimensions exacting crime (social interaction, value systems, and cultural factors shaping the nature of learning), it is considered the first *general theory* of crime. As a general theory, differential association moved beyond the question of why individuals commit crime to explaining variation in crime rates across places (countries and cities) and social groups. Differential association is so ingrained in both academic and popular cultural understandings of crime that we readily accept that a delinquent peer group and a community characterized by procriminal definitions of values generate criminality.

AKERS'S SOCIAL LEARNING THEORY

One criticism of differential association theory is that it fails to explain exactly *how* people learn to commit crime. By the 1960s, researchers had made many advances about learning processes, and some criminologists saw the need to update differential association theory to reflect new knowledge on learning. Ronald Akers (collaborating with Robert Burgess) developed perhaps the most significant revision of differential association theory. Differential association remains a significant cornerstone of social learning theory, but Akers's theory incorporates reinforcement/punishment and observational learning as well.

As in Sutherland's theory, everyone is differentially exposed to "procriminal" and "proconforming" values. The people with whom we spend most of our time shape our reality (or how we interpret the world around us), reward and punish behavior, and provide the models for behavior. For differential association to have the best likelihood of an effect on one's behavior, a group has to have the opportunity to shape a person's behavior early, have a lengthier time to work on the individual, and have more frequent contact of a more intense quality. Family and close friends are the most likely sources of influence, but other sources may include teachers, neighbors, and even the media.

Definitions simply refer to how you define a situation. Many things have symbolic value that influences our thought processes and behavior. Think, for instance, of a miniskirt. To a Martian, a leather miniskirt is simply a piece of fabric with no symbolic value. If a miniskirt is being worn by a male football player around campus, some people might define the situation as inappropriate or positively weird. Martians, of course, would wonder what the fuss is about because they were not socialized about the meaning of the miniskirt. More specifically to social learning theory, definitions refer to all the attitudes and values we have about what is right and wrong, pleasurable and unpleasurable, and so forth. Both our own definitions as well as those belonging to others important to us can influence behavior. Definitions even provide us with our own justifications or excuses for committing crime under certain circumstances. For example, if a person does not define marijuana use as wrong, or problematic, then he or she may be able to use the drug without remorse or restraint.

Learning theory maintains that the continuation of a behavior depends on its consequences. Behavior associated with pleasure is more likely to be continued, but behavior that typically brings pain will be very short-lived indeed, a basic logic quite similar to deterrence and control theories. We will discuss four categories of reinforcement/punishment: positive reinforcement, negative reinforcement, positive punishment, and negative punishment. Reinforcement occurs when you try to get a behavior to continue, while punishment refers to anything that discourages a behavior. The notions of *positive* and *negative* are easy to get mixed up, since we normally think of *positive* as something good and *negative* as something bad. Instead, we suggest that you think of *positive* and *negative* in mathematical terms, where *positive* refers to giving, adding, or introducing something. *Negative* would indicate a situation in which you take something away.

If one wants a behavior to persist in someone, learning theory indicates that one way to accomplish this is to reward the behavior whenever it occurs (such as through approval or money). If you do something and the action or the reaction of others is to give you something you like, that is *positive reinforcement*. If you do something that causes others to take away something you didn't like (say, chores), then that would be *negative reinforcement*. But let's say that you want to get someone to stop doing something you don't like. You could inflict pain on that person (by hitting her or yelling), which would be *positive punishment*. Or you might consider punishing the person by taking away something she likes (such as your friendship), which would be *negative punishment*. Someone who has consistently experienced these rewards and punishments in the past is likely to associate them with present and future behavior, thus influencing whether he or she engages in them at all. So if someone associates crime with pleasure and the punishments are few and inconsistent, he or she is more likely to commit crime in the right situation. Conversely, someone who figures that the rewards of crime aren't worth it in view of the punishments will be less likely to commit crime.

Imitation occurs when one observes behavior in others and mimics it without necessarily understanding the consequences of the behavior. According to Akers, this is how novel behavior begins in the individual. (Remember that according to learning theories people do not spontaneously commit crime or deviance; they have to pick it up from somewhere.) Whether the behavior continues depends on the consequences. One of the authors, for example, knew a colleague who repeatedly used the "f-word" and was unsuccessful at guarding his language around his toddler. Swearing in a moment of frustration made him feel good, which the child apparently noticed. Consistent with the notion of imitation, the child began using the word, too. As is the case with toddlers, the child chose probably the most embarrassing moment to loudly and repeatedly imitate his father—in this case, in the middle of a church sermon. You can probably guess the consequences of the behavior!

Social learning theory thus offers ideas for explaining why people become violent. People observe violence in their environment and imitate it. They learn that some situations call for violence, and they learn the rules for when violence is acceptable and when it is not. Their violence is reinforced, and the punishments are of relatively less consequence than the rewards. While differential association and social learning theories dwell on the processes whereby people become criminal or law abiding, the remainder of this chapter will focus on the cultures themselves, which are the contexts in which socialization occurs.

AKERS' SOCIAL LEARNING AND SOCIAL STRUCTURE THEORY (SLSS)

In an effort to expand social learning theory by incorporating some of the key concepts and ideas from macro, or structural, criminology, Akers introduced social learning and social structure (SLSS) theory (Akers, 1998, 2009). Though social learning and its precursor, differential association, were originally framed as micro-level, or individual-level, theories, much of criminological thought and research has focused on macro-level, or structural, correlates of crime. In fact, an extensive line of empirical research has shown that both macro factors such as neighborhood conditions and micro factors such as delinquent peers are important to fully understanding the causes and context of criminal and delinquent behavior. Since we know that both do matter, a comprehensive theory will incorporate both of these types of variables. Akers' revised theory, called SLSS theory, does just that.

The basic proposition of Akers' revised theory is that variations in the social structure, culture, and locations of individuals and groups in the social system account for differences in the crime rates of different neighborhoods or cities. These variations in the social structure impact crime through their influence on differences among individuals on the key social learning variables—differential association, imitation, definitions, and reinforcements (Akers, 1998, p. 322). In this way, structural variables impact crime because they work through social learning variables. Essentially, depending on where people live and to which influences they are exposed, they are either more or less likely to experience learning environments conducive to criminal behavior. Simply put, the environment in which one is raised (e.g., neighborhood quality and family structure) affects the types of associations, definitions, and reinforcements they experience. These, in turn, impact the likelihood of individual crime and delinquency.

Take, for example, the issue of gangs. Gang membership is one of the most salient correlates of criminal and delinquent activity among adolescents. Gangs are not, of course, equally distributed throughout cities and neighborhoods; that is, not every neighborhood has gang activity. So, in order for an adolescent to be a member of a gang, and thus more likely to engage in crime and delinquency, he or she must first be exposed to gangs either in school or in the neighborhood. This can happen only if he or she happens to live in a neighborhood or attend a school where gangs are present.

CULTURAL TRANSMISSION THEORIES

Cultural studies inform us that *ideas* form the essence of both cultures and subcultures, the primary difference between the two being that their definitive idea sets are dissimilar and often in conflict. The very term *sub* suggests a separate reality—a distinct set of norms, values, mores, and attitudes that contrast with those of a larger and more dominant culture. In fact, values that conflict with mainstream normative standards characterize the *subcultural* or *cultural transmission* approach to crime.

Cultural transmission theories focus, then, on the ideas that form values and beliefs that differ from conventional ideas. Value systems that conflict with conventional standards largely define subcultures. The values, beliefs, and norms of deviant subcultures are thought to predispose people to commit crime while simultaneously providing a rationalization for being criminal. This rationalization is essentially a technique for neutralizing or minimizing the guilt associated with criminal offending (Sykes & Matza, 1957). Guilt associated with committing crime may be minimal or nonexistent, however, for subcultural members whose social learning process conveys the message that crime is normal.

Sometimes, subcultural group members see their behavior as altogether normal and noncriminal—the criminality involved is attached externally from the dominant culture. Think, for example, of the recent highly publicized manhunt and capture of Warren Jeffs, the fugitive leader of the Fundamental

Latter Day Saints (FLDS) who was on the FBI's Most Wanted list for facilitating the marriage and sexual coercion of underage girls. At the heart of this case was the issue of polygamy, which, while illegal, is normal practice for members of the FLDS. The involvement of Jeffs and his followers in polygamy, as illustrated in the popular HBO series *Big Love*, is considered a cornerstone of their religion, and FLDS members are socialized in polygamist families, wherein multiple wives and the marriage of underage teenage girls is commonplace. In this example, it is obvious that criminal behavior is not considered such within the context of the subculture and the behavior culturally transmitted through the family, community, and church from one generation to another.

The Rise of the Subcultural Perspective

Subcultural theories emerged as the dominant perspective on crime during the 1950s and, along with the differential association theory discussed earlier in this chapter, are among the earliest of the criminological theories. The 1950s were perhaps the foremost period during which middle-class values defined social norms and dominated social institutions. Freedom of expression and a widespread liberalization of social behavior and attitudes did not unfold on a national level until the 1960s and 1970s, and variation from traditional behavior was still viewed negatively, especially in the context of juvenile delinquency.

Social change usually occurs over time, and attitudes and behavior, particularly by teenagers, during the 1950s moved society away from its traditions. For the first time in American history, middle-class youth owned or had access to automobiles, and thus freedom. The rise of rock and roll in popular culture fostered rebellion, greater independence, and outright disobedience. The result was unprecedented levels of juvenile delinquency. Criminologists usually reject the notion that the rise in juvenile delinquency during this era resulted from a general societal moral decay, submitting instead that the delinquency rise was a result of the combination of greater freedom from parents (i.e., being less "homebound"); money from part-time jobs; and popular cultural endorsement of rebellion through drinking, indifference toward school performance, and sexual promiscuity.

Cultural transmission theories of crime and delinquency are based on the idea that people *internalize* values and beliefs. Learning shapes and perpetuates values that constitute a belief system representing social attitudes, preferences, and a sense of group identification. Belief systems come to characterize social environments, but some environments are distinguished by atypical, criminogenic value and normative systems wherein crime is encouraged or at least condoned. *Cultural variation* is thus a fundamental assumption, as is the power of conformity. Subscription to the unconventional is rewarded through increased social status and self-esteem that is denied to subgroup members elsewhere in the larger society.

Similarly situated people face social rejection because of their family's socioeconomic status or their race, ethnicity, religion, or place of geographic origin. It is common practice and seems only natural, for example, that people from the same state or region choose to identify and bond together. This reality becomes more pronounced when the group is outside its native environment, largely because its culturally specific practices and patterns of speech and behavior stand out as different. Noticeable differences in dialect, manners, and political or religious attitudes seem to simultaneously push nonnatives outside the mainstream and pull them into social groups and settings with which they are more familiar and feel more comfortable.

Associating with similar others happens all the time and doesn't necessarily involve deviance or crime. College students from the northeast region of the country enrolled in southern universities readily identify with one another and form peer groups that replicate practices reflecting their socialization processes and regional attitudes. The same social pattern holds true for southern students at northern schools, as people use culture as a means of defining themselves and to engage in social interaction. College students, regardless of where they are from, have a lot in common that dissuades them from crime; they are investing in themselves through education and preparing to compete in the economic arena and therefore are likely to realize upward social and economic mobility. Within subcultures, which are typically found in lower-class settings, college or preparation for college is not the norm. Rather, focus on meeting the more immediate necessities of daily life blocks upward-mobility opportunities for various groups situated throughout the lower class.

Cultural Norms and Legal Process

The study of subcultures from a criminological orientation is necessarily integrated with the study of *legal process*. While the production of law has been more aligned with special interests than those of the populace (Lynch & Groves, 1986), the criminal law is generally regarded (ironically, by the populace) as a product of normative consensus, a parallel reinforced by both the myths and realities of democratic ideals (Lynch & Groves, 1986). The law thus denotes the conventional or *dominant culture*. But an important, and paradoxical, feature of the legal process is the disjuncture between the moral normative value system held by lawmakers and the positional norms of various societal groups.

Positional norms, defined by values correlated with combinations of class status, sex, age, race and ethnicity, religious affiliation, and similar variables, are often underrepresented in the formal definition of authority. A simpler way to state this is that what is considered normal, appropriate, popular, or wrong varies considerably across different social groups throughout society. Repudiation of other groups' societal standards and norms, as formally specified in law and the rules governing societal institutions, fosters greater group cohesion, thus amplifying differences between the value systems of the subculture and the larger society. Thus, another defining characteristic of a subculture is **cultural conflict.**

It is important to make the conceptual distinction between subculture and population segment. The subcultural values of a gang, for example, may intensify, although membership is reduced through criminal justice system actions. In short, normative conflict is inherent in social structure; subcultures are very much a manifestation of this conflict. Because American society is so multifaceted and groups often disagree about appropriate standards, the criminal law becomes a kind of glue that holds society together in lieu of the absence of informal standards. Next, we examine the leading theories of lower-class crime that are known by a number of names, most commonly subcultural theory, cultural transmission theory, and cultural conflict theory.

Cohen's Middle-Class Measuring Rod

Most criminology and criminal justice text authors begin discussion of subculture theory with the work of Albert K. Cohen (Lilly, Cullen, & Ball, 1989; Martin, Mutchnick, & Austin, 1990; Reid, 1990; Shoemaker, 2004). Others, however, have chosen to either ignore (Bartol, 1980; Vold & Bernard, 1986) or minimize Cohen's contribution. This lack of consensus raises the question of whether Cohen's theory stands alone as a cultural accounting of crime or is more of an extension and synthesis of previously established theories. The answer lies in examination of not just Cohen's writings but also his academic background.

Perhaps no student of sociology has ever enjoyed exposure to the high quality of instruction as Albert Cohen. He enrolled in courses taught by prominent sociologists, most notably Talcott Parsons and Robert K. Merton, while an undergraduate during the 1930s at Harvard. While pursuing a master's degree at Indiana University, Cohen studied under Edwin Sutherland. After service in the army during World War II, he returned to Harvard as a doctoral student, where he was mentored by the famous sociologist George Homans (Martin et al., 1990). Of these scholars, Merton and Sutherland substantially molded Cohen's interests with their strain and differential association theories, respectively. It is because of these influences that his works have occasionally been omitted from reviews of subculture literature. Specifically, it has been alleged that Cohen focuses on internal social conditions of subcultures, culminating in a strain theory dependent on social structural forces, instead of a more appropriate focus on the essence of a subculture, ideas ((Bernard, Snipes & Gerould, 2009). This once dissenting view gained momentum throughout the discipline, evident by Thomas O'Connor's paper, "Is Albert Cohen a Strain Theorist?"—a 1992 American Society of Criminology Gene Carte Paper Competition winner (*The Criminologist*, 1992). Today, criminological theory texts often discuss

Cohen in the context of strain rather than subculture. Nonetheless, Cohen remains a founding pioneer of subcultural theory.

Cohen's repute as the founder of a distinct subcultural theory is based on his most famous work, *Delinquent Boys: The Culture of the Gang* (1955). In this revised version of his doctoral dissertation, Cohen developed a general theory of subcultures through a detailed commentary on delinquent gangs that features five major causal factors: *prevalence, origins, process, purpose,* and *problem.* Prevalence refers to the uneven distribution of delinquency across class sectors in society. From a strain theory orientation, Cohen concluded that some groups were more anomic and moved toward deviance due to societal constraints. The delinquent-prone groups were predominantly from working-class backgrounds.

From a symbolic interactionism perspective, Cohen postulated that individuals from the bottom end of the socioeconomic scale shared difficulty in conforming to the dominant society that largely rejected them. The emergence of subcultures, then, is an alternative created by various people to deal with their mutual rejection, a collective response to shared problems. The process by which subcultures form and evolve is one of trial and error, a redefining of accepted norms likened to crowd behavior. Cohen notes that while "collective outbursts" as a way of solving problems are usually temporary and soon wane, they often succeed in establishing subcultures that, once created, assume a life of their own (1955).

The purpose of the subculture is individual benefit via interaction with the subgroup. The benefit may be material, but also psychological in terms of positive reinforcement, a necessary ingredient for continued group existence. Precisely, individuals may profit by increased self-esteem and social status. These micro-level advantages foster greater group cohesion, making the differences in value systems of the subculture and the larger society pronounced. Repudiation of societal standards and norms thus become a defining characteristic of a subculture and necessarily result in cultural conflict, often referred to as *cultural resistance* (Vetter & Silverman, 1978).

In his focus on delinquent gangs, Cohen noticed class-differentiated degrees of drive and ambition that manifested themselves in individual responsibility. Due to social structural constraints largely beyond their control, lower-class youths experience a socialization process that devalues success in the classroom, deferred gratification, long-term planning, and the cultivation of etiquette mandatory for survival in the business and social arenas (Cohen, 1955). Cohen also observed that working-class juveniles generally did not participate in wholesome leisure activity, opting instead for activities typified by physical aggression, consequently stunting the development of intellectual and social skills valued in the mainstream culture.

The overall learning experience of lower-class males leaves them ill prepared, says Cohen (1955, p. 129), to compete in a world gauged by a **middle-class measuring rod.** The deficiencies of lower-class youth are most noticeable in the classroom, where working-class youth are frequently overshadowed and belittled by their middle-class counterparts. Turning to membership in a delinquent gang is a normal adaptation to status frustration resulting from clashing cultures.

Reviews of Cohen's gang theory of delinquency have been comparatively favorable, one early exception being an *American Sociological Review* article (Kitsuse & Dietrick, 1959) that took issue with methodological considerations. It contended that Cohen failed to present adequate support for what was basically an untestable theory. In response to this criticism, others (Martin et al., 1990) have considered the matter an issue of perspective. The criticism of verification has merit from a positivistic viewpoint, but Cohen's book is a theoretical commentary with an objective of recognizing qualitative distinctions between juvenile and adult crime and the uneven distribution of delinquency throughout society that prompts the creation of gangs (Shoemaker, 2004).

Cloward and Ohlin's Gang Typology

Whereas a correct chronological listing of subculture theories would move from Cohen (1955) to Miller (1958), Richard Cloward and Lloyd Ohlin's subcultural theory of delinquency (1960) is naturally paired with Cohen's, for it too is sometimes classified as a strain theory. Like most criminological theories of this era, Cloward and Ohlin focused on the delinquent behavior of gangs (Williams & McShane, 1988). Not dissimilar from Cohen, their major work, *Delinquency and Opportunity: A Theory of Delinquent Gangs* (1960), is rooted in Merton's anomie and Sutherland's differential association.

In several respects, Cloward and Ohlin further Cohen's hypothesis by offering a more detailed accounting of both subculture emergence and the nature of defiant outgroups via a typology of gangs. Often termed an *opportunity theory* (Bartol, 1980; Lilly et al., 1989; Shoemaker, 2004), the basic assumptions are that *limited and blocked economic aspirations lead to frustration and negative self-esteem* and that *these frustrations move youth to form gangs that vary in type.* The ratio of conventional and criminal values to which a juvenile is consistently exposed accounts for the differences in the character of the gangs. Cloward and Ohlin's thesis is that lower-class teenagers realize they have little chance for future success by conventional standards and consequently resort to membership in one of three types of gangs whose different activities result from a shared subcultural perspective.

The typology of gangs is a hierarchy, with the *criminal gang* at the top. Individuals reacting to frustration from failure may blame society rather than themselves. Part of this rationalization includes justifying successful illegal activity. Success models for lower-class youth are not the bankers and lawyers that middle-class youth seek to emulate, but rather thieves and drug dealers whom they observe daily. This suggests an ecological influence as described by Shaw and McKay (1942) wherein children grow into crime, which appears to be an attractive option in depressed environments.

Cloward and Ohlin note that not all have the skills and composure to integrate into the criminal gang, which screens potential members for certain abilities and willingness to conform to a code of values necessary to the unit's success. Mandatory skills include self-control, demonstrated solidarity to the group, and desire to cultivate one's criminal ability (Bartol, 1980, pp. 98–99). The criminal gang revolves around stealing in a social context, the deviant act itself serving to positively reinforce the mutual codependence between the juvenile and the gang.

Because some strained youth are precluded from gangs that primarily steal, they congregate around violent behavior. This type of subgroup is called a *conflict gang* (Cloward & Ohlin, 1960) and is often the result of an absence of adult role models that are involved in utilitarian criminal behavior. Violent behavior, such as fighting, arson, and serious vandalism, is attributable to a sociological factor, lack of social control. A lack of interest by adults in the future success or failure of their sons and other young males in the neighborhood symbolizes rejection, the adaptation to which is "exploration of nonconformist alternatives" (Cloward & Ohlin, 1960, p. 86).

Cloward and Ohlin also observed that some youth were neither violent nor successful in criminal endeavors. Having failed in both conventional and multiple deviant sectors of society, they formed a third variety of gang, the *retreatist gang*, largely characterized by drug use (Cloward & Ohlin, 1960, p. 183). Members of this kind of comparatively unorganized gang turn to drugs as an escape from status frustration that comes from falling short of both middle-class standards and those of others within their own social class.

While all three gang types emerge in lower-socioeconomic neighborhoods, the particular form they assume is related to the degree of organization of both licit and illicit activity in an area. Although Cloward and Ohlin framed a theory that is more descriptive than Cohen's, it has been crit-icized for its unnaturalistic rigidity (Empey, 1982, p. 250; Lilly et al., 1989). Delinquents do not choose between theft, vandalism, or drug use through a conscious affiliation with gang types. Instead, any one of the gang types may engage in all or a combination of these behaviors.

In sum, Cloward and Ohlin followed a strain tradition to view society as a constraining mechanism that prompted lower-class juveniles to respond by forming gangs. The type of gang a frustrated youth joins depends on the opportunity structure of a neighborhood, particularly the mixture of criminal and law-abiding values held by adult role models. The delinquent acts of gang members are considered normal in that they are responses of conformity by young males to their environment.

Miller's Focal Concerns

Unlike the delinquency theories of Cohen and of Cloward and Ohlin, Walter B. Miller envisioned a pure cultural theory explaining gang delinquency. His theory, presented in an article titled "Lower-Class Culture as a Generating

Milieu of Gang Delinquency" (1958), argued the existence of a distinct and observable lower-class culture. Whereas the middle class has values, the lower class has defining **focal concerns**: *trouble, toughness, smartness, excitement, fate,* and *autonomy.*

Trouble, the first of Miller's focal concerns, refers to getting into and staying out of trouble; primarily this can relate to "official" forms of trouble that involve law enforcement, but can also be understood as a tendency for problematic behavior more generally (e.g., missing work, domestic problems, and consequences of alcohol and drug use). Toughness involves an overemphasis on masculinity, endurance, and strength, what is often referred to in Latino cultures as *machismo.* Miller attributed this exaggerated sense of masculinity to a lack of adult male role models. In many disadvantaged neighborhoods, young boys do not have role models to learn from and imitate and thus their behavior becomes extreme expressions of what they perceive to be a correct representation of manhood. A focus on toughness can lead to a hypersensitivity toward perceived challenges to one's manliness, often resulting in a greater likelihood for interpersonal conflict.

Smartness denotes a skill for outsmarting others toward the goal of taking advantage of someone; it refers to a street sense or street smarts as opposed to educational attainment. Excitement involves the constant search for thrills and stimulation (a characteristic frequently observed among the criminal element). Fate is the belief that individuals are not in control of what happens to them; instead, events simply unfold with no rhyme or reason. It is of course easier to alleviate one's own guilt or anxiety over their own behavior and life circumstances if that person believes things have just happened to them. Finally, autonomy infers a resentment and rejection of authority and rules, be it at school with teachers or in the streets with law enforcement.

These concerns advocate the formation of street-corner gangs, while undermining the positive reinforcement needed for the development of conventional values. Smartness, for example, is a skill that warrants respect in the lower-class culture. This refers to the ability to con someone in real-life situations, rather than formal knowledge that is relatively inapplicable and even resented in poorer areas. The notion of fate discourages the work ethic and minimizes hope for self-improvement. Deviance is normal and to be expected in lower-class cultures because the focal concerns make conformity to criminal behavior as natural as acceptance of conventional mores for the middle class. Miller observes that juveniles accepting a preponderance of these "cultural practices which comprise essential elements of the total life pattern of lower class culture automatically violate legal norms" (1958, pp. 5–19).

Miller's theory is an explanation of delinquency situated in depressed inner cities, wherein the majority of households were headed by females. Evaluation of the theory has centered on two significant criticisms. First, some of the focal concerns contended to be exclusive to the lower class are also observable in the middle class (Shoemaker, 2004). A second and more controversial issue concerns the use of race rather than class in assessing the relationship between delinquency, matriarchal households, and an exaggerated sense of masculinity associated with physical aggression (Berger & Simon, 1974; Moynihan, 1967). Unfortunately, a focus on blacks and atypical family structure moves discussion away from the veracity of a lower-class value system to differences in racial groups.

The impact of the theories of Cohen, Cloward and Ohlin, and Miller was significant in two respects. First, they developed a general subcultural theory around what was perceived to be a timely issue. Second, the early studies as a whole focused on what was then a novel problem, the emergence of gangs. Gangs in the future were to be defined as delinquent and subcultures considered inherently deviant. Moreover, subculture became a major concept in sociology, a convenient comparative device for highlighting normative standards.

Subculture theories dominated criminological thought during the 1950s and 1960s. In stressing that deviant behavior was more or less normal for those within the subculture, several theorists built on the initial efforts of Cohen (1955), Miller (1958), Cloward and Ohlin (1960), and Wolfgang and Ferracuti (1967). New approaches developed systematic descriptions of the generating processes and patterns of delinquency, often in a gang context (Arnold, 1965; Bordua, 1961; Kobrin, Puntil, & Peluso, 1967). Policing gangs was equated with addressing the larger issue of delinquency, and research funding to address gang delinquency was plentiful. Major studies thus focused on the gang and both relied on and built on subculture explanations of delinquency. In short, the rise of the subculture perspective was aided by the circumstances of social transition, a point that also explains, in part, its decline.

The Demise of the Subcultural Perspective

By the 1960s a number of interrelated social movements (including the civil rights crusade, anti-Vietnam protest, and the counterculture) were under way. In varying degrees they expressed the same themes: distrust and defiance of authority. As the criminal justice system came to be perceived as an instrument of exploitation, theorists' attention shifted to opposing the oppressiveness of the criminal justice system (see Chapter 9).

As bandwagon shifts to the political left transpired, labeling theory soon replaced cultural transmission as the leading approach to explaining crime (Bookin-Weiner & Horowitz, 1983). The main thrust of labeling theory was that crime and delinquency are definitions and labels that are assigned to people and events by operatives of the criminal justice system. Explaining crime and delinquency from this perspective, then, means explaining how the labeling process works and how it singles out certain people for labeling and not others.

In its more extreme formulations, labeling theory was not concerned with explaining the behavior we call crime and delinquency, because criminals and delinquents were not assumed to differ very much in their behavior from other people. Rather, the real difference is said to be the degree of vulnerability to the labeling activities of the criminal justice system.

During this period of interest in labeling, theoretically oriented research on the relationship between crime and culture languished, but did not disappear. More moderate versions of labeling theory propelled some research (such as research on gang behavior and emphasis on the role of official processing and labeling in the development of that behavior), but the leading cause of crime and delinquency was considered the criminal justice system itself (Armstrong & Wilson, 1973; Werthman, 1967). Specifically, criminal and delinquent behavior was portrayed as a rational and justified response to social inequality and class oppression (Bookin, 1980).

Much of the contemporary literature of the 1970s, not just on gangs but on social problems generally, was not only indifferent to subculture theory but actively opposed to it. This literature included works such as Chambliss's "The Saints and the Roughnecks" (1973), which emphasized a conflict perspective that viewed the subculture perspective as too conservative. Social control was deemed reactionary because crime and delinquency were considered direct, reasonable, and even justifiable adaptations to injustice.

The rise of social control theory (see Hirschi, 1969) did not seriously factor into the subculture perspective either, though seemingly well-suited to do so (Bookin-Weiner & Horowitz, 1983; Vold & Bernard, 1986). The central elements of attachment to others, degrees of commitment to conventionality, daily routine, and belief in a moral order speak to why subcultures exist and have implications for criminal behavior therein (see Chapter 8). Ensuing research interests moved toward macro-level determinants of crime and further away from culture and group behavior. Consequently, subcultures were largely ignored until the mid-1980s, when they were seriously connected with gang-related drug and violence problems (Curry & Spergel, 1988).

While historical developments set into motion a chain of events that moved criminological theorizing away from the subculture, the theory was further marred by paradigm shifts in social science research methodology. The rise of positivism delivered subculture theory a would-be deathblow. There was suddenly a disjuncture between the strategy of observation-based data gathering used by most subcultural theorists and a newer preferred theoretical–methodological symmetry involving variable assignment, measurement, and analysis congruent with causality as established by levels of statistical correlation. Critics of subculture theory (see Ball-Rokeach, 1973; Kitsuse & Dietrick, 1959; Kornhauser, 1978) focused on the growing belief that acceptable science must subscribe to particular precepts that subculture explanations did not meet.

The cultural transmission theories could not be adequately tested through the dominant variable analysis methodology that largely defines what is and is not considered acceptable social science. Most central to this discussion is the difficulty that social scientists experienced concerning how to adequately measure subculture and its effects. Another fundamental criticism concerned the problem of *tautological reasoning,* that is, an unclear separation of cause and effect. Does subculture (as an independent variable) generate crime (the dependent variable), or vice versa? For many, the inability to answer this question in terms of statistical clarity moved attention away from the causal effects of the cultural transmission of criminogenic values.

Subcultures of Violence and the Rerise of the Cultural Perspective

A main reason that cultural transmission theory survived intellectual extinction is the work of Wolfgang and Ferracuti (1967), who extended the subcultural perspective beyond a gang context. They argued that homicide resulted from acceptance of a value system that endorsed violence, observing that "Groups with the highest rates of homicide have in the most intense degree a subculture of violence" (p. 78). *Subcultures of violence* were identified by Wolfgang and Ferracuti throughout the social strata. Subcultures are identifiable at the small-group or micro level—for example, delinquent and criminal gangs. They are also recognized at larger social levels, often certain communities labeled "bad parts of town" or even an entire region of the country such as the American South.

Wolfgang and Ferracuti's attention to regional variation in high rates of violence and particularly homicide prompted criminologists to focus on the American South, where violence was far more commonplace. Accordingly, *southern subculture of violence theory* emerged and revitalized the cultural transmission approach to explaining crime. Criminologists have debated whether disproportionately high rates of southern violence stem from cultural or structural properties. Those making the structural argument have focused on the high level of poverty in the region that, when coupled with the related factors of crowded households and a hot climate, seemingly explain frustration and aggravated conditions ripe for violent outbursts. While these factors apply to southern settings, they are also applicable to other areas, such as the Southwest, and thus fail to adequately account for the southern crime phenomenon.

Cultural theorists point, instead, to the South's retention of a distinct identity that characterizes a subsociety or general subculture (Gastil, 1971; Hackney, 1969; Huff-Corzine, Corzine, & Moore, 1991). The high value placed on autonomy, reputation, the glorification of military skills, high levels of gun ownership, and, particularly, the South's history foster a regional subculture of violence. The South's history as a frontier region in the 1700s and 1800s necessitated independence and informal social control realized through vigilante justice. The practice of slavery, the custom of dispute resolution through dueling in the upper class and family feuds in the lower class, high levels of gun ownership, and, most significantly, subscription to a culture of honor came to characterize a distinct culture (Reed, 1972). The southern sub-culture of violence theorists argued that southern culture and the premium placed on honor moved southerners to approve of violence—but not under all circumstances. Violence is considered a normal response, and thus more likely, only in response to challenge of one's honor and in defensive contexts.

Nisbett and Cohen (1996) have recently presented a **culture of honor** theory that addresses southern crime and extends the general knowledge base on the causal effects of subcultural value systems. They observe that the South is heavily populated by the Scots–Irish, who primarily occupy the highland areas of the region, also where the majority of homicides occur. These groups are physically isolated in remote, rural settings, very homogeneous, and experience little migration in or out, and their social attitudes and standards of behavior are less challenged by changing times or outside ideas. It is contended that the same values of their Celtic ancestors—independence, close-knit kinship groups, defense of personal and family honor, and freedom were transmitted from one generation to the next to generate contemporary values. By comparing levels of violence across lowland, rolling hills, and mountainous areas, the culture of honor theory illustrates that violence is most common in places where the high value placed on honor has been least diffused. Researchers further note that in such places the criminal law reflects ideas that endorse violence, such as support for the death penalty.

Criminologists are considering the effects of migration on the southern subculture of violence, generally concluding that greater exposure to outside influence will weaken beliefs and values that support violence. It is uncertain if this is altogether correct, however, due to the fundamental subcultural assumption of cultural conflict. As traditional southern attitudes and practices begin to erode somewhat proportionally to immigration and the aging of older generations, those still subscribing to the traditional ways will likely "solidify the core" as a reaction to outside pressures and challenges to their way of life.

Criminologists have certainly recognized the importance of youth subcultures in a more general manner recently, largely due to the well-known Columbine High School shootings. Whereas previous attention to culture and crime was limited to lower-class criminality, gangs, or the American South, the Columbine incident portrayed the gothic subculture as a facilitating context in the tragedy.

Elijah Anderson's *Code of the Street* (1999) is perhaps the foremost contemporary statement on subculture and crime. This work interestingly focuses on lower-class and inner-city criminality like the 1950s cultural transmission theories, arguing that it is largely a function of a subcultural norming process. Like Miller (1958), Anderson suggests that distinct culturally based values or elements generate crime and, like Cohen (1955), he suggests that a lack of competitiveness in conventional arenas leads to reaction formations involving and valuing criminal behavior. The street culture or "code" prescribes violent responses to personal attacks and shows of disrespect. The fundamental assumption that defines the code is that no sign of weakness can be displayed, for doing so invites additional attacks. A major element of this logic is status insecurity, which, similar to Miller's focal concerns, is specific to the lower class. Lacking affluence, occupational status, and professional prestige, young males in depressed socioeconomic urban areas believe that physical aggression is vital to their survival while also bolstering their self-esteem and reputation in the neighborhood.

Anderson's subcultural theory is more complex than the 1950s versions in that, while illustrating deviant values and a socialization process favorable to crime, adoption of the code is adaptation to the immediate environment. Accordingly, the "code" largely applies to public life but carries over to private settings only for those most alienated and socially isolated within high-crime communities. The code is problematic beyond its advocacy of violent retaliation, promoting a "generalized contempt" for the wider society on the perception that the society carries a mutual contempt for inner-city youth. Though based on ethnography conducted during the 1990s, Anderson's attention to a street code is defined, partially, in comparison to a "decent" moral code of the inner city, which is a prosocial and conventional reference point akin to Cohen's utilization of the middle-class measuring rod. Whereas Cohen used the measuring-rod metaphor to accentuate differences between social classes, Anderson's contribution should be credited with calling attention to value differences specific to criminality within the lower social class.

Recent research has attempted to test Anderson's *Code of the Street* thesis. For example, the work of Stewart and his colleagues (Stewart, Schreck, & Brunson, 2008; Stewart, Schreck, & Simons, 2006; Stewart & Simons, 2006) has explored the influence of the street code on both violent crime and violent victimization among African American adolescents. These studies found that the neighborhoods in which adolescents reside, the characteristics of their families (e.g., single-parent–headed households), and their experiences with racial discrimination all impact the likelihood of adopting the street code. Adoption of the street code, in turn, increases adolescents' likelihood of both committing violent crime and being the victim of violence. Stewart's contributions are unique in that they examine both the effects of living in a disadvantaged, disorganized neighborhood (macro-level, structural factors) and individual adoption of the street code mentality (micro-level).

SUMMARY

According to learning and cultural transmission theories, crime, like all behavior, results from a socialization process that encourages crime. Learning theories focus on the social processes wherein youth are exposed to behavioral definitions favorable to crime. Role models and peer groups are important facilitators in the learning process, reflecting the significance of differential association. Cultural transmission theories focus less on the learning process and more on the values characterizing the (sub)culture; the subculture both provides a context in which learning occurs and shapes what is learned through establishing normative behavior.

Social learning theories have become increasingly complex, with Akers's version being the most general learning-based explanation of crime with strong empirical support. Subcultural theories emerged as a major force in criminology during the 1950s and 1960s, were largely ignored during the 1970s, and have reemerged since. Cultural theories have primarily focused on lower-class culture, especially in urban and gang contexts. Attention to subcultures of violence is applicable outside urban settings, most notably the southern subculture of violence thesis emphasizing a code of honor prescribing violent retaliation to threats and insults. Most recently, Anderson's *Code of the Streets* reiterates a code of honor-based value system while returning to the applicability of the culture and crime relationship to urban crime.

KEY TERMS

cultural conflict a repudiation of other groups' societal standards and norms fostering greater group cohesion as a reaction formation ideologically rooted in cultural resistence; conflictual processes typically accentuate differences between groups as a justificatory reference point for group validation

cultural transmission theory a theory that contends that group values, historical customs, and the ethnocentric nature of social learning are intergenerationally transferred normative standards; values that accentuate the role of violence are associated with gangs, the lower class, the American South, inner-city minorities, and fringe social groups

culture of honor a value system of requisite retaliatory and defensive violence for protection and defense of social status threats and personal insults; contextually based in family and immediate group interaction; often identified with southern culture and high violent crime rates

differential association a concept developed by Edwin Sutherland that emphasizes the group nature of delinquency as characterized by the interaction of similarly suited individuals, particularly those with severed ties to conventional social institutions and practices

focal concerns Miller's subcultural elements that combine to characterize lower-class culture; considered less conceptually sophisticated than middle-class values; these elements (smartness, toughness, trouble, autonomy, fate, and excitement) condition the behavioral

norms that define a value system con-
doning and encouraging crime

imitation mimicking observed behavior,
often without much understanding of
direct consequences

learning theories a strand of criminological
theory emphasizing the socialization
processes involving level of definitions
favorable to crime versus conventional
definitions; reference group, subculture,
and environment are important, additionally relevant factors; differential
association is a fundamental assumption; Akers is one of the leading contemporary learning theorists

middle-class measuring rod a metaphor
coined by Albert Cohen, a leading
pioneer of the subcultural approach,
that references middle-class values,
norms, and expected standards of
academic, social, and civic achievement against which lower-class youth
experience status frustration and
strain that is reduced through crime
and gang affiliation

SLSS theory a theoretical elaboration of
Akers' original social learning theory
emphasizing focus on environmental
and support elements at macro-level
analysis.

DISCUSSION QUESTIONS

1. What is meant by the term *differential association*, and how is this
concept significant to the learning
process?

2. Why doesn't everyone who is socialized in a deviant subcultural setting
become criminal?

3. How does Cohen's middle-class
measuring rod have current applicability for lower-class criminality as

a reaction formation to status frustration?

4. Do you think W. B. Miller's focal
concerns are useful for explaining
lower-class criminality today?

5. Will migration patterns in the
American South lessen or worsen
violent crime, according to the logic
put forth by the culture of honor
thesis?

REFERENCES

Akers, R. L. (1998). *Social learning and social structure: A general theory of crime and deviance.* Boston: Northeastern University Press.

Akers, R. L. (2009). *Social learning and social structure: A general theory of crime and deviance* (2nd ed.). Boston: Northeastern University Press.

Anderson, E. (1999). *Code of the street: Decency, violence and the moral life of the inner city.* New York: Norton.

Andrews, D. A., & Bonta, J. (1998). *Psychology of criminal conduct* (2nd ed.). Cincinnati, OH: Anderson.

Armstrong, G., & Wilson, M. (1973). City politics and deviance amplification. In I. Taylor & L. Taylor (Eds.), *Politics and deviance.* New York: Penguin Books.

Arnold, W. R. (1965). The concept of the gang. *Sociological Quarterly, 7,* 59–75.

Ball-Rokeach, S. J. (1973). Values and violence: A test of the subculture of violence thesis. *American Sociological Review, 38,* 736–749.

Bandura, A. (1962). *Social learning through interaction.* Lincoln: University of Nebraska Press.

Bartol, C. R. (1980). *Criminal behavior: A psychosocial approach.* Upper Saddle River, NJ: Prentice Hall.

Berger, A. S., & Simon, W. (1974). Black families and the Moynihan Report: A research evaluation. *Social Problems, 22,* 145–161.

Bernard, T. J., Snipes, J. B. & Gerould, A. L. (2009). *Vold's Theoretical Criminology* (6th ed.). New York: Oxford University Press.

Bookin, H. (August 1980). *The gangs that didn't go straight.* Paper presented to the Society for the Study of Social Problems, New York.

Bookin-Weiner, H., & Horowitz, R. (1983). The end of the youth gang: Fad or fact? *Criminology, 21,* 585–602.

Bordua, D. J. (1961). Delinquent subcultures: Sociological interpretations of gang delinquency. *Annals of the American Academy of Social Science, 338,* 119–136.

Chambliss, W. J. (1973). The saints and the roughnecks. *Society, 11*(1), 24–31.

Cloward, R. A., & Ohlin, L. E. (1960). *Delinquency and opportunity: A theory of delinquent gangs.* Glencoe, IL: Free Press.

Cohen, A. K. (1955). *Delinquent boys: The culture of the gang.* Glencoe, IL: Free Press.

Curry, G. D., & Spergel, I. A. (1988). Gang homicide, delinquency and community. *Criminology, 26*(3), 381–406.

Empey, L. (1982). *American delinquency: Its meaning and construction.* Homewood, IL: Dorsey.

Gastil, R. (1971). Homicide and a regional culture of violence. *American Sociological Review, 36,* 412–427.

Hackney, S. (1969). Southern violence. *American Historical Review, 74,* 906–925.

Hirschi, T. (1969). *Causes of delinquency.* Berkeley: University of California Press.

Huff-Corzine, L., Corzine, J., & Moore, D. (1991). Deadly connections: Culture, poverty, and the direction of lethal violence. *Social Forces, 69*(3), 715–732.

Kitsuse, J., & Dietrick, D. C. (1959). Delinquent boys: A critique. *American Sociological Review, 24,* 208–215.

Kobrin, S., Puntil, J., & Peluso, E. (1967). Criteria of status among street groups. *Journal of Research in Crime and Delinquency, 4*(1), 98–118.

Kornhauser, R. R. (1978). *Social sources of delinquency: An appraisal of analytic models.* Chicago: University of Chicago Press.

Lilly, J. R., Cullen, F. T., & Ball, R. A. (1989). *Criminological theory: Context and consequences.* Newbury Park, CA: Sage.

Lynch, M. J., & Groves, W. B. (1986). *A primer in radical criminology.* New York: Harrow & Heston.

Martin, R., Mutchnick, R. J., & Austin, W. T. (1990). *Criminological thought: Pioneers past and present.* New York: Macmillan.

Miller, W. B. (1958). Lower-class culture as a generating milieu of gang delinquency. *Journal of Social Issues, 14*(3), 5–19.

Moynihan, D. P. (1967). *The Negro family: The case for national action.* Washington, DC: Government Printing Office.

Nisbett, R. E., & Cohen, D. (1996). *Culture of honor: The psychology of violence in the South.* Boulder, CO: Westview Press.

Reed, J. S. (1972). *The enduring South: Subcultural persistence in mass society.* Lexington, MA: Lexington Books.

Reid, S. T. (1990). *Crime and criminology.* Fort Worth, TX: Holt, Rinehart & Winston.

Shaw, C. R., & McKay, H. D. (1942). *Juvenile delinquency and urban areas.* Chicago: University of Chicago Press.

Shoemaker, D. J. (2004). *Theories of delinquency: An examination of explanations of delinquent behavior* (5th ed.). New York: Oxford University Press.

Stewart, E. A., Schreck, C. J., & Brunson, R. K. (2008). Lessons of the street code: Policy implications for reducing violent victimization among disadvantaged citizens. *Journal of Contemporary Criminal Justice, 24*(2), 137–147.

Stewart, E. A., Schreck, C. J., & Simons, R. L. (2006). I ain't gonna let no one disrespect me: Does the code of the street reduce or increase violent victimization among African-American adolescents? *Journal of Research in Crime and Delinquency, 43*(4), 427–458.

Stewart, E. A., & Simons, R. L. (2006). Structure and culture in African-American adolescent violence: A partial test of the "Code of the Street" thesis. *Justice Quarterly, 23*(1), 1–33.

Sutherland, E. (1947). *Principles of criminology* (4th ed.). Philadelphia: J.B. Lippincott.

Sykes, G. & Matza, D. (1957). Techniques of neutralization: A theory of delinquency. *American Sociological Review. 22*(6).

The criminologist. (1992). *Official Newsletter of the American Society of Criminology, 17*(6), 13.

Vetter, H. J., & Silverman, I. J. (1978). *The nature of crime.* Philadelphia: Saunders.

Vold, G. B., & Bernard, T. J. (1986). *Theoretical criminology* (3rd ed.). New York: Oxford University Press.

Werthman, C. (1967). The function of social definitions in the development of delinquent careers. In P. G. Garabedian & D. C. Gibbons (Eds.), *Becoming delinquent: Young offenders and the correctional process.* Chicago: Aldine.

Williams, F. P., III, & McShane, M. D. (1988). *Criminological theory.* Upper Saddle River, NJ: Prentice Hall.

Wolfgang, M. E., & Ferracuti, F. (1967). *The subculture of violence: Towards an integrated theory in criminology.* London: Tavistock.

Wolfgang, M. E., Figlio, R. M., & Sellin, T. (1972). *Delinquency in a birth cohort.* Chicago: University of Chicago Press.

CHAPTER 7

STRAIN THEORIES OF CRIME

As the revision of this textbook was nearing completion, a remarkable homicide took place. The killer was 57-year-old George Zinkhan, who was a professor at the University of Georgia. College professors are usually perceived as timid, retiring types—indeed, Zinkhan's neighbors described him as such. Although anecdotal student comments did not indicate much liking for Professor Zinkhan, his supervisors characterized him to news reporters as "a respected professor on campus" with an "impeccable" record. Colleagues who knew him well would have been surprised to hear that Zinkhan ever raised his voice, let alone got mad. But one day he did. On April 25, 2009, he arrived at the Athens (Georgia) Community Theater and got into an argument with his wife. News stories so far have not reported what the argument was about, but friends and family speculated that Marie Bruce, Zinkhan's wife, might have been considering divorce (which is plausible enough, as colleagues reported that he spoke little of his wife and only talked about his children). But whatever the argument was about, afterward Zinkhan walked away for a few moments. And then he returned with two handguns and opened fire. Three people, including his wife, were killed and two others were injured. So far as anyone could determine, Zinkhan was last seen alive when he dropped off his two children at a neighbor's house afterward. He then evidently drove to a forest, where a week later authorities found his wrecked and abandoned Jeep Liberty. A week after finding the Jeep, police dogs found Zinkhan's body buried in thick woods 10 miles west of Athens. And, so ended a man's prolific academic career, his life, as well as the lives of three others—tragic outcomes of a simple argument.

Zinkhan's slaying of three people is unusual in many respects, especially since most arguments fortunately do not end in violence. But the basic motivation behind his crime is one that many folks can relate to. Does it seem reasonable to you that crime is more likely to occur when someone fails to get something he or she wants or needs, or else when placed under a great deal of stress? For instance, students in financial difficulties might feel frustrated and turn to stealing food, beer, or clothes from their roommates. The stress of taking exams or having to find a job after graduation makes drinking alcohol—in sufficient quantities to forget one's troubles—appealing, in order to alleviate the stress. Strain theories, the focus of this chapter, generally make the case that if people get frustrated in their desires, or experience stress, they will be more likely to commit crime.

Strain theories are among the older criminological theories in the literature, and it says something that they still hold currency for today. Robert Merton, a sociologist, formulated a theory of "anomie" (later called "strain theory" by others) during the 1930s, and in the subsequent decades his version of strain theory has seen many refinements (see Cloward & Ohlin, 1960; Cohen, 1955). After a long period as the dominant and influential theory of crime, strain theory waned in importance during the 1970s and 1980s before being revived by such criminologists as Robert Agnew (1992) and Steven Messner and Richard Rosenfeld (1994). Over the years, the various versions of strain theory have received considerable testing, and Agnew's version of strain theory is one of the most frequently tested theories in the literature today.

WHAT DO STRAIN THEORIES ASSUME?

You may have noticed that some theories, such as deterrence and control theories, allege that people are naturally inclined to commit crime and that the reason many people don't is because they are under some sort of restraint. That is, they are afraid for some reason to commit crime or else are unable to do so. In this case, we don't need frustration or stress to explain the causation of crime since people are naturally inclined to do it anyway (or put another way, these theories might say that everyone is pretty much continually frustrated, and whether they act on any given frustration depends on whether the advantages outweigh the costs). Some other theories, however, say that crime is not natural to human beings. Rather, something externally imposed on us must push, prod, or compel us to commit crime. Strain theories take the latter approach, saying that we wouldn't normally commit crime but do so because of external circumstances that place us in a situation we don't like. That is, we generally would like to be law abiding and live in the manner society would expect us to; however, we encounter obstacles that prevent us from fulfilling this wish. For example, I would like to obey the speed limit, but the construction I ran into earlier will make me late for class if I don't hurry to make up for the lost time. The obstacles we encounter, or else our inability to satisfy our desires, are what push us to commit crime. As you might imagine, not all obstacles are of equal importance. The job of the strain theorist, then, is to locate those that are most important for producing crime or else the conditions that make otherwise innocuous inconveniences (like getting bumped into or threatened with divorce) a motive for a criminal response.

While all this talk of stress and inability to satisfy desires may sound psychological, strain theorists do not usually use ideas originating in psychology. Rather, strain theorists explain how the frustration of our wants leads to crime, using sociological concepts like *anomie,* coined by the French sociologist Emile Durkheim (1897/1951). *Anomie* comes from the French word *anomique,* meaning, roughly, "normlessness." Durkheim believed that people naturally thrive in societies where their desires and wants are socially well regulated. For example, everyone may have a desire for sex, but social institutions such as the church can regulate when and where sexual activity is appropriate and thereby impose a limit on that particular desire. When a lack of adequate regulation or social guidance exists because of some breakdown or malfunction in society, then anomie develops (i.e., a state of normlessness) and people are more likely to deviate. Durkheim only emphasized the link between anomie and suicide, but strain theorists building from his work suggested that a lack of adequate social regulation, such as regulation of economic desires, leads to crime as well. More specifically, early strain theorists such as Robert Merton argued that anomie was caused by poor integration of the goals of a particular culture with the means available for achieving these goals, as well as with the existing social structure. Culture fails to set limits, and the social structure fails to adequately assist people in achieving culturally valued objectives. All this may sound dry and abstract for now, but the theory will make pretty good sense as we look at it. For now, let us look at Merton's theory and discuss each of the pieces that—working together—lead to crime. Namely, we will focus on the American Dream (or, the culture) and the American social class system. Later in this chapter, we will consider some of the revisions to strain theory by later theorists in response to empirical research and further thinking.

MERTON'S STRAIN THEORY AND ITS VARIANTS
The American Culture

Remember that strain theorists attempt to figure out the conditions that give rise to the frustration of wants and, thus, crime. The culture that Americans live in represents a starting point for some strain theorists to explain why America has the highest crime rates of any industrialized country. Merton was the first to look closely at American culture, or what Messner and Rosenfeld (1994) call the **American Dream,** which he believed placed excessive emphasis on material and monetary success and too little emphasis on the "proper" way of achieving success. Precisely what our *culture* emphasizes is important, because individual people are presumed to be not naturally capable of working out the value of material objects on their own; people need the help of culture. For instance, we are not born with any desire for money and the material trappings of success. Money, after all, can't be eaten, so it—in and of itself—doesn't satisfy perfectly natural hunger. Neither is it likely that infants will know anything about the vast difference in prestige between a woolen Brioni business suit and, say, a polyester suit from JC Penney's. Babies, after all, will spit up on either with equal enthusiasm. The rest of us, however, have learned that Brioni suits are ridiculously expensive and can only be worn by successful people like that famous fictional British agent James Bond, whereas you can buy a JC Penney suit for less than a hundred dollars and—fairly or unfairly—be judged as being one of the common riffraff as a result. So the fact that we take for granted that money is important and that there is a vast difference in prestige among clothing labels, automobiles, and even ink pens and watches is because of our culture, and the American Dream is a convenient label for American culture. The aspects of American culture that are relevant for crime concern (1) the "goals," or what we are socialized to want, and (2) the "means," or the rules we're expected to follow while striving to achieve the goals.

Let us first look at the goals. In order to understand what Americans are socialized to desire, one place to begin might be to focus on what the media tells us we're supposed to desire. With few notable exceptions, prime-time sitcoms and "reality" programs show people who live in stylishly appointed houses or high-rise apartments, sport designer clothing, and are fashionably groomed in the latest trendy hairstyles. If anyone was to take the time to price out all this, we would find that the typical American cannot usually afford any aspect of the lifestyle portrayed on television. Many television commercials—at least before our recent economic crash—peddled big-ticket items that only a tiny fraction of the population even has a remote chance of affording. Yet ownership of prestigious material things, such as clothes and cars, is a sign that we've "made it," and many Americans will stretch their finances to the breaking point and beyond to imitate the style of the successful, to advertise their success to others, and to make themselves feel good. Other Americans aren't there yet, and do everything they can to make their dream an eventual reality. Whether or not one can actually achieve the American Dream, our culture bestows on everyone the desire to imitate the style of the successful. It is interesting to note that the alleged materialism of American society is not a recent phenomenon; Merton, working during the 1930s, made the same characterization of society that critics make about American culture today. (Merton wrote during the Great Depression, the period when nearly 25 percent of the population was out of work and when Americans were supposedly happy just to have enough to eat and a roof over their heads.)

Besides socializing us about what to want in life, the American Dream also specifies how one should go about achieving success. Americans are expected to work hard, be honest, defer gratification, become educated, and so forth. By going to college and not slacking off, you are following the ideals set forth about how one is supposed to go about achieving the American Dream. One is also expected to be competitive and to stand out in front of one's peers. If you get angry with yourself when you score a 96 on a test and somebody else gets a 98, then you have a pretty good idea of how the American Dream works. Should one play by these rules, then the eventual ability to enjoy material success should be all but assured.

So far, so good. But the problem, as Merton saw it, was that the goals of American society are emphasized at the expense of encouraging people to follow the rules. Put more simply, our society stresses that the only important thing is that you are successful—if you fail gracefully (read: by trying hard and following the rules), then you're still a failure. There are plenty of easy examples of this to which you might be able to relate. Professional football aficionados will recall that the Buffalo Bills had some of the strongest teams during the early 1990s, making it to four Super Bowls in a row. But they also lost every one of those Super Bowls. Therefore, the Bills are not remembered for destroying opponents during the regular season, but rather—if anyone thinks of them much at all—for the fact that they couldn't win the "Big One." The New England Patriots, on the other hand, had very similar success during the regular football season, but they were referred to as a "dynasty" for having won, as of this writing, three of the past eight Super Bowls (including an undefeated regular season in 2007, which ended in a surprising loss in the Super Bowl). Clearly, winning is very important, and it is not enough to merely make a good showing if the result is not victory. Given this emphasis on winning and the very little to be gained by following the rules, there is a natural tendency to shift to "winning at all costs." When only the results matter to us, then we follow the rules only as long as it is convenient for us to do so; as soon as they become an impediment on the way to the American Dream, they get jettisoned. In short, while the culture itself does not encourage us to be criminal, the seeds of crime are present and are likely to bear fruit when one is unable to achieve the American Dream. As Merton (1968, p. 200) wrote, things we normally consider "virtue"—such as ambition—lead to "vice," such as deviant behavior.

The American Social Structure

Merton thus turned to what the impediments to the American Dream might be. The American Dream promises equal opportunity for all. American history has many examples of people who raised themselves out of the dirt to become millionaires. If real-life successes were not enough, there were also Horatio Alger stories and other similar American-produced fiction to reinforce the belief that *anyone* can achieve the American Dream as long as one has the necessary pluck and ability. The only impediment our society acknowledges is variation in individual ability, and a lack of ability does not excuse the failure to achieve the American Dream. Some of us are smarter, cleverer, and harder working, but those who lack these skills are viewed with scorn because they have failed to take advantage of opportunities.

Unfortunately, reality is crueler to most of us. Depending on where you are in the socioeconomic structure, according to Merton, your road to success can be absurdly easy or impossible. Think of the advantages that rich folks have on the way to success, compared to those people with less economic wherewithal. Rich people have the luxury of not having to practice triage with their budgets—for example, they need not ask themselves, "Do I go to college and get the credentials I need for a better job, or do I buy groceries?" Rich people do not have to worry so much about such dilemmas. Politicians are also more likely to listen to rich people, and thus make laws that are to their advantage. Moreover, rich families have useful social connections that allow them to place even their most mediocre children in the finest colleges and universities, as well as in business and in government. Poor families, on the other hand, are unlikely to have wealthy or influential patrons who are eagerly willing to look out for them, since such families are unable to reciprocate in any consequential way. Merton thus believed that the reality of inequality in America was perhaps the biggest impediment to achieving the American Dream. Things might not be so bad, however, if only the poor had lower and more realistic expectations; but the American Dream (the need to have expensive stuff), according to Merton, resonates across the *entire* economic spectrum of our society. The poor, like the rich, are socialized to desire pricey cars, plasma TVs, nice watches, and fancy clothes—all of the material trappings of the good life. But the already rich are in the best position to achieve success, while the poor labor at a serious disadvantage where their success is not guaranteed or even likely even after enormous effort, honesty, and dedication. People with doctorate degrees do work as cashiers at Wal-Mart. In view of this unfortunate reality, Merton hypothesized that a disproportionate amount of strain falls on the lower social classes.

Responses to Strain

When faced with an obstacle to achieving one's desires, anomie (or strain) occurs, and one has to respond to it somehow. Merton proposed that there were five ways people can cope with strain. A person experiencing strain need not necessarily fall into any one particular category.

Conformity. In **conformity,** the individual continues to strive for the American Dream as well as obey the rules of society. For example, imagine that you sent an application for the post of chief executive officer (CEO) of a major company. Obviously, being a highly paid CEO would go a long way toward achieving the American Dream; but you later received a letter informing you that you were not selected for the job because only Harvard Business School graduates will do for them and you're not good enough. You thus followed legitimate channels toward success and failed. If you continue to strive for similar jobs, sending applications and following all of the rules and working hard, then you have responded to the strain through conformity. Merton believed that most Americans experiencing strain continued to conform.

Innovation.   This response to strain is somewhat misleadingly titled. We normally think of **innovation** as a good thing, and something to encourage; however, Merton uses this term to describe those who want to achieve the American Dream but who have rejected the "accepted" and legal means for doing so. Put differently, let's say you are part of a team playing soccer and you lose playing fair. Rather than continuing to play fair, you decide to break the rules in order to improve your chances of winning (like breaking the kneecaps of the other side's star player—an action that is not allowed in the rules). In other words, in response to the strain, you continue to strive for success, but no longer employ the socially approved means for doing so. One would expect that crime occurring because of innovation would improve the economic standing of the criminal. The best examples of the innovator would be the white-collar criminal, the "robber barons" of the nineteenth century, and con artists.

Ritualism.   After experiencing strain, some individuals lose their ambition and merely hope to hold on to what little they have. Lack of ambition is handy for another reason: It is hard to experience crushing disappointment if your expectations are low. College students actually quite frequently encounter ritualists. Think of how many students take a difficult class (like calculus). They are expected to get an "*A*" just like in any other class, but even after working hard many folks are unable to even come close to an "*A*." A "*C*," or any minimally passing grade, then, is acceptable because, many students reason, "the class is calculus and no one is supposed to do well in that." Those who employ **ritualism** might still exert effort, but merely for dogmatic reasons (it's all they know) or out of habit; they no longer really strive for the American Dream or believe that their effort will lead to any greater rewards. The lifelong bureaucrat, tired of his or her work and life, might be one example. Ritualists do not commit crime.

Retreatism.   Followers of **retreatism** abandon both the American Dream and the effort or ambition expected of citizens. After experiencing strain, their purpose is simply to escape or drop out from society, often through alcohol or drug use. If you have a roommate or a significant other who has no job and who sits on the sofa all day watching reruns on the Cartoon Network and drinking beer, then you have a good sense of what a retreatist is like. Merton (1938) himself described retreatists using such labels as "pariahs, outcasts, vagrants, vagabonds, tramps, chronic drunkards, and drug addicts."

Rebellion. The rebel rejects the American system and replaces it with a different set of goals and means. In a sense, these are innovators of a different sort, as their purpose is to change the system. Albert Cohen, for instance, talked about how strained lower-class teenage boys reject the American Dream and replace it with the anti–American Dream (which is basically anything that might offend middle-class sensitivities). The **rebellion** response can be seen in revolutionaries and militants. Rebels may commit crime, but the crime is not intended to promote the economic interests of the rebel so much as to advance society toward the ends the rebel sees as legitimate. Here is a summary table of possible responses to strain, according to Merton:

RESPONSE TO STRAIN	GOALS	RULES
Conformity	Accept	Accept
Innovation	Accept	Reject
Ritualism	Reject	Accept
Retreatism	Reject	Reject
Rebellion	Replace	Replace

Later Work on Merton's Theory

While Merton's theory of social structure and anomie is widely cited in criminology and sociology, it did not receive much further attention for approximately two decades after its publication in 1938. The reason was more political and ideological than scientific. Murray (1984) observed that poverty, to thinkers in the mid-twentieth century, was wholly a product of individual abilities and deficiencies. By the 1960s, however, the idea that individuals are not necessarily at fault for their poverty but that the system creates and maintains inequality began to gain momentum among scholars. Indeed, the civil rights movement borrowed from these ideas, arguing that the poverty of minorities had less to do with inherent lack of ability than a system designed to guarantee that minorities have virtually no chance to succeed on their own. Strain theory then began to garner considerable attention. Another lesson here is that many good or interesting ideas in criminology go unnoticed, sometimes for years, not because these ideas were found scientifically inadequate, but because the changing political and ideological landscape made them suddenly fashionable.

In 1960, sociologists Richard Cloward and Lloyd Ohlin proposed one of the major extensions of Merton's theory, what they called "differential opportunity" theory, which considers access to delinquent opportunities as well as legitimate opportunities. This underlying premise of Cloward and Ohlin's work—that delinquency requires opportunities—certainly makes sense if you think about it. One of the authors, during the early 2000s, lived in Craighead County in northeast Arkansas. This particular area had a large number of tiny farming hamlets seemingly isolated from the rest of the world. One of these is a little place in the middle of an endless expanse of rice and cotton fields named Egypt, Arkansas, which consists of a single street scattered with tiny houses and mobile homes all landscaped (in the local style) with rusty appliances. There was also a rather dirty-looking fire station and a couple of other buildings in varying degrees of neglect. To be sure, this is not the place where it would be possible to achieve the American Dream through legitimate means, as a visual inspection of the town suggested that there was no sign of even the modest economic activity afforded by a gas station or convenience store. Presumably, residents here would be inclined to turn to crime in order to live the good life. If this is so, it is difficult to imagine how residents of Egypt could achieve the American Dream through illegitimate means, either. The monetary value of everything in the town, right down to the metal door hinges and copper electrical wiring, even if it all could be plundered from every building, would likely amount to a pitiful haul more suitable for a shabby flea market than the good life. In view of the limited options for success, criminal or otherwise, in many areas of our country, how can one then cope with strain arising from the failure to achieve the American Dream?

Cloward and Ohlin attempted to extend Merton's theory by answering this question. They indicated that the community in which one lives determines the kind and degree of crime present. Economically beneficial crimes require skill and training and are more likely to occur in communities that provide suitable learning environments, such as the presence of criminal role models. Cloward and Ohlin clearly drew these insights from Sutherland's (1947) differential association theory and other work (see Sutherland, 1937) and integrated it with Merton's version of strain theory. The two sociologists also sought to answer the problem of why individuals selected one adaptation to strain over another, which was a question that Merton did not attempt to answer.

Three criminal subcultures can emerge, depending on the environmental circumstances. The **criminal subculture** comes about when there are no opportunities for legitimate gain, but illegitimate opportunities are still open—that is, strained residents can respond with innovation. Youth gangs form in order to perform income-generating crimes, such as selling drugs, hustling stolen merchandise, and so forth. Economic conditions are such that there are buyers aplenty for these goods. Other forms of organized crime exist, and youth who are blocked off from the American Dream can consult the criminal element and receive training and mentorship that will allow them to live the high life through crime. If you are affluent, then you might have access to the executive positions necessary to execute white-collar crimes. The **violent subculture** emerges in locations like Egypt, Arkansas, where strain exists but there are no means—legitimate or illegitimate—to deal with the strain. Cloward and Ohlin's theory would indicate that it is highly improbable that an individual from this town, or from another area lacking in income-generating criminal opportunities, will become a wealthy drug distributor or a corrupt CEO of a major company. Consequently, the crime occurring among those in the subculture tends to be of a violent sort—when status cannot be earned through money, being tough becomes the way to have a reputation. Borrowing from the work of Shaw and McKay (1942) on social disorganization theory, Cloward and Ohlin reasoned that the violent subculture is most likely to be an adaptation in disorganized communities. Finally, there is the **retreatist subculture,** for the double failures, who were ineffective at achieving the American Dream through crime or conformity. As Merton indicated, the retreatists self-medicate their strain with alcohol and drugs. In short, the opportunity circumstances surrounding where one lives go a long way toward determining what adaptation one takes in adjusting to strain.

Empirical Support

Merton's theory, and some of the subsequent updates, generally suggests a certain image of the criminal offender. Criminal offenders are essentially ambitious people—made so by the American Dream—who are no different from upper-class people in terms of their natural abilities, but who are denied material success because of their disadvantageous location in the social structure. Because the social structure gets in the way of material success for the lower class, one might thus reasonably expect that crime would be heavily concentrated among the lower class. Official records of youthful and adult offenders seem to bear this out. Additionally, in areas where a criminal subculture could form, crime should be economically rewarding. As noted earlier, this theory made a great deal of sense to criminologists starting in the 1960s, and was influential in both criminology and in policy.

The theory did have its critics. Some questioned whether American culture was as single minded as strain theorists allege. For instance, many of you might look with disgust, rather than admiration or envy, upon the multimillion-dollar salaries of professional athletes or corporate executives. Others (see Pfohl, 1985) felt that the contradiction in American society between the culture and the class structure was a worthwhile beginning, but that Merton and others never addressed the question of how this contradiction formed and why it continues. In other words, why America, of all places, and why have Americans for so long been unsuccessful at tackling the problems arising from a purportedly flawed combination of culture and social structure?

Critics have also cited scientific research as a reason why strain theory might not be an adequate explanation of crime. It may seem strange to us, but strain theory was not subjected to extensive empirical testing until the late 1960s (nearly three decades after Merton first published the theory). The growth of self-report surveys at this time suggested that the causes of crime were very different from those envisioned by strain theorists. First, social class turned out to be a very weak predictor of criminal activity, apparently refuting the notion that the American social structure was a key facilitator of high crime (see Hirschi, 1969). That is, these studies showed that the poor are only marginally more likely to be delinquent than the rich. These studies also found that criminals lack ambition, and their educational achievements tend to substantially trail those of their peers within the same social class. Moreover, research has found that crime in fact does not pay very well, offering more in the way of short-term gratification than long-term financial gain (Gottfredson & Hirschi, 1990). Strain theorists would suggest, for example, that offenders steal beer in order to sell it and make money. Instead, it appears that offenders steal beer in order to drink it, obviously negating any long-term economic advantage they might have obtained. And even crimes like burglary and robbery net the offender very little from fences and pawnshops. Through the 1970s, criminologists began to believe that strain theory was wrong, and they consequently abandoned it for many years.

More recently, however, scholars have begun to argue whether this research has adequately tested strain theory (see Bernard, 1984). Some scholars measured Merton's idea of strain in terms of the distance between one's goals and what one actually achieves (presumably indicating the availability of means). One would ask questions such as the following: "How much do you want to get a full-time job?" and, then, "How well are you doing at that?" The idea seems reasonable: those who are ambitious relative to their actual accomplishments will feel the motivation to innovate more intensely than a person who aims low and accomplishes little. People who feel that they are underpaid relative to their skill and effort should commit more crime. Burton and Cullen (1992) reviewed 50 studies over a 30-year period and found that this was how researchers typically measured strain. However, one might ask whether the actual performance of the measure justified so many studies over such a long period: The disjuncture between expectations and achievements was not a significant predictor of offending.

Other research considers whether individuals actually experience strain. Following this idea, if one can measure the strength of someone's belief that his or her opportunity to achieve success has been blocked, it should correspond more strongly with breaking the law. Burton and Cullen (1992) found this to be the case. Other researchers in recent years have proposed or turned to other indicators of strain, such as **relative deprivation** (Burton, Cullen, Evans, & Dunaway, 1994) and satisfaction with monetary status (Agnew, Cullen, Burton, Evans, & Dunaway, 1996). These studies find that those who feel deprived and who are dissatisfied with their economic situation are more apt to engage in crime. The lesson here is that measurement is important and that changes to how strain gets measured in research have given new life to strain theory. More recently, researchers have continued the strain tradition by moving beyond Merton's theory and taking strain theory in new directions, some of which we discuss next.

AGNEW'S GENERAL STRAIN THEORY

During the 1980s and early 1990s, however, scholars began work that indicated that strain theory could be rehabilitated (e.g., Burton & Cullen, 1992; Cullen, 1988). Robert Agnew is probably the most successful, having revived the concept of strain as a cause of crime and then formulating a theory he termed "general strain theory" (GST). This theory would become one of the currently influential theories of criminal behavior. Earlier versions of strain theory emphasized how people are socialized to want something—typically material success—but are unable to get what they want. Agnew expanded strain theory beyond this. Agnew's theory broadens the range of the causes of strain and departs from Merton's adaptations to strain, developing more general means of coping.

Types of Strain

Agnew's theory expands the sources of strain from one cause to three. Note that GST does not make specific predictions about what type of strain among the three is "worse" or more likely to result in crime. Moreover, Agnew (1992) stated that it is unlikely that a single instance of strain would necessarily be a problem, but rather an accumulation of events fitting into the categories below would increase the chances someone will break the law.

The *failure to achieve positively valued goals,* which is a staple of earlier strain theories, is present in GST as well. While earlier strain theories emphasized the failure to achieve the American Dream, Agnew's theory focuses less on culture than on the individual. We may experience strain when we fail to win the approval of a person whose approval genuinely matters to us. And strain does not need to be linked with economic advancement, though economic concerns can also be a source of pain and frustration that might lead to crime. Indeed, the popular music industry has long profited from articulating into sometimes disturbing songs the emotions resulting from failed romances and consequent deviant responses. Examples of these run the gamut from stalking (The Police, "Every Breath You Take") to murder (The Beatles, "Run for Your Life"). Other examples of this type of strain might include not making the football team or even not getting to work on time. People may break the law to get what they desire, such as by speeding to make up lost time getting to work.

Strain might also occur when *something positively valued is removed from us.* Imagine how you might feel if your teacher told you that the A you received on a test was a mistake, and that your actual grade was a D! You would likely feel badly at having "lost" your *A*, and would justifiably feel a great deal of stress and frustration. More generally, this type of strain can occur when parents take away the privileges of their children, when one gets fired from work, or when a relationship ends. Responses to having something desirable taken away would be aimed at restoring whatever had been lost. Conventional responses to the preceding scenarios might include starting a new relationship or getting a new job. There are deviant responses as well. Children have been known to sneak out of their houses at night in response to being grounded by their parents, for instance. The movie *Office Space* details how one employee dealt with his termination (and, worse still, the loss of his red Swingline stapler) by burning down his employer's building.

Strain also occurs if people impose on us *stimuli that we find noxious.* Most people resent it if others ask them to do something, such as clean their room, take on an extra assignment, or take a test. Behaviors in response to this strain would tend to emphasize removing the individual from this situation. For instance, a noncriminal response might be to negotiate with a demanding teacher for reduced work or extended deadlines. Crimes also can deal with noxious situations. For instance, one can shut up another person who is being insulting by punching that individual in the mouth. Being bullied or victimized would also fit into this category of strain (Agnew, 2002).

In short, Agnew reasoned that strain occurs for more reasons that just expecting something and not getting it. Because Agnew's theory does not focus on social structure or make claims about what Americans want, it is applicable to a broader range of crimes than just those committed by the lower classes for their own economic advantage. This is why Agnew refers to his theory as *general* strain theory. Crime nevertheless has a purpose to it, being intended to alleviate the strain in some way. We next discuss coping with strain in greater detail, as strain need not necessarily lead to a criminal response.

Types of Coping

Like other strain theories, Agnew's version does not assert that crime is a necessary consequence of stress. Many of us feel bad, angry, and frustrated, and many people are pretty much miserable most of the time. And yet they do not always turn to crime. As Merton's strain theory suggests, coping with strain can lead to legal as well as illegal consequences. Agnew proposed several ways that people cope with strain.

First, people can cognitively reinterpret the situation (**cognitive coping**). Suppose that you get into a wreck, and your automobile is destroyed. Normally, this event would cause a considerable degree of stress and frustration, but what if you really do feel that "I was driving carelessly, so I deserve it," or "At least I got out of it with my life; the car is not so important," or, even, "I'm glad to not have to drive that old beater anymore." By minimizing your failures, indignities, or inconveniences, or accepting your responsibility for them, you may still feel unhappy but at the same time you no longer have a reason to act out against others.

We can also deal with strain by using **behavioral coping** strategies. These strategies entail taking some sort of action to deal with the source of the strain, which *might* include delinquency. For instance, if you don't have enough money to live in the style that you would prefer, you might get a job that allows you to afford your lifestyle, or else you might steal the money. People who fail their thesis defense in graduate school might cope by revising their work and thus attempt to satisfy the criticisms of their thesis committee. Legitimate coping is not always successful, however, as is reflected in an old graduate school urban legend where a graduate student had dealt with a stubborn thesis advisor by putting a ball-peen hammer through his head (thus negating the source of the strain by forestalling future objections to the thesis, at least from that particular faculty member).

Finally, one can deal with strain through **emotional coping.** In this case, one does not reinterpret the situation or attempt to deal with the strain, but rather attempts to neutralize the unpleasant emotions that follow from the strain. Do you hate how you feel if you do not do well on a test? Some people take out their anger on the racquetball court. Some pray or go to church. Others go get seriously drunk after finding out their test score. While emotional coping can include deviant or delinquent activity, the common characteristic is the tendency to not deal with the source of the strain but rather to counteract its negative emotional consequences.

When Does Strain Lead to Delinquent Coping?

While there are clearly different ways that people can cope with strain, there is still the question of why some people elect to cope using legitimate strategies while others turn to crime. Under what conditions will strain lead someone to commit crime?

First, Agnew reasoned that strain is more likely to lead to crime *if the strain affects areas that you consider important.* This assertion goes beyond Merton's claim that money—or material success—is the only issue people consider important enough to possibly turn them toward crime. In Agnew's theory, money could be very important to some people, but other people might highly value grades, their masculinity or femininity, their success in sports, and so on. If I don't care about grades, then getting a poor grade on a test is not likely to lead me to assault the teacher, cheat on future tests, or drown my sorrows with Mad Dog 20/20. If grades represent a substantial part of my self-worth, on the other hand, then a low grade is going to have an exaggerated effect on my level of stress and frustration, and that deviance might appear a very tempting response.

Second, those possessing *poor coping skills and resources* are more likely to turn to crime. Some people are better prepared to mitigate potential sources of strain. Those who are diplomatic are in a better position to resolve stressful situations than those who lack tact, for instance. Indeed, a lack of social skills can further aggravate a situation and possibly lead to a physical confrontation. The presence of financial resources can likewise alleviate strain. Money gives us access to therapists, who can make us feel better after a setback. The presence of money also enables us to better deal with financial setbacks.

Third, the *absence of conventional social supports* in one's life makes strain more difficult to deal with legitimately. These social supports include friends, family, and others who might listen to your feelings or give advice and assistance. Conversely, those lacking in social support have no one with whom they can safely vent their frustration, and neither can they expect to receive any assistance through their troubles. Consequently, they are more prone to crime.

Fourth, one is more likely to cope with strain through delinquency if the *advantages of crime are high and the risks are low*. Essentially, when faced with criminal temptation while experiencing strain, the person considers both "What's in it for me?" and "Will I get caught?" If you can get even with an irritating roommate by sabotaging his noisy stereo with an axe, and you can do so without his knowledge, then you are more likely to respond to the strain criminally.

Fifth, strain will tend to lead to crime among those *already predisposed to delinquency*. Agnew's GST borrows from other theories of crime at this point, arguing that such traits as low self-control, criminal beliefs, and exposure to criminal role models predispose some people to react to strain in a criminal way.

Empirical Support

To the extent that researcher attention is a gauge of a successful theory, few can question that Agnew's GST is a successful theory. Since 1992, GST has received considerable empirical testing (see Agnew & White, 1992; Brezina, 1996; Hoffman & Miller, 1998; Katz, 2000; Mazerolle & Maahs, 2000). Studies testing GST have generally relied on survey data, including self-reports and third-party observations of respondents (which is quite handy, since people sometimes can do a poor job describing what they are really like). Researchers have measured strain using such indicators as neighborhood problems, negative life events, hassles with peers, negative relations with adults, and experience of abuse (e.g., Paternoster & Mazerolle, 1994; Piquero & Sealock, 2001). The research literature is extensive enough to suggest several conclusions about the empirical support for strain theory.

There has been consistent empirical support for GST, but Agnew has also periodically revised GST in light of those research findings that were not in accord with his original work on the theory. For instance, research on GST tends to find that the three sources of strain noted earlier have only a limited ability to predict who will offend and who will not (e.g., Agnew, Brezina, Wright, & Cullen, 2002). In that case, it is natural enough to wonder under what conditions might experiencing strain lead someone to commit a crime.

Agnew thus proposed a number of "conditioning" factors that would make some people more susceptible to breaking the law while under strain. Many of those Agnew mentioned in 1992 did not work as well as expected (see Agnew et al., 2002). Agnew and his colleagues (2002) recognized this and turned to personality factors as the most important contributor to crime among strained persons. Specifically, "negative emotionality" was identified as perhaps the biggest reason strain led to crime. Negative emotionality refers to the tendency to take the darkest and most sinister interpretation of events. If you fail a test, it was because the teacher was unfair. If you get a speeding ticket, it was because the traffic cop hated you. Sometimes these interpretations are true. Teachers are sometimes unfair, and cops do sometimes hate people. Negative emotionality, however, refers to a personality type that readily and habitually draws these conclusions about events. A second personality type—"constraint"—also could condition the effects of strain. Constraint simply describes the ability to control one's impulses, to avoid stupid risks, consider the feelings of others, and so forth. Negative emotionality and a lack of constraint would increase the likelihood of a criminal response to strain. Agnew and his colleagues (2002) found stronger research support for these conditioning factors than with Agnew's (1992) original predictions.

Research also showed that not all negative events had significant relationship to crime. Many did, like being abused as a child (Piquero & Sealock, 2001), but some did not—like failure to achieve educational and occupational goals (Agnew, 1995). Agnew (2001) then attempted to be more specific about what types of strain are most likely to lead to criminal behavior. Agnew made a distinction between "objective" and "subjective" types of strain. Objective strain refers to situations where there is reasonable consensus in a group or among a variety of groups that a situation is undesirable. Few people enjoy starvation and having fingernails ripped out and the mutilated fingers then dunked in lemon juice, for example. Subjective strain, on the other hand, is more particular to the individual. Some people might view divorce as especially nasty, but others can perceive it as a rite of liberation! Agnew in fact criticized research on GST for measuring what the researchers believed to be strain-inducing events, but which the individual being studied might not have seen that way. To better resolve the issue, Agnew reasoned that there are four characteristics to those types of strain connected with crime: (1) when the strain is seen as unjust, (2) when the strain is high in magnitude, (3) when the strain is caused by or associated with low social control, and (4) when the strain creates an incentive to commit crime.

Agnew's GST mainly focuses on strains and the responses they caused from the point of view of the individual. But would it not make sense to say that strain is shaped by structural factors, just as the earlier strain theorists have proposed? Some of Agnew's work (1999, 2006) has looked at this possibility and formulated a macro-version of GST, although it has not yet received extensive testing. But perhaps the reason why African Americans have higher arrest rates might be due to the fact that they are more likely to live or exist in conditions that generate strain and where resources for dealing with strain are relatively limited. Recall from Chapter 5 ("The Social Ecology of Crime") that disorganized areas, where African Americans are more likely to be concentrated, tend to have more concentrated noxious stimuli (e.g., disorder and decay), denial of positively valued goals (e.g., fewer jobs), and frequent removal of positive stimuli (e.g., divorce or parents being sent to jail).

While there is a growing number of data sets available that can test modern formulations of social disorganization theory—one of GST's major theoretical competitors—these data sets typically do not measure feelings or emotions among residents very well. Nevertheless, some research does exist. John Hoffman (2002), using data from over 10,000 students living in over 1,600 communities, found that the connection between stressful events and crime is much more pronounced when male joblessness in the area is high. Put another way, the student didn't have to be stressed out from having no job (10th graders are not usually employed in large numbers), but the fact that there was a high level of joblessness seemed to combine with already existing stress to result in more crime. A few other studies exist indicating that higher-order factors make stress more likely to result in crime (e.g., Brezina, Piquero, & Mazerolle, 2001; Warner & Fowler, 2003), but there is otherwise not enough research to draw many conclusions.

MESSNER AND ROSENFELD'S THEORY OF INSTITUTIONAL ANOMIE

In 1994, Steven Messner and Richard Rosenfeld published work on strain theory that builds more directly from Merton's original theory than was the case with Agnew's GST. Messner and Rosenfeld specifically focused on institutions that are responsible for regulating our behavior and how many of these institutions have been subverted and rendered ineffective (leading to anomie). Anomie arises as the unbounded desire to succeed pushes people apart, which causes the breakdown of communities and benevolent social institutions, like families and school. The combination of the breakdown of these institutions and a desire for success that can never be sated (at least through legitimate channels) leads to crime.

When talking about Merton's ideas about the American Dream, we focused primarily on the goals (namely, the desire for money and/or material success) and the means (the rules we're supposed to go by to achieve the American Dream). For Messner and Rosenfeld, the American Dream has four distinctive value orientations: achievement, individualism, universalism, and the money fetish. Many of these ideas were touched on earlier in the chapter, but the theory of **institutional anomie** further develops Merton's ideas.

First, America values *achievement;* Americans are expected to set and achieve goals. Actual achievement is clearly important, since the prestige you have depends very much on the successful outcome of your efforts. If you are a failure, you have little value; if you are a success, then you have great value. Second, *individualism* is an essential trait of American culture. Individuals are expected to make it on their own, overcoming others competing for the same rewards. Those who relied on luck or help from others will see their prestige tarnished somewhat even if they enjoy achievement. In this respect, achievement is most culturally satisfying when taking the best an opponent offers and still winning on one's own merits. For instance, pretend your favorite baseball team is playing a rival that is more than a match for your own team. If your team wins by outplaying the opposition, the victory is all the sweeter than if your team won because the other team played the game without its best hitter. Third, the values of America are *universal.* That is, everyone in society is expected to strive for success. Finally, there is the *money fetish,* in which success is specifically the consequence of getting lots of money. Money, as Messner and Rosenfeld argued, has value beyond its ability to buy things. The acquisition of money is a source of status and prestige in and of itself. How else could one explain why boorish professional athletes and pop stars always seem to be fighting off armies of groupies when the rest of us—who lack the impressive salaries—have to pathetically beg for a date? But there is more to the fetish than getting money. There is the fact that our society sets no upper bound on how much money one gets. As long as somebody out there is doing better than we are, we will be resentful. In short, Americans, one and all, are socialized to desire money and, moreover, are expected to achieve wealth through the abilities that they have.

The theory of institutional anomie goes beyond Merton's emphasis on the class system of the United States, arguing for a more general examination of the social structure and its institutions. Institutions normally exist to help the society function better, like the organs within our own body. Each organ—the heart, the brain, and so forth—helps us survive, and so it is with society's institutions. More specifically, Messner and Rosenfeld argued that institutions address the need of the society and its people to adapt to the environment, gather and deploy resources for collective purposes, and socialize members of the society. Four important types of institutions are most relevant for understanding crime: economic, political, family, and education. Economic institutions are concerned with providing goods and services. At a minimum, they are responsible for meeting basic human needs: food, shelter, and clothing. Political institutions are responsible for activities that benefit the community as a whole, such as organizing the police so that everyone is safer. Educational and familial institutions share responsibility for socializing children. These institutions are interdependent, like bodily organs, and the actions, relative importance, and failure of one may have consequences for the others.

Messner and Rosenfeld make the case that the economy holds disproportionate power. One reason for this is that the other institutions are "devalued" relative to strictly economic pursuits. Those responsible for educating and socializing our children, for instance, are paid low salaries or not at all (as in the case with stay-at-home parents). Additionally, other institutions are expected to "accommodate" economic institution needs, rather than the other way around. For example, have your bosses ever demanded that you schedule your classes around your work day? If you do this, then you are accommodating your life to your work rather than to your learning. Even universities are under pressure from economic interests to provide the kind of education that will help students get jobs, and many students go to college not so much to learn or acquire interests of a higher order than partying, but rather to obtain the credentials they need to get a better paying job. Thus, even higher education is expected to have a financial payoff and must therefore accommodate economic interests. Finally, the business mentality "penetrates" into other institutions. Economic institutions are characterized by competition and a concern for the bottom line. This may sound like the business world is fundamentally amoral, and it is; however, businesses that make decisions that aren't profitable usually fail to survive. So while the business world is brutal, it must be. But what if business values seep into such institutions as government, family, and education? Schools would not be interested so much in educating students as in keeping them happy (and keeping their tuition dollars coming). Parents would spend more time at work, because having and raising their children is not "cost-effective." Government would abandon programs that lose money, including programs that are altruistic in nature—for example, social assistance programs to the poor, such as welfare and food stamps. Indeed, people in an anomic society become deeply cynical and hardly feel morally to blame for taking advantage of opportunities for corruption. Heck, everyone else seems to be doing it. The recent spate of ethical problems in the United States Congress leading to a number of resignations as well as criminal indictments and convictions (e.g., the cases of Tom Delay, Bob Ney, William Jefferson, and Duke Cunningham) illustrates this point very well.

What does all this have to do with more crime? The economic institutions are less concerned with following rules than getting profits. Again, following the rules is okay as long as there is some advantage to it, but ultimately getting the money is what really matters. Crime would naturally be very tempting. Consequently, it is up to the remaining institutions to teach people to follow the rules. But if economic institutions devalue and penetrate into other institutions, and force others to accommodate, then the emphasis on social control is less likely to occur within these institutions except superficially and ineffectively. Additionally, families with dual-wage earners necessarily have less time to spend socializing their children, so the ability of institutions to socialize people about the rules is lacking even if the willingness is there. Put differently, we have to make choices: Do you give your all to that high-paying job and neglect your family, or do you raise your family and lose the job? If economic ideals predominate, then you would elect to let your family slide while you chase the big bucks. Meantime, your children are taught the rules of the business world—get ahead, whatever it takes. Thus, the overwhelming importance of economic institutions, and the accompanying mindset, means that the other institutions are ineffective at countering the socializing of children into the business mentality. Serious crime is the result.

Unlike Agnew's GST, Messner and Rosenfeld's theory of institutional anomie has not received as much empirical testing. A basic thesis is that a dominant economic institution should produce a higher crime rate. But it is difficult to measure precisely how much business values predominate and how strongly have they penetrated into other institutions. One has to infer it from evidence indicating the level of vitality of noneconomic institutions—or their decay relative to economic forces. From this vantage, there does appear to be some support for the theory. Messner and Rosenfeld (1997) comparing crime and social data from 45 countries found support for the idea that those countries that had more social safety nets, and thus did more to insulate citizens from the capitalist markets, tended to have less homicide. These social safety nets included such items as the presence of publicly available health care. Interestingly, the presence of these safety nets reduced crime even in those countries with greater economic inequality.

Other research finds similar results. Chamlin and Cochran (1995), for instance, using state-level data from 1980, found that poverty had a stronger effect on crime in those states where church membership was low and divorce rates were high. This is consistent with institutional anomie theory—if religious authorities are unable to motivate people to show up and the institution of marriage is unable to persuade people to remain married, then it is difficult to make a case that these institutions are especially effective. Poverty was not a direct influence on crime, but those states that had a combination of poverty and failed institutions had more significant problems with crime than those economically poor states where marriage and church membership were relatively strong.

Jukka Savolainen (2000), a Finnish scholar, found in Eastern European countries that income inequality was less connected with homicide in those countries that took steps to protect their poor from economic catastrophe. These studies differ from those testing Agnew's GST in that the focus is on political units (like states and countries) and their activities and characteristics rather than individuals. Beyond this, there are not many studies and little in the way of generally approved indicators of institutional anomie.[1]

SUMMARY

Strain theory has a long and influential tradition in criminology, starting with the work of Merton through the recent developments of Agnew's GST and Messner and Rosenfeld's theory of institutional anomie. The underlying premise of strain theory is that people who fail to get what they want are more likely to turn to crime, and that they would obey the law if they could, but are forced into crime by various dysfunctions in their society or circumstances.

Strain theories have influenced public policy. Merton's theory suggests that to reduce crime, one might help level the playing field between the poor and the rich in terms of opportunities for success, or else somehow get American culture to better regulate our desires and do so in such a way as to be more realistic. President Lyndon Johnson's war on poverty was an attempt to address the lack of opportunities that poor people faced that might lead them to crime. Examples include welfare and food stamp programs. While Merton and the war on poverty have faded in terms of importance, the resurgence of strain theories may redirect attention toward addressing social class and institutional issues that foster higher rates of crime in the United States.

KEY TERMS

American Dream a convenient label for American culture; specifically, the American Dream maintains that all Americans should strive to achieve wealth

behavioral coping in general strain theory, attempting to resolve the strain through actual behaviors—for instance, assaulting someone who is being insulting

cognitive coping in general strain theory, reinterpreting a situation in order to deemphasize the strain in one's own mind or to accept personal responsibility for its happening

conformity a response to strain in Merton's anomie theory, whereby the individual experiencing strain continues to pursue legitimate ends through legitimate means

---

[1]Contrast this situation with that of, say, Hirschi's (1969) social control theory or Gottfredson and Hirschi's (1990) self-control theory, where the theoretical measures are quite well developed and understood. See Chapter 8 for more information.

criminal subculture in Cloward and Ohlin's theory, the subculture that emerges in areas where criminal role models and financially rewarding crimes are available; offenders tend to focus on using criminal means to make money

emotional coping in general strain theory, resolving the emotional consequences of strain, though not necessarily the underlying reasons for the strain, for instance, crying after experiencing disappointment

innovation a response to strain in Merton's anomie theory, whereby the individual experiencing strain continues to pursue legitimate ends while rejecting legitimate means; crime is one example

institutional anomie the imbalance between institutions essential for a functioning nation; in the United States, in particular, institutional anomie results when economic interests receive precedence over other institutions (such as the family and education), even to the point where other institutions view their roles in economic terms

rebellion a response to strain in Merton's anomie theory whereby the individual experiencing strain rejects both legitimate means and ends, replacing them with something else

relative deprivation the notion that one's neighbor or peer has more than oneself, resulting in strain. This differs from ideas of "absolute deprivation" (where one is lacking wealth in an objective sense) in that one can, conceivably, be wealthy and still feel inadequate in comparison to his or her peers in terms of wealth

retreatism a response to strain whereby the individual experiencing strain no longer strives to achieve legitimate goals, and abandons legitimate means as well; examples are drug use and alcoholism

retreatist subculture in Cloward and Ohlin's theory, the subculture that emerges when individuals fail at both crime and conformity; retreatists, as in Merton's theory, engage in drinking and drugs

ritualism a response to strain in Merton's anomie theory whereby the individual experiencing strain continues to follow legitimate rules, but has abandoned hope of achieving legitimate goals

violent subculture in Cloward and Ohlin's theory, the subculture that emerges when there are no opportunities for financially rewarding crime; consequently, the only means by which individuals can earn status is through toughness

DISCUSSION QUESTIONS

1. Use each of the strain theories discussed here to explain George Zinkhan's murder spree. Which theory appears to make the most sense?

2. What role do you think the family might play in Merton's strain theory? What about Agnew's general strain theory?

3. How do you feel about the way Merton and other strain theorists view the American Dream?

4. What kind of person would be most likely to respond to strain with crime, according to Agnew's general strain theory?

5. Where does the American Dream fit in Agnew's strain theory?

REFERENCES

Agnew, R. (1992). Foundation for a general strain theory of crime and delinquency. *Criminology, 30*, 47–87.

Agnew, R. (1995). Strain and subcultural theories of criminality. In J. F. Sheley (Ed.), *Criminology: A Contemporary Handbook*. Belmont, CA: Wadsworth.

Agnew, R. (1999). A general strain theory of community differences in crime rates. *Journal of Research in Crime and Delinquency, 36*, 123–155.

Agnew, R. (2001). Building on the foundation of general strain theory: Specifying the types of strain most likely to lead to delinquency. *Journal of Research in Crime and Delinquency, 38*, 319–361.

Agnew, R. (2002). Experienced, vicarious, and anticipated strain: An exploratory study on physical victimization and delinquency. *Justice Quarterly, 19*, 603–632.

Agnew, R. (2006). *Pressured into Crime: An Overview of General Strain Theory*. Los Angeles: Roxbury.

Agnew, R., Brezina, T., Wright, J. P., & Cullen, F. T. (2002). Strain, personality traits, and delinquency: Extending general strain theory. *Criminology, 40*, 43–72.

Agnew, R., Cullen, F. T., Burton, V. S., Evans, T. D., & Dunaway, R. G. (1996). A new test of classic strain theory. *Justice Quarterly, 13*, 681–704.

Agnew, R., & White, H. R. (1992). An empirical test of general strain theory. *Criminology, 30*, 475–499.

Bernard, T. (1984). Control criticisms of strain theories: An assessment of theoretical and empirical adequacy. *Journal of Research in Crime and Delinquency, 21*, 353–372.

Brezina, T. (1996). Adapting to strain: An examination of delinquent coping strategies. *Criminology, 34*, 213–239.

Brezina, T., Piquero, A. R., & Mazerolle, P. (2001). Student anger and aggressive behavior in school: An initial test of Agnew's macro-level strain theory. *Journal of Research in Crime and Delinquency, 38*, 362–386.

Burton, V. S., & Cullen, F. T. (1992). The empirical status of strain theory. *Journal of Crime and Justice, 15*, 1–30.

Burton, V. S., Cullen, F. T., Evans, D., & Dunaway, R. G. (1994). Reconsidering strain theory: Operationalization, rival theories, and adult criminality. *Journal of Quantitative Criminology, 10*, 213–239.

Chamlin, M. B., & Cochran, J. (1995). Assessing Messner and Rosenfeld's institutional-anomie theory: A partial test. *Criminology, 33*, 411–429.

Cloward, R. A., & Ohlin, L. E. (1960). *Delinquency and opportunity: A theory of delinquent gangs*. Glencoe, IL: Free Press.

Cohen, A. K. (1955). *Delinquent boys: The culture of the gang*. Glencoe, IL: Free Press.

Cullen, F. T. (1988). Were Cloward and Ohlin strain theorists? *Journal of Research in Crime and Delinquency, 42*, 80–82.

Durkheim, E. (1951). *Suicide: A study in sociology*. New York: Free Press. (Original work published 1897)

Gottfredson, M.R. & Hirschi, T. (1990). *A general theory of crime*. Stanford, CA: Stanford University Press.

Hirschi, T. (1969). *Causes of delinquency*. Berkeley: University of California Press.

Hoffman, J. (2002). A contextual analysis of differential association, social control, and strain theories of delinquency. *Social Forces, 81*, 753–785.

Hoffman, J., & Miller, A. S. (1998). A latent variable analysis of general strain theory. *Journal of Quantitative Criminology, 14*, 83–110.

Katz, R. (2000). Explaining girls' and women's crime and desistance in the context of their victimization experiences. *Violence Against Women, 6*, 633–660.

Mazerolle, P., & Maahs, J. (2000). General strain and delinquency: An alternative examination of conditioning influences. *Justice Quarterly, 17*, 753–778.

Merton, R. K. (1968). *Social theory and social structure*. New York: Free Press.

Merton, R. K. (1938). Social structure and anomie. *American Sociological Review, 3*, 672–682.

Messner, S., & Rosenfeld, R. (1994). *Crime and the American Dream*. Belmont, CA: Wadsworth.

Messner, S., & Rosenfeld, R. (1997). Political restraint of the market and levels of criminal homicide: A cross-national application of institutional-anomie theory. *Social Forces, 75*, 1393–1416.

Murray, C. (1984). *Losing ground: American social policy, 1950–1980.* New York: Basic Books.

Paternoster, R., & Mazerolle, P. (1994). General strain theory and delinquency: A replication and extension. *Journal of Research in Crime and Delinquency, 31*, 235–263.

Pfohl, S. J. (1985). *Images of deviance and social control: A sociological history.* New York: McGraw-Hill.

Piquero, N., & Sealock, M. D. (2001). Generalizing general strain theory: An examination of an offending population. *Justice Quarterly, 17*, 449–484.

Savolainen, J. (2000). Inequality, welfare state, and homicide: Further support for institutional anomie. *Criminology, 38*, 983–1020.

Shaw, C. R., & McKay, H. D. (1942). *Juvenile delinquency and urban areas.* Chicago: University of Chicago Press.

Sutherland, E. H. (1937). *The professional thief.* Chicago: University of Chicago Press.

Sutherland, E. H. (1947). *Principles of criminology.* Philadelphia: J.B. Lippencott.

Warner, B. D., & Fowler, S. K. (2003). Strain and violence: Testing a general strain theory model of community violence. *Journal of Criminal Justice, 31*, 511–521.

■ ■ ■ ■ ■

CHAPTER 8

CONTROL THEORIES
OF CRIME

Ashley Slonina was a student at the University of Florida. Between October 13, 2007, and early April of 2008, Ashley ran up over $3,000 in credit card debt. This in itself isn't unusual, as many college students—innocent of the perils of credit—put balances on their cards far in excess of what they can pay. What was unusual in this case was that Ms. Slonina was killed on October 12, 2007, in a motorcycle accident, as she was riding with a member of Florida's football team, Michael Guilford, who also died from injuries in that accident. That charges were nevertheless still appearing on the monthly credit card statement puzzled her parents, who reported them to the authorities. Within a month, Jamar Hornsby, a 21-year-old defensive back and teammate of Guilford, was accused by police of having stolen the card the day after Slonina died. That day, with the tragedy still fresh, Hornsby and a fellow teammate were helping to pack up the woman's belongings at her apartment. It was there that Hornsby helped himself to her card. Hornsby then wasted no time impersonating a member of Congress, ultimately using the card 70 times.

While many athletes get into trouble with the law, Hornsby's theft is noteworthy in that he stood to lose much more than what he gained if his crime was discovered. Jamar Hornsby was a scholarship football player, meaning that he could take full advantage of the educational opportunities at the University of Florida at no cost. Moreover, he was projected to be a starting defensive back on a team that would, during the 2008 season, win the national championship. The national spotlight might have assured him a lucrative career in the National Football League. Instead Hornsby was kicked off the team and placed on probation after a plea bargain. He eventually joined the University of Mississippi's football team after the 2008 season, but in March 2009, he may have squandered that opportunity as well when he was arrested for attacking a man with brass knuckles after an argument over a traffic accident at a McDonald's drive-through. Hornsby also allegedly took $6 from the man after fracturing his nose. At the time this textbook was being revised, Hornsby's criminal case was only in the preliminary stages; he has not been formally proven guilty of the assault. But the circumstances so far lead one to wonder why a man who had so many opportunities to build a future potentially worth millions of dollars would foolishly throw it all away for approximately $3,006. The control perspective, which this chapter will present, will attempt to answer this question.

The control perspective is among the oldest and most popular to have explored the causes of criminality. The basic idea behind the control perspective—which is that people are fundamentally selfish pleasure seekers—dates as far back as the work of the English social philosopher Thomas Hobbes during the seventeenth century. The control perspective also draws insight, or at least shares remarkable similarities with, the ideas of such thinkers and social scientists as Jeremy Bentham, Sigmund Freud, and Emile Durkheim. But not until the 1950s did criminologists begin to give control theory much more than cursory scholarly attention (see Nye, 1958; Reckless, 1955; Reiss, 1951; Toby, 1957). At the time, however, strain theory was at the peak of its influence, and so criminologists tended to focus their thinking and research on strain theories rather than control theories. In 1969, however, Travis Hirschi published a book that integrated the ideas of the early control theorists and presented research supporting his theory. Hirschi's version of social control theory became the definitive social control model as well as the most frequently tested theory of crime during the 1970s and 1980s.

While Hirschi's social control theory continues to shape crime research even today, the 1990s witnessed the advent of self-control theory (Gottfredson & Hirschi, 1990). Although there are many modern varieties of control theory (see Sampson & Laub, 1993; Tittle, 1995), this chapter will focus on the two versions that have been the most influential at shaping criminological research.

WHAT DO CONTROL THEORIES ASSUME ABOUT HUMAN NATURE?

We begin with a discussion about what makes control theories distinct from the others that we cover in this book, particularly strain and differential association theories. Many theories of crime assume that something must cause, compel, or push people to commit crime. If something must cause crime, then it follows that crime cannot be a *natural* thing for people to do. People can commit crime, for example, only if someone or something else teaches them, or they experience the failure to achieve the American Dream, or they have a biological or psychological "problem." In either case, these theories suggest that people do not decide to commit crime on their own. The idea that criminality is not a normal part of human nature makes so much sense that whenever we hear of a brutal crimes, the first question that often pops into our head is, "What caused that person to do it?" After all, thinking back to the Hornsby case, it cannot possibly be normal for someone to offer to help clean out a dead woman's apartment—a woman who was a friend of one's teammates—and then steal her credit card. Something must have been seriously wrong with him, right? Put another way, we tend to think that it is natural for us to behave ourselves and obey the law and it is unnatural for us to commit crime.

Control theories, in contrast, usually assume that the desire to commit crime is natural to all human beings and what needs to be explained is why people resist criminal temptation. Control theories begin with the view that crime is simply a consequence of the rational and self-interested nature with which *everyone* is born. Learning the motivation to commit crime from others is not necessary. We can all naturally anticipate the benefits and costs of our actions, and we choose to behave in whichever way yields the most advantage. Our self-interested nature means that we consider costs and benefits as they relate specifically to our own pleasure. Now imagine the kind of person you might be in your "natural" state, which is how you would be if you did anything and everything that gave you pleasure or advantage. Marriage vows would mean nothing, provided that you had an opportunity for sex and you thought that you could escape undetected or unpunished. Nor would you hesitate to use force, if doing so would get you what you wanted and the risk to yourself was not too high. You also might be quick to lie to others, manipulate, cheat, or steal your way to what you wanted if you felt you could get away with it. You would be drawn to eat any food, drink any beverage, or inhale, inject, or snort any substances that made you feel good. This does not mean that everyone is essentially evil or bad—after all, control theory assumes that we are capable of obeying societal rules (at least when it is to our advantage; virtue, as they say, is its own reward). Instead, the assumption is that we are amoral and that both good and bad actions can ultimately be traced to personal self-interest. Control theory says that when we get right down to it, none of us (at the core) are really very nice. We may, of course, see some advantage to giving other people the impression that we are otherwise, however. This is the control theorist's picture of humanity at its most fundamental. Given this somewhat gloomy view of human nature, the basic question for the control theorist thus is *not* "Why do some people commit crime?" but instead "How do people stop themselves from committing crime when it would have been to their own advantage?" After all, not all of us hit, steal, or rob even when doing so might appear beneficial.

Another factor commonly assumed in control theories is the idea that there is general agreement in the world about what constitutes socially unacceptable behavior. That is, crime is not simply an arbitrary product of moral entrepreneurs (as suggested by labeling theory) or powerful people (as implied in differential association and social conflict theories). As one might expect from the examples in the preceding paragraph, it is not unreasonable to think that people who simply act out their gross desires regardless of the rights of others create chaos and instability in any society. For instance, trust would be foolish if we expected our neighbors to steal from us if they thought they would not get caught. Societies therefore create formal and informal methods of enforcing rules, so as to protect order and ensure a smoothly running society. While there may be gray-area behaviors that are sometimes tolerated and sometimes not—smoking and substance use (e.g., alcohol) come to mind—this viewpoint maintains that no society can function very well when its citizens are free to rob, steal, and kill one another. What all this means is that, unlike differential association and labeling theories, control theories first assume that what crime is does not vary in meaningful ways from one culture to another, and second, that criminal law is not merely a tool used by some people so that they can maintain their positions of power and privilege.

So, on the one hand we can expect that people will act in their self-interest and that sometimes crime will be in one's self-interest to commit. On the other hand, even as crime is beneficial to the individual, everyone else will readily observe that crime harms them in multitudinous ways and so will oppose it. One can predict from this that society will invent barriers in order to dissuade its members from taking advantage of criminal opportunities. We noted earlier that society has adopted formal and informal methods of keeping us from freely acting on our desires. Modern control theories focus on trying to identify which kinds of restraints are most effective at preventing people from committing crime. Social control theories often emphasize how connectedness with society deters crime or eliminates opportunities for crime. Self-control theory, in contrast, focuses almost entirely on an acquired fear of long-term consequences for criminal actions.

As a final note, some people may be able to relate to these assumptions about human nature and find them believable, while others might not. You should be aware, however, that assumptions are not the same things as proven facts. Assumptions—by definition—cannot be scientifically proven, which means that you are under no obligation to accept them. But knowing and understanding the underlying assumptions behind theories is essential for being able to distinguish between and understand individual theories.

EARLY CONTROL THEORIES

To begin the presentation of the major control theories themselves, we present some of the founders of the modern control perspective. The ideas of these founders provide the basis of contemporary thinking about where social control emanates from. Today, most of these ideas are not used by themselves, but instead have been revised and added to for contemporary use. It is important, however, to first review these "older" ideas for a couple of reasons. First, this can show us how some of the major modern theories developed. Theorists do not pull their ideas out of thin air, but work creatively with the ideas available to them at the time. Second, a historical understanding shows where the dead ends are as far as explaining crime. This latter point is particularly important, as all of us have our own beliefs and opinions about what causes crime—and we may not recognize that these ideas and beliefs may have been considered, tested, and found to be inadequate. As the saying goes, if we fail to understand history, we doom ourselves to repeat it.

This is not to say that control theories historically have been failures like Lombroso's theory of atavism or the explanations of the phrenologists. Rather, the history of control theories has been slowly gathering momentum. The perspective began with only a few isolated studies—but these few ideas continue to influence thinking today. Now, more than a half century later, control theories clearly are among the most important modern explanations of crime.

Albert Reiss (1951) was perhaps the first American criminologist to discuss the idea of "controls," distinguishing between "personal" and "social" forms of control. Personal controls refer to our individual ability to resist temptation, whereas social controls compel us to resist temptation out of fear of what others may do to us—for instance, fear of arrest. A few years later, Jackson Toby (1957) wrote about **stakes in conformity,** a type of control in which people resist criminal temptation because their very conformity up to the present had led to rewards (such as reputation, job prospects, or educational opportunities) that might be jeopardized were they to engage in crime. Those with few stakes in conformity, on the other hand, have fewer reasons for resisting when faced with the opportunity for crime. F. Ivan Nye (1958) added to control theory, proposing two types of external control: direct (for instance, when you elect to not hit your sibling because your parents are watching you) and indirect (when you worry about the embarrassment you might cause others by failing to resist temptation and getting caught). Internal controls, on the other hand, refer to the guilt that we anticipate feeling were we to engage in delinquency. Such a control essentially takes the fun out of whatever pleasure we might have obtained by giving in to temptation. Of these three types of controls, Nye felt that informal controls were the most efficacious at restraining criminal activity.

During the same period (the 1950s and 1960s), Walter Reckless developed a major branch of control theory called *containment theory.* After going through several rounds of revisions and modifications, the final version of containment theory (see Reckless, 1967) lays out a fairly complex model of "pushes" and "pulls" that might lead to crime as well as "inner" and "outer" **containments,** the forces that might buffer or insulate the individual from succumbing to criminal pushes and pulls. Pushes to crime are generally internal in focus (some have argued these to be psychological or biological), though sometimes the push might ultimately originate from a social event, structure, or experience, such as poverty or discrimination. Pushes include the need for sex, aggression, frustration, rebelliousness, and a need or desire for immediate gratification. Pulls, on the other hand, refer to social invitations or encouragements to crime originating from other people. Pulls often come from our role models or companions. For example, you might be at a party where someone is passing a marijuana joint around. The encouragements of your friends to take a puff might pull you into smoking the joint and thus engaging in an illegal activity.

You probably realize that pushes and pulls toward crime are all around us, but that not all of us commit crime. Recall that Reckless identified two types of containments that help us resist pressures to commit crime—inner and outer. Inner containment is our **self-concept,** our conscience, which he believed was formed by about age 12 or so. Individuals with a negative self-concept will be more likely to commit crime. Outer containment is most effective when we receive supervision and discipline. The responsibility for outer containment does not rest so much on the individual as on the ability of the community and the family to provide an effective structure and organization that can provide observation and control. This argument is much the same as that in social disorganization theory (Shaw & McKay, 1942). Indeed, many of the same ideas that Reiss and Nye proposed are evident in Reckless's work—inner containment and self-concept resemble internal control, whereas external containment is similar to social control. The basic idea behind these theoretical terms is very similar.

In some ways, Reckless's theory went beyond the common assumptions of control theory as we know it today, and his theory tends to overlap with some of the other theoretical explanations that we cover in this text (namely, learning and strain theories). Strain theory, for instance, is clearly a theory that emphasizes pushes. One version of strain theory, advanced by Robert Merton (1938), argues that the lack of access to economic opportunities that some people must endure causes them to violate the rules in order to get what they want. As we noted earlier in the discussion on the assumptions behind control theories, this perspective assumes that we need no outside push to commit crime. Differential association theory, which would emphasize how we learn to become criminal from the people closest to us, is clearly one example of a pull theory. Control theories, in contrast, argue that we do not "learn" crime nor do we necessarily imitate criminal role models.

Reckless' theory, however, is not used much today. Although his work seemed to show that having a high self-concept (or high self-esteem) insulated children from delinquency, for his results to be scientifically credible there had to be independent verification of his findings. Science, after all, cannot simply take someone's word that their theory works. Unfortunately for containment theory, such results were not forthcoming (e.g., Orcutt, 1980). Even policies designed specifically with Reckless' theory in mind, such as an attempt to improve the self-concept of a group of Ohio boys, produced little reduction in delinquency (Reckless & Dinitz, 1972). Reckless' theory is, at present, only significant insofar as it identifies a false trail and, more importantly, sets the stage for later work.

HIRSCHI'S SOCIAL CONTROL THEORY

As noted earlier, the control theory formulated by Travis Hirschi has assumed the position as the primary and most frequently drawn-on form of social control theory. Hirschi's conceptualization focuses on the idea of individuals' **social bond** as a means for imposing a variety of restraints on our behavior. The social bond is simply our connectedness to society, and crime—according to Hirschi—is more likely to occur among those with weakened connections to others. Social bonds act as barriers to opportunities for crime, as well as restraints. Thus, criminals are not socialized into crime as other theories might say, but are in fact *undersocialized* into conformity. The social bond consists of four elements: attachment, commitment, involvement, and belief. While each of these bonds may vary independently (i.e., it is possible to conceive of somebody with strong commitment but few attachments), Hirschi hypothesized that the four elements of the social bond are interconnected. Note that people with weakened bonds to society are not in any way destined to become criminals. They can still be considerate most of the time, because there are advantages to virtuous behavior; however, criminal temptation will often speak more persuasively to such people, because they would sacrifice less should they get caught.

Attachment

Imagine that you had the opportunity to cheat on a test at school, but you realized that if your professor caught you, your actions would humiliate your parents. If the thought of causing your parents embarrassment, combined with expectation of a loss of their affection, would deter you from cheating, then **attachment**—feelings of sensitivity and affection for others—was what compelled you to take your test honestly. People with strong bonds of attachment genuinely care about what other people think and appreciate the possibility that people they love and admire will think badly of them. Faced with the opportunity for crime, those with strong attachment to others consider the embarrassment or inconvenience their actions would cause those who are close to them.

This consideration of the feelings for others is even true, according to the theory, for those who are strongly attached to criminal friends or parents! Remember what we said about there being general agreement about what constitutes legal and illegal behavior? This means that criminals share the same basic beliefs as noncriminals. They may of course take a more lax view when it comes to their own conduct, but, because they can presumably foresee themselves as victims of crime, they would disapprove of the thefts and murders committed by others and would withdraw their friendship. And so, according to the theory, anyone who truly cares what these delinquents think will actually be less—rather than more—likely to commit crime. This is a very different position than that of differential association theory. But, given that these delinquent friends are by definition engaging in behavior that is not exactly admirable, one can expect that there will be very few people who are genuinely attached to them enough to care about their sentiments concerning crime. But regardless of who one is attached to, strong attachment should act as a barrier to offending.

On the other hand, Hirschi's theory suggests that if you know someone who is sincere when she says, "I don't care what anyone thinks of me," you might want to guard your wallet or purse, because she is not particularly troubled with the thought that her criminal actions might damage her relationships. People who lack attachment are more likely to succumb to criminal opportunity because they risk less when they participate in crime. We should also note that attachments might lead to greater direct control (as we tend to spend more time around the people we like, who then are in a position to regulate our behavior), but that people who possess strong attachment do not require observation in order to be deterred from crime. Attachment, as Hirschi thinks of it, is something like an "internal parent."

Commitment

The bond of **commitment** refers to stakes we have in following the rules, stakes that we could lose if we were to commit crime. Commitment is somewhat different from attachment in that commitment is more selfish. Commitment means that we care about what people think of us, but only insofar as their having a negative opinion of us impairs our enjoyment of something we *do* care about: wealth, status, or a job. We might not worry about disappointing a teacher by cheating on a test, but we do fear failing the class (and ruining future job prospects) if we are caught. A person who has no long-term job, few educational achievements, and no reputation worth acknowledging would be more likely to be a delinquent; this person would have little to lose by engaging in crime.

Try to think of commitment like this. One person has a stable high-paying job, while another has a low-paying temporary job. The consequences of crime for both would be the same: Many bosses take a dim view of crime. They, after all, can foresee that criminal employees might not scruple even when it comes to victimizing their employers. And so, employees who get arrested and convicted can expect in many cases to lose their jobs. Of the two people just mentioned, who would you guess would be most likely to be deterred from committing crime that may lead to losing the job?

Involvement

The third element of the social bond, **involvement,** looks at how time acts as a restraint. Many of us feel that we are so busy that it would be hard to take on additional activities. Perhaps the same is true of crime. If we are too busy and engrossed in conventional activity, there should be much less time left for criminal activity. Those who spend more time doing homework have less time to commit crime. Those teenagers who spend more time practicing at sports or working at jobs will have that much less time to commit crime. Even simply watching television should serve to tie up one's time. In contrast, people who do not spend a whole lot of time engaged in conventional activity, such as by idling on the street corner or in a vacant lot, would have lots of time and opportunity to commit crime.

Belief

Social control theory is a "consensus" theory, as we described earlier. The basic assumption is that everyone intuitively believes that crime is wrong because they understand the havoc for society that would follow should crime be allowed to go unchecked. But they may differ in how strongly they believe in the rules against crime, at least when it comes to their own actions. Take killing, for example. Do you believe that killing is wrong under all circumstances? If not, when is it permitted? Any time your own life is in danger? Any time someone threatens your child? Any time someone does something to provoke you beyond your limit? Any time someone you don't like is walking down the street? Whenever it might be fun? In all cases, there is no suggestion that killing people is positively valued. But clearly, some of these excuses or justifications set aside more room, morally speaking, for killing someone than others.

Hirschi's theory maintains that those who have a strong **belief** that crime is wrong are less likely to take advantage of criminal opportunities. The less we think that rules have moral authority, the more easily we can find excuses and rationalizations for our criminal actions. If you don't think that your parents or your government has the right to make rules for you, are you likely to follow them anyway? Possibly, but these rules will have a weak hold over you. Weak beliefs do not require that we commit crime, but weak beliefs in the moral wrongness of certain acts function as a poor or weak restraint. It may be more accurate to say that those with weak belief in conventional rules have an ambivalent attitude toward the law. On one hand, people with weak beliefs may not consider crime to be necessarily a good thing. But at the same time, there are many situations when illegal acts would not necessarily be seen as wrong, either. A relative of one of the authors frequently tailgates other cars and feels justified doing such a reckless act [saying, "Well I'm in a hurry (so the rules don't apply to me right now)!"], and yet speaks disparagingly of others when they tailgate. People we know who practice such "situational ethics" can be seen as weakly bonded to conventional beliefs and are thus more likely to commit crime. In contrast, strong beliefs—in which we believe that there is no excuse or justification for crime—mean we are more likely to overcome our natural tendency to commit crime.

The element of belief is often thought of as the most difficult to understand. Why would our beliefs not both push and restrain people from crime? After all, we sometimes hear that criminals were taught the "wrong" beliefs at some point in their life—such as from running with a "bad crowd"— and these bad beliefs somehow *pushed* people into crime. This understanding of belief, however, makes sense only if people are not naturally predisposed toward crime (as assumed by control theories). In Hirschi's social control theory, the few people who seemingly hold procriminal beliefs were simply never socialized into conventional values. Their amoral human nature, moreover, means that no push toward crime in the form of beliefs or anything else is even needed. In other words, their procriminal belief system only mirrors what one would expect from those who feel justified to commit crime any time it is to their advantage—that is, people who are completely unsocialized.

Empirical Testing

For at least the first 25 years after publication, Hirschi's social control theory was subjected to empirical testing more frequently than perhaps any theory of crime (Stitt & Giacopassi, 1992). Hirschi (1969) himself recognized the importance of testing his theory and provided the first test in the book in which he outlined social control theory. He drew on self-reported delinquency survey data from a sample of more than 4,000 juveniles living in California during the mid-1960s.

So how did Hirschi (and other later researchers) measure such ideas as attachment, commitment, involvement, and belief? This is worth knowing, because if you are going to be able to critically evaluate the results of theory-tests, you need to see the measures and ask yourself if they seem reasonable. We should note that Hirschi did not invent his measures out of thin air. Even though large-scale data collection efforts were uncommon before the 1960s, many of Hirschi's measures were derived from the work of Sheldon and Eleanor Glueck (1950) and F. Ivan Nye (1958).

Hirschi gave the high school kids living in Contra Costa County a survey asking all of the questions he thought were relevant to his theory. We cannot provide an exhaustive list of everything he asked here, but we can give you a sampling. He measured attachment with questions like "Do you share your thoughts and feelings with your parents?" and "Do you care what teachers think of you?" The participants in the survey would record responses like, for instance, "often," "sometimes," or "never." Examples of commitment questions included "How much schooling would you like to get eventually?" and items relating to the sort of job they aspired for (e.g., "professional," "white collar," or "manual labor"). Involvement in conventional activity measured things like participation in school-related activities and organizations as well as work and dating. Belief was measured with items including "I have a lot of respect for the police" and "It's all right to get around the law if you can get away with it." Hirschi then conducted statistical analyses to see if these items and others like them were connected in any way with the delinquency items asked on the same questionnaire.

His results supported his argument that criminal offenders tended to have weaker attachments, commitments, and belief in the moral authority of rules than nondelinquents. The effects of these elements of the social bond on offending tended to be stronger than more traditional crime correlates such as race or social class. One weakness in the theory that emerged, however, is that Hirschi did not find that spending time doing conventional activities had any consistent relationship with crime. Indeed, involvement in many activities had no influence one way or the other on crime. More interesting still, conventional activity like working and dating tended to predict delinquency in the opposite manner to what the theory predicted: people who dated or worked were more likely to be delinquents. (Remember this when you have children someday and they argue with you about dating and working.) Later tests of Hirschi's theory also tended to confirm these findings (see Kempf-Leonard, 1993).

Empirical testing has also uncovered some other possible weaknesses in Hirschi's version of social control theory. First, Hirschi's own initial test found that juveniles who associated with delinquent peers were significantly more likely to be delinquent as well, and that this predictor tended to have a stronger influence than the elements of the social bond. Other researchers have also confirmed this through other tests through the years (see Conger, 1976; Warr, 2002). Criminologists often interpret this finding about the importance of delinquent peers as evidence of support for social learning theory, which argues that children model themselves on others and learn behaviors based on whether that behavior gets reinforced or punished (see Akers & Sellers, 2004).

As the use of self-report surveys to study delinquency proliferated since 1969, researchers have also examined the questions Hirschi asked on his survey and explored other possible ways to measure his concepts more effectively. One issue with surveys is that the researcher has to trust what the respondent is saying. This doesn't mean that people will lie on surveys. Lying does happen, but people also forget. For instance, if I were to ask you how often you have eaten pizza in the last six months, you might find it hard to answer accurately. Another problem, which involves neither lying nor forgetting, is known as the "Dunning–Kruger Effect," which was reported by Justin Kruger and David Dunning in an article in the *Journal of Personality and Social Psychology* in 1999. The two psychologists found that people who were incompetent tended to be oblivious to their own incompetence, rating themselves "above average" on skills in which they in fact ranked at the very bottom. Your professors encounter the Dunning–Kruger effect when students who are struggling in their classes nevertheless give the strongest assurances that they are "A" and "B" students. But the implication here is that people who are incompetent at relationships may rate their ties with others as being better than in fact they are, simply because they are clueless about what a strong relationship looks like. The moral of this lesson is that what people say about themselves is not always in agreement with reality. One must be appropriately skeptical of how we measure things.

So to address this potential problem, at least with respect to attachment toward others, some researchers have turned toward direct observation. This involves recording parent–child interactions using video cameras and classifying the interactions in terms of warmth, emotional closeness, and openness of communication (e.g., Stewart, Simons, & Conger, 2002). Such techniques provide a more objective index of such concepts as attachment, unfiltered by deception or forgetfulness on the part of the respondent. Although using direct observation offers a more pure way to measure attachment, the results produced appear to mirror those of survey research. Parent–child interactions indicative of attachment predict less delinquency. Many researchers have made other measurement refinements to other elements of the social bond as well, such as by measuring religiosity or commitment to religion and relating it to delinquency (e.g., Chard-Wierschem, 1998; Hirschi & Stark, 1969).

One question that you might ask regarding social control theory—and it's a good question—is, "where do bonds come from in the first place?" Hirschi (1969) stated that bonds are meaningful only when acquired through personal investment and exertion, not when society gives them away to an individual. But not all people are inclined to exert themselves in order to secure something that has long-term advantage. For instance, colleges and universities frequently award scholarships to those in need, to those who have records of academic and/or civic excellence, and for athletic achievement. Most of us would look on a scholarship as something of great advantage. But who do you suppose would value the scholarship more, and thus be more afraid to lose it by stupidly stealing a book from the university bookstore and/or using school as an opportunity to get away from annoying parents in order to party for a few years: someone who worked hard to get the scholarship and sees the value of obtaining a degree, or someone who did little to earn it? Clearly, opportunities to fashion stronger bonds do not always mean the same thing to different people, and we can probably think of many examples of people squandering opportunities to better their lives. Thus, we have Jamar Hornsby's circumstances, described at the beginning of the chapter. Something else appears to be at work.

SELF-CONTROL THEORY

Some 20 years after Hirschi published *Causes of Delinquency* (1969), Gottfredson and Hirschi (1990) published a revision of control theory in a book titled *A General Theory of Crime.* Apart from the question about what creates bonds in the first place, research had uncovered other reasons why social control theory needed an update (see Hirschi & Gottfredson, 2002). Interestingly, their book in fact said little about social bonds, and instead focused attention on a concept they called **self-control.** Self-control refers to the habit of refraining from grabbing at short-term pleasure out of fear of the long-term consequences. The authors noted that much short-term pleasure has negative long-term pain. For example, pretend you like cheese fries with bacon and ranch dressing. Cheese fries taste really good, and many of us can eat a lot of them. But a single plate of cheese fries also typically contains more than a day's worth of calories. That's *one* plate. If we grab at the short-term pleasure of eating a lot of something that tastes really good, we must ignore the long-term fact that (1) we will get fat and will have to exercise and diet to make up for our cheese fries binge if we still wish to fit into our clothes, and (2) that our health will suffer. Clearly, an appreciation of the long-term consequences (self-control) would affect many behaviors besides crime, which is why Gottfredson and Hirschi refer to their theory as a "general" theory. More generally, some forms of pleasure can be reckless (i.e., can get us hurt or killed), immoral (offend people), or illegal (criminal). Self-control theory assumes that pleasure appeals to all of us; however, for many of us, our fear of the consequences helps keep us from engaging in such activity. But what makes us fear the consequences? That is where self-control comes in—lots of bad things can happen if we do not take long-term negative consequences into account.

For some people, it is difficult to put the long-term consequences into perspective, because the consequences are not always immediately apparent or even certain. Obeying a stop sign, for example, makes sense because we risk our lives and those of other people if we violently collide with another car. But this possibility of a collision is only a *maybe.* We have all probably run stop signs without getting into an accident; the long-term consequences, while obviously potentially negative, sometimes happen very infrequently. Moreover, running a stop sign is *immediately* advantageous to us (contrast this with the merely *potential* negative consequences). Without a doubt, we can get to where we want to go faster if we do not have to stop anywhere along the way or yield to other cars. So what do you do when you come up to a stop sign? If you have low self-control, you may think about how much of a hurry you are in, dismiss the risk of accident, and go through the intersection without stopping. If you have more self-control, you are more likely to shudder at what *might* happen if a car hits you, and therefore stop.

What would a person be like who had low self-control? Gottfredson and Hirschi suggested that low self-control leads to distinctive personality characteristics. In particular, those with low self-control tend to be impulsive, self-centered, belligerent, lazy, and unable to defer gratification. One common thread in each characteristic of low self-control is that all of them are potentially self-destructive. Yet the following traits would be how all of us are naturally inclined to behave if we did not appreciate the potentially negative impact of our actions:

- *Impulsivity.* Do you know anyone who goes out and buys things on the spur of the moment, expensive things such as designer clothes, running up huge credit card debt without even thinking about it? Impulsivity, according to self-control theory, comes naturally and without effort. It takes effort to do things deliberately and with forethought about what the consequences might be whenever temptation (whatever it may be) is beckoning.
- *Adventure seeking.* We all naturally prefer to do things that are exciting, but many exciting things can get us into trouble (such as promiscuous sex or lying down on the median of a busy highway for laughs). People with low self-control therefore have a passion for doing thrilling things. Having high self-control and exercising due caution, on the other hand, would have the unexciting—but potentially life-saving— benefit of discouraging us from taking foolish risks.
- *Self-centeredness.* Have you ever known somebody who acts as if he or she is the only person who matters in the world? Self-control theory argues that we all are basically selfish; we are naturally inclined to look out for ourselves first. In other words, our natural inclination is not to care what others think, except insofar as manipulating other people's feelings can help us to get what we want. It takes self-control to be able to put other people first—genuine empathy toward others takes effort.
- *Minimal tolerance for frustration.* When a boss or friend yells at you, what is your first reaction? Do you say, "I deserved it"? Probably not. Your first reaction is likely to get angry, and maybe imagine how pleasurable it would be to tell your tormentor where to get off or even deliver a punch to that person's mouth. Frequently venting anger toward someone simply feels good, universally so, and it takes effort not to lash out at those who frustrate us.
- *Lack of diligence.* Self-control theory says that people naturally prefer to do things that bring pleasure quickly and easily, even if there are potential long-term costs to taking the easy way. Tasks that are more complicated and require effort are more likely to discourage us. A willingness to undertake difficult tasks rather than take the easy way requires effort.

- *Inability to defer gratification.* Not many people have an easy time waiting for something pleasurable to occur. Nevertheless, many of us can be patient and wait, but patience sometimes takes a great deal of effort. Inability to wait is an indicator of low self-control.

While low self-control includes all these different traits, self-control is at the same time unidimensional. That is, these personality traits are *symptoms* of having low self-control, and all traits should appear in people possessing low self-control. So if someone is unusually selfish, you should also expect that on average this person is also impulsive, lazy, risk seeking, belligerent, and unable to defer gratification. What do you suppose the life of someone like this must be like? As fun as having low self-control might seem to be, the theory tells us that low self-control is not a ticket for a happy or stable life. Ignoring consequences would lead to, among other things, accidents, disease, employment instability, brief and volatile social relationships, and even victimization. Kristy Holtfreter and her colleagues (2008) even showed that those with low self-control are more likely to be ripped off by scam artists. It is here where social bonds fit in, too: People with low self-control have a habit of frittering away opportunities to form bonds. For example, it is fair to say that most people feel tired when the 7 A.M. alarm for an early class goes off. Who is more likely to sleep in and risk failing the class—someone who cares about the long-term consequences of not getting ready for class or someone who does not even think about them? If the thought of failing does not trouble you, then sleeping in sounds like a much better idea than hurrying to get to class. As implied in this example, developing social bonds sometimes requires short-term sacrifice and inconvenience, which someone with low self-control is generally not too willing to make. So Gottfredson and Hirschi would say that social bonds are by-products of self-control.

Besides unpleasant life outcomes and weak social bonds, crime clearly would appeal to someone with low self-control. First, people habitually unable to defer gratification are unlikely to have the kind of patience to wait until they can pay for something; therefore, they are more likely to simply take it (especially if they think they can get away without paying). Moreover, most crimes take very little training or skill, which is wonderful if one doesn't have much patience. Anyone, even an uneducated and unskilled person, can thrust a knife at somebody or pull the trigger on a loaded handgun. Second, most crimes really do not require much effort to commit. After all, how much effort does it take to push a handgun in someone's face and demand his or her money (as opposed to working eight hours a day at a job)? Third, Gottfredson and Hirschi (1990) reported that a great deal of crime is spontaneous—very little time elapses between recognition of an opportunity and the actual carrying out of the crime (see also Felson, 1998). Contrary to what television and movies seem to show, the average bank robbery, for instance, undergoes very rudimentary planning, if any. Most crimes simply do not involve much, if any, real planning or thought. Fourth, since crime can lead to inconvenience (if not pain) for a victim, commiting crime is less likely to appeal to someone who genuinely cares about the feelings of others. A person who has low self-control will not worry so much about those he or she hurts. Fifth, although not in every instance, but in many, the danger associated with crime makes it exciting. Finally, committing crime can be a very satisfying way of coping with our frustration. While we would not expect people with low self-control to go out of their way to seek out crime—since that would be a little too much like work—neither would we expect them to resist opportunities for crime, either.

So where does self-control come from? Self-control is an acquired characteristic, so we are not born with it. Gottfredson and Hirschi specifically emphasized child rearing in the family as the primary agent for the development of self-control. In contrast, social learning theories give no particularly important role to the family, and classic versions of strain theory and labeling theory hardly acknowledge the family at all. In self-control theory, childhood socialization is the process of educating individuals about the consequences of their actions and teaching children that others have rights. Borrowing from the work of Gerald Patterson (1980), Gottfredson and Hirschi reasoned that three factors must be present before self-control becomes a habit. First, parents must be able and willing to supervise their children. The level of supervision children receive thus substantially depends on how intact the family is, as well as the bonds of love between parent and child. Second, parents must also be able and willing to recognize deviant behavior when it occurs. This does not always happen, even when parents love their children. For instance, parents sometimes resent people who tell them that their child is acting up and punish the messenger; as a result, the child receives no disciplining. Third, parents must punish the deviant behavior. Parents, perhaps surprisingly, sometimes do everything they can to avoid punishing their children—or they take punishment too far. Yet once self-control becomes evident in children, approximately around age eight, differences in self-control remain relatively stable—older children who frequently ignore the consequences of their behavior will show similar tendencies as adults and will engage in more antisocial and self-destructive behavior relative to their same-age peers.

Empirical Research and Criticisms of Self-Control Theory

Since 1990, few theories have garnered as much research attention and discussion as self-control theory (Pratt & Cullen, 2000). Dozens of empirical tests of the theory took place in the two decades after *A General Theory of Crime* was published (see Baron, 2003; Grasmick, Tittle, Bursik, & Arneklev, 1993; Keane, Maxim, & Teevan, 1993; LaGrange & Silverman, 1999; Sellers, 1999). The theory is still going strong as a basis for research.

How do criminologists usually test self-control theory? As with many other theories, the most usual method uses self-report surveys (where people are asked to fill out a questionnaire, and researchers then conduct a statistical analysis of the responses they provided). One issue that made measuring self-control tricky for researchers is that Gottfredson and Hirschi (1990) did not spell out exactly how they thought self-control ought to be measured. In 1993, Harold Grasmick and his colleagues developed what came to be called "the Grasmick scale" for measuring self-control. It consisted of a battery of 24 questions that psychologists had used to measure personality—namely, impulsivity, preference for simple tasks, risk seeking, preference for physical activities, self-centeredness, and temper. People were typically asked questions about how much they agreed with such statements as, "I try to look out for myself first, even if it means making things difficult for other people," "When I'm angry, other people better stay away from me," and "I sometimes take a risk just for the fun of it." The responses would then be combined and researchers would statistically correlate peoples' self-control scores with their self-reported delinquency.

Hirschi and Gottfredson (1993) noted a danger in using such measures as the Grasmick scale. The two theorists felt that the Grasmick scale would imply that some aspects of personality caused crime, such as risk seeking and impulsivity (when, in fact, these—like crime—were simply by-products of low self-control). Hirschi and Gottfredson instead endorsed behavioral measures of low self-control, such as those used by Carl Keane and his colleagues. Keane et al. (1993) were interested in explaining drinking and driving, so their measures of self-control included questions about wearing seatbelts, how much they drank in the past week, and whether or not anyone had pled with the respondent to not drive after drinking. Hirschi and Gottfredson also recommended indicators of childhood misconduct, frequency of accidents, and so forth. The field of criminology, however, has preferred the Grasmick approach by a substantial margin (Pratt & Cullen, 2000).

The results of these tests have generally been supportive of the theory—those with low self-control tend to engage in more crime. While significant, the effect of self-control on crime is not huge (Pratt & Cullen, 2000). Research has also explored whether self-control links to crime-analogous outcomes, as Gottfredson and Hirschi had speculated. Indeed, there is evidence linking low self-control with adverse circumstances such as contact with delinquent friends, spotty work histories, accidents, and even street and fraud victimization (see Evans, Culleu, & Burton, 1997; Holtfreter et al., 2008; Jones & Quisenberry, 2004; Schreck, 1999). Consistent with Gottfredson and Hirschi's claims, low self-control does appear to have general effects.

Self-control theory has not lacked for critics, however (see Goode, 2008). Notwithstanding the research showing that self-control predicts many unpleasant outcomes for people, researchers have expressed concern about whether the theory is suitable for explaining specific types of crime. Some research suggests that the "general theory" of crime may not be very effective for explaining such crime as white-collar crime, where offenders typically must have high self-control in order to achieve the positions necessary to make their crimes possible (e.g., Friedrichs & Schwartz, 2008). Other critics have made similar claims about other types of crimes, such as for violence (Felson & Osgood, 2008).

Critics have also homed in on how one measures self-control. Unlike Hirschi's earlier book, *Causes of Delinquency* (1969), where he provided a detailed guide for measuring the four elements of the social bond, *A General Theory of Crime*, as just mentioned, did not make positive statements about how to best measure self-control (Akers, 1991). Gottfredson and Hirschi (1990) claimed that once one has a suitable measure of low self-control, then the statistical correlation between all of the by-products of low self-control (e.g., marriage, strong social bonds, having deviant friends) and crime should disappear. This so far has not been the case (Pratt & Cullen, 2000), as many of these measures stubbornly remain predictive of crime, notwithstanding controls for the Grasmick scale or alternative measures of self-control. This is actually quite an important problem, as self-control theory has no way of accounting for the significance of many of these other variables. If marriage, for instance, exerts an effect on offending that is independent of self-control, well, what could it possibly mean except that the theory is wrong? We will look at that question in the next section! If delinquent friends still contribute to offending independently of self-control, then does this mean that social learning theory is correct? We can at least address that question now.

Gottfredson and Hirschi (1990) tackled the delinquent peer issue head-on, arguing that the traditional way of measuring it—for example, questions like: "How many of your friends have stolen something"—was seriously flawed. They posited that respondents often attributed their own qualities onto their friends. That is, if a kid is delinquent, then Gottfredson and Hirschi believed that he or she will tend to describe friends as being delinquent whether really they are or not. Moreover, they asked, how do the respondents know about the delinquency of their friends? How much did they actually see? How much was just hearsay? Much research on self-control theory, including the 94 studies summarized in Pratt and Cullen (2000), used the traditional peer deviance measure anyway. Dana Haynie and Wayne Osgood (2005), looking at peer deviance data provided by the peers themselves, found that Gottfredson and Hirschi were in fact correct; the deviant peer effect was quite modest and was sometimes accounted for by other theories' measures. One lesson you can draw from this example is that one has to treat supposed facts very carefully and not just uncritically accept what the textbook tells you. Long-established facts can undergo a serious challenge owing to better data collection. In the meantime, tests of self-control theory still appear in the literature, indicating that the theory continues to have vitality and excite the interest of researchers (e.g., Chapple, 2005; Goode, 2008; Longshore, Chang, & Messina, 2005; Reisig, Pratt, & Holtfreter, 2009).

Sampson and Laub's Life Course Theory

One of self-control theory's more controversial positions is its claim that by late childhood individual differences in self-control remain relatively stable. A concrete example might clarify what the theory is talking about. Let's say that you take three of your best friends, Moe, Larry, and Curly, and rank order them based on their level of self-control at age 10; this rank ordering (assuming you have a good measure of self-control) should hold true at any age thereafter. The chart below graphically shows what this basic pattern ought to look like from age 10 to 21, if the theory is accurate:

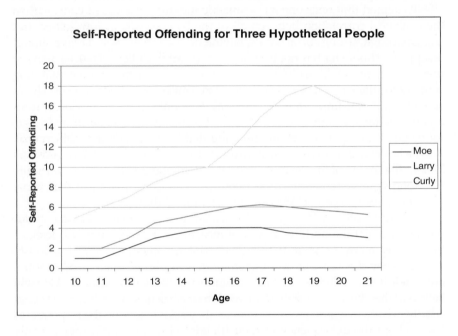

For purposes of this example, we're going to pretend that Curly has the least self-control, Larry has more self-control, and Moe has the most self-control. You can see that if Curly is very obnoxious relative to Moe and Larry at age 10, he will generally make more of a mess of things at age 21 as well. If we extended the chart all the way out to age 80, an 80-year-old Curly would commit less crime than he did as a teenager (because criminal activity generally decreases for everyone from early adulthood onward, as the chart begins to show), but he would still commit more crime than an 80-year-old Moe or Larry. Put another way, there is nothing society can do to influence these relative rank orderings after childhood. Rehabilitation won't work, and neither would incarceration, marriage, military service, or parenthood. So sorry, but if your prospective spouse is a slovenly jerk now, self-control theory would argue he or she will still be one after you are married!

The life course perspective, however, takes a very different view. Robert Sampson and John Laub's 1993 book, *Crime in the Making*, is perhaps the most influential book to shape research and theory on crime over the life course. In this book, Sampson and Laub reanalyzed data from 500 delinquents and 500 nondelinquents that earlier criminologists Sheldon and Eleanor Glueck had collected over a period of several decades starting in the 1930s. The Glueck data, which contained highly detailed information about the subjects, had been collecting dust in boxes for many decades until John Laub reconstructed and computerized the data set.

From this information, Sampson and Laub developed a theory that could account for why juveniles become offenders in the first place as well as how and why transitions take place between adolescence and adulthood that can shape adult offending. Like self-control theory, family context shapes juvenile offending tendencies. What is especially interesting, however, is the argument about stability and change over the life course. Sampson and Laub's theory recognizes that most adult offenders have lengthy juvenile rap sheets. Feeding this stability is the idea that early offending blocks opportunities to develop strong bonds. After all, how many of us want to be friends with an obnoxious troublemaker? How many people will hire a kid who has been arrested for stealing and assaulting people? But meaningful friendships and jobs are what social control theory asserts as being restraints on crime. Offenders are unable to develop strong bonds, even if they really want to do so, and so will often find themselves with little to lose.

But now the paradox: Not every kid that has a run-in with the police becomes an adult offender. Clearly, there is much stability in troublemaking behavior, but it is not absolute. Some people change as they enter adulthood. Social bonds are a big reason, according to Sampson and Laub. One social bond that typically is not available until adulthood is marriage, and Sampson and Laub found that a meaningful marriage has a long-term effect at reducing crime even after we take into account how much of a troublemaker the person was in the years leading up to the marriage.

In many ways, Sampson and Laub's theory is not original—they explicitly built from Travis Hirschi's (1969) social control theory, and so their theory has assumptions that are closely related to the control theories discussed in this chapter (e.g., that people are naturally capable of crime and to explain patterns of offending we have to think in terms of restraints). Their emphasis on and detailed discussion of how the nature and strength of social bonds changed over the life course, however, was an important original development.

So both stability and change characterize the lives of people in Sampson and Laub's theory. The theory recognizes that, for the most part, people are remarkably consistent in their behavior. This consistency over the life course is a *trajectory*. One's life circumstances determine the arc of one's trajectory. If you have parents who drank and used drugs while they were pregnant with you, then your crime trajectory will start higher than others and go farther. Over the life course, one's trajectory will open and close opportunities to strengthen social bonds and become a decent law-abiding citizen. For instance, many of you had to acknowledge on your college applications whether you had ever been arrested and/or charged with a felony. Do you think your college would have been very eager to give you a chance if they knew that you had mugged somebody and tried to kill him? What do you think your likelihood of a stable marriage would be if you had a background of being in and out of prison? For these reasons, trajectories tend to be relatively resistant to alterations.

Over the life course, however, there are particular turning points of such power that they can alter one's trajectory. Sampson and Laub (1993) argued that many of these potential turning points are age graded. Let us see a show of hands—how many of you refrain from crime right now because you would disappoint your kindergarten teacher? (No one raises hands, probably.) Strange! Upsetting your kindergarten teacher perhaps mattered when you were in kindergarten, but not now. And, likewise, it is improbable that marriage would successfully control an unruly five-year-old American, largely because marriage is not legally permissible in most states until at least the onset of puberty. The starting and ending of compulsory education (at roughly ages 5 through 16 and 18) also represents a potential turning point. Military service is not possible until age 17. In short, opportunities to build or destroy social bonds change over the life course. There is research support for the existence of Sampson and Laub's idea of turning points. Alex Piquero and his colleagues (2002) indeed found that marriage and a good full-time job seemed to reduce recidivism among parolees who are young adults. Christopher Uggen (2000) found the same thing, except that work affected the behavior of those 27 and older and not young parolees. Other studies have found that life events like work, incarceration, and relationships result in at least short-term fluctuations in criminal behavior (e.g., Horney, Osgood, & Marshall, 1995). Laub and Sampson (2003) returned to their Glueck data to study their sample of delinquents at age 70 and find out what led them to change their ways and obey the law. The elderly sample, looking back on their lives, indicated that getting married, entering into the military, and finding a career were what kept them out of jail. Laub and Sampson interpreted this as indications that the delinquents were cut off from the environments and immediate factors that made crime likely and placed in contexts where social control was much more effective.

Self-Control Theory Revised?

Recently, Travis Hirschi (2004) published a book chapter in an edited volume where he reconsiders self-control and how it ought to be measured. As we mentioned earlier, Gottfredson and Hirschi (1990) saw self-control as our ability to respect the long-term consequences of our actions. Hirschi, however, expanded self-control to include the *totality* of consequences an individual considers when tempted by crime, whether short or long term. Social bonds (attachment, commitment, and belief) are, in reality, these consequences. If you have a person in your life, a job, and a reputation, these would be what you would stake if you committed a crime and somebody (it need not be the police) found out. Of course, these consequences have to matter to you, and there has to be a chance that these others whose opinions matter to you will find out what you have done. So people, in their usual imprecise way, add up what they might risk by committing crime and act appropriately.

Rather than using a series of personality questions to measure self-control (the Grasmick scale, mentioned earlier), Hirschi proposed simply that those people who were aware of more consequences to their behavior would be less likely to commit crime. In his own test of the revised theory, Hirschi used the same questions he had used to test social control but modified to reflect the theory. For instance, if a person answered in response to "Do you like or dislike school?" that they "liked it," they got a point. There were eight other questions like this, so members of the sample could get anywhere from 0 to 9 points. He used two data sets collected three decades apart to test his measurement strategy and found indeed that those who had more consequences that they considered were less likely to commit crime. These consequences in fact had a cumulative effect on the likelihood that a teenager would commit a crime. A kid who scored a 9 was less likely to commit a crime and had fewer friends who had been arrested than one who scored an 8.

Hirschi's revised version of self-control theory is too recent a development to have received extensive testing yet. Piquero and Bouffard (2007) were the first and so far only researchers to have examined whether Hirschi's revised theory offered added value to the work on self-control theory that had preceded his revision. They tested his new theory using hypothetical scenarios—that is, they gave male college students a questionnaire containing scenarios where the student would describe the likelihood that he would engage in drinking and sexual assault. The students were then free to describe negative consequences on their own as well as how important they are. It turned out that those people who listed a lot of bad things that might happen to them (and who described these "bad things" as being really important to them) were significantly less likely to say that they might engage in these behaviors. Piquero and Bouffard also conducted a comparative test of the earlier conception of self-control as concern about long-term consequences versus Hirschi's more recent focus on all consequences, and they found that a narrow focus on clearly long-term consequences did not predict the likelihood that the respondent would commit a crime as well as Hirschi's (2004) modification. This is, to date, the only test of Hirschi's revision of self-control theory, but these early results indicate empirical validity. Further independent analyses are needed, however, before anyone can draw clear conclusions about this theory.

POLICY IMPLICATIONS OF CONTROL THEORY

As control theories assume that offenders are undersocialized, much like a dog that has not been housetrained, the most effective policies to make people less criminal will strengthen the ability of society to socialize its members and successfully integrate people into society. Social control theory in particular suggests policies that would strengthen bonds between individuals and society, especially with such institutions as the family and the school. *Big Brothers/Big Sisters* programs likewise strive to create a bond between two people—a youth and an adult role model. Among adults, policies should provide adults with stable employment and community involvement.

Self-control theory indicates that the most far-reaching programs for reducing crime with the greatest long-term benefits would be those that successfully promote development of self-control in children, such as early intervention programs. Programs such as these train parents how to raise children who have impulse control and self-discipline, for instance. These efforts to develop self-control in children should target families that are struggling in terms of their ability to supervise and socialize children (see Hirschi, 1995). To assist families, the general theory advocates society's striving to maximize the number of caregivers available to each child. Moreover, programs should address the sources of weakened or broken families, in particular, teenage pregnancy. We described the successful instilling of self-control as "far-reaching" a moment ago. Remember that low self-control is likely to lead to all manner of self-destructive consequences; instilling self-control in youth can therefore be expected to lead to less crime as well as fewer automobile accidents, teenage pregnancies, drug overdoses, and so on. Children in the habit of behaving as if consequences mattered might be less likely to encounter problems such as these.

As with many theories explored in this book, social control theory questions the usefulness of prison. The specific reasoning is that long-term incarceration is very likely to undermine social bonds. Loved ones might drift away, forming new relationships with others outside prison. Additionally, incarceration disrupts education and employment. Hence, if social bonds are important for keeping individuals from committing crime, incarcerating people—where they are likely to have their bonds of attachment, commitment, and involvement weakened—might actually make them *more* likely to be involved in crime. In short, prison could give offenders less to lose.

Self-control theory is also critical of the emphasis of current policy on the courts and corrections systems. First, the theory indicates that the individuals that these policies seek to protect society from are less capable of appreciating the long-term consequences of their decisions and will simply ignore the tougher sanctions. Thus, threats of exceedingly punitive sanctions are of no value if a person is not in the habit of considering them. Second, the theory also does not recommend efforts to rehabilitate offenders. Self-control, as noted earlier, stabilizes in late childhood, which means that efforts to teach self-control would have no effect in later years. Not surprisingly, rehabilitation programs have been notoriously unsuccessful at providing any long-term effective solution to crime. Self-control theory indicates that the formal justice system offers little crime prevention in return for huge tax expenditures.

SUMMARY

Control theories are recent developments building from ideas that originated long ago. At the core of the control theory perspectives are the ideas of Thomas Hobbes, who believed that people are naturally inclined to be deviant because they are rational and pleasure seeking. This idea is central to understanding control theory and how it differs from other theories. Indeed, the purpose of the control theorist is to make sense of why we do not commit crime in circumstances where doing so would be so gratifying. Hirschi's social control theory says that a person's investment in society creates bonds that make crime impossible or not worth committing. Gottfredson and Hirschi's self-control theory says that during childhood we learn that negative long-term consequences follow from reckless, immoral, illegal, or sinful activity, and so those who learn self-control more or less lose their taste for such activities because they fear the consequences. Hirschi's social control theory and Gottfredson and Hirschi's self-control theory represent the two leading control perspectives today.

Social control theories are distinguished from other theories in that they assume that we are all perfectly capable of crime from birth. In contrast, these other theories argue that crime is a characteristic that is not natural to people (or at least not to "normal" people). You may have noticed that the assumptions behind the control perspective share remarkable similarities to that of classical theory, and this insight would be correct. The key difference is that Beccaria and other classical thinkers were attempting to reform eighteenth-century legal systems and, not surprisingly, argued that the fear of legal sanctions for crime—certainty, swiftness, and severity— were key to promoting order in society. The control perspective, on the other hand, tends to place greater importance on other types of sanctions. Hirschi's control theory, for instance, emphasizes social sanctions. In fact, there is a lot to recommend social sanctions as being more important than legal sanctions. In the legal system, you enjoy (at least nominally) due process protections. You have the right to a formal trial, where you can potentially be exonerated for the crime you are charged with, and you might appeal if proper procedure was not followed in the courtroom. When it comes to what other people think of you, however, you are probably aware that there is no formal trial, no due process, no delays or continuances, and no appeal. The opinions of those who matter to us can be certain, swift, and severe indeed! Self-control theory goes further, adding natural sanctions; however, none—no matter how gruesome—are effective at stopping us if we are not in the habit of thinking about them. At least in these respects, the control perspective offers unique insights.

KEY TERMS

attachment   an element of Hirschi's social bond, referring to the degree of sensitivity that an individual has for the feelings of others, particularly those whom he or she respects or admires

belief   an element of Hirschi's social bond, referring to the degree in which an individual believes that a particular rule of society ought to be obeyed

commitment   an element of Hirschi's social bond, referring to the conventional investments an individual risks losing by engaging in crime

containment   a component of Reckless's containment theory; containment can be both "inner" and "outer," with each insulating individuals from pushes and pulls toward crime

involvement   an element of Hirschi's social bond, referring to how engaged an individual is in conventional activity

self-concept   a component of Reckless's containment theory; a form of inner containment that insulates the individual from pushes and pulls toward crime

self-control   the central component of Gottfredson and Hirschi's self-control theory; refers to the habit of individuals to behave as if long-term negative consequences matter

social bond   in Hirschi's theory, a bond that consists of attachment, commitment, involvement, and belief; it collectively acts to restrain individuals faced with criminal temptation

stakes in conformity   a term coined by Jackson Toby; refers to the stakes (benefits) individuals gain by obeying society's rules—stakes that risk being lost by engaging in crime; a central component in Hirschi's concept of attachment

DISCUSSION QUESTIONS

1. What makes control theories different from differential association and strain theories?

2. Why do you suppose that low self-control would influence crime as well as "crime-analogous" acts?

3. How can one create stronger social bonds in a person who is, right now, an offender?

4. What would you do to create people with more self-control?

5. Relate the story of Jamar Hornsby to the theories discussed in this chapter. How would each theory make sense of Hornsby's behavior?

REFERENCES

Akers, R. (1991). Self-control as a general theory of crime. *Journal of Quantitative Criminology, 7,* 201–211.

Akers, R., & Sellers, C. (2004). *Criminological theories: Introduction, evaluation, and application.* Thousand Oaks, CA: Roxbury.

Baron, S. (2003). Self-control, social consequences, and criminal behavior: Street youth and the general theory of crime. *Journal of Research in Crime and Delinquency, 40,* 403–425.

Chapple, C. L. (2005). Self-control, peer relations, and delinquency. *Justice Quarterly, 22,* 89–106.

Chard-Wierschem, D. J. (1998). *In pursuit of the "True" relationship: A longitudinal study of the effects of religiosity on delinquency and substance use.* Unpublished doctoral dissertation. Albany, NY: State University of New York.

Conger, R. (1976). Social control and social learning models of delinquency: A synthesis. *Criminology, 14,* 17–40.

Evans, D. T., Culleu, F. T., & Burton, V. S. (1997). The social consequences of self-control: Testing the general theory of crime. *Criminology, 35*(3), 475–504.

Felson, M. (1998). *Crime and everyday life.* Thousand Oaks, CA: Pine Forge Press.

Felson, R. B., & Osgood, D. W. (2008). Violent crime. In E. Goode (Ed.), *Out of control? Assessing the general theory of crime* (pp. 160–172). Stanford, CA: Stanford University Press.

Friedrichs, D. O., & Schwartz, M. D. (2008). Low self-control and high organizational control: The paradoxes of white collar crime. In E. Goode (Ed.), *Out of control? Assessing the general theory of crime* (pp. 145–159). Stanford, CA: Stanford University Press.

Glueck, S., & Glueck, E. (1950). *Unraveling Juvenile Delinquency.* New York: Commonwealth Fund.

Goode, E. (2008). *Out of control? assessing the general theory of crime.* Stanford, CA: Stanford University Press.

Gottfredson, M. R., & Hirschi, T. (1990). *A general theory of crime.* Stanford, CA: Stanford University Press.

Grasmick, H., Tittle, C., Bursik, R., & Arneklev, B. (1993). Testing the core implications of Gottfredson and Hirschi's general theory of crime. *Journal of Research in Crime and Delinquency, 30,* 5–29.

Haynie, D. L., & Osgood, D. W. (2005). Reconsidering peers and delinquency: How do peers matter? *Social Forces, 84,* 1109–1130.

Hirschi, T. (1969). *Causes of delinquency.* Berkeley: University of California Press.

Hirschi, T. (1995). The family. In J. Q. Wilson & J. Petersilia (Eds.), *Crime.* San Francisco: ICS.

Hirschi, T. (2004). Self-control and crime. In R. F. Baumeister & K. D. Vohs (Eds.), *Handbook of self-regulation: Research, theory, and applications.* New York: Guilford Press.

Hirschi, T., & Gottfredson, M. R. (1993). Commentary: Testing the general theory of crime. *Journal of Research in Crime and Delinquency, 30,* 47–54.

Hirschi, T., & Gottfredson, M. R. (2002). Self-control theory. In R. Paternoster & R. Bachman (Eds.), *Explaining criminals and crime: Essays in contemporary criminological theory.* Thousand Oaks, CA: Roxbury.

Hirschi, T., & Stark, R. (1969). Hellfire and delinquency. *Social Problems, 17,* 202–213.

Holtfreter, K., Reisig, M. D., & Pratt, T. C. (2008). Routine activities, low self-control, and fraud victimization. *Criminology, 46,* 189–220.

Horney, J., Osgood, D. W., & Marshall, I. H. (1995). Criminal careers in the short-term: Intra-individual variability in crime and its relation to local life circumstances. *American Sociological Review, 60,* 655–673.

Jones, S., & Quisenberry, N. (2004). The general theory of crime: How general is it? *Deviant Behavior, 25,* 401–426.

LaGrange, T., & Silverman, R. (1999). Low self-control and opportunity: Testing the general theory of crime as an explanation of gender differences in delinquency. *Criminology, 37*, 41–72.

Laub, J. H., & Sampson, R. (2003). *Shared beginnings, divergent lives: Delinquent boys to age 70*. Cambridge, MA: Harvard University Press.

Longshore, D., Chang, E., & Messina, N. (2005). Self-control and social bonds: A combined control perspective on juvenile offending. *Journal of Quantitative Criminology, 21*, 419–437.

Keane, C., Maxim, P., & Teevan, J. (1993). Drinking and driving, self-control, and gender. *Journal of Research in Crime and Delinquency, 30*, 30–46.

Kempf-Leonard, K. (1993). The empirical status of Hirschi's control theory. In F. Adler & W. S. Laufer (Eds.), *New directions in criminological theory: Advances in criminological theory*. New Brunswick, NJ: Transaction.

Kruger, J., & Dunning, D. (1999). Unskilled and unaware of it: How difficulties in recognizing one's own incompetence lead to inflated self-assessments. *Journal of Personality and Social Psychology, 77*, 1121–1134.

Merton, R.K. (1938). Social structure and anomie. *American Sociological Review, 3*, 672–682.

Nye, F. I. (1958). *Family relationships and delinquent behavior*. New York: Wiley.

Orcutt, J. D. (1980). Self-concept and insulation against delinquency: Some crucial notes. *Sociological Quarterly, 2*, 381–390.

Patterson, G. (1980). Children who steal. In T. Hirschi & M. Gottfredson (Eds.), *Understanding crime* (pp. 73–90). Beverly Hills, CA: Sage.

Piquero, A. R., & Bouffard, J. (2007). Something old, something new: A preliminary investigation of Hirschi's redefined self-control. *Justice Quarterly, 24*, 1–27.

Piquero, A. R., Brame, R., Mazerolle, P., & Happanen, R. (2002). Crime in emerging adulthood. *Criminology, 40*, 137–170.

Pratt, T. C., & Cullen, F. T. (2000). The empirical status of Gottfredson and Hirschi's general theory of crime: A meta-analysis. *Criminology, 38*, 931–964.

Reckless, W. (1955). *The crime problem* (2nd ed.). New York: Appleton-Century-Crofts.

Reckless, W. (1967). *The crime problem* (4th ed.). New York: Appleton-Century-Crofts.

Reckless, W., & Dinitz, S. (1972). *The prevention of juvenile delinquency*. Columbus, OH: University of Ohio Press.

Reisig, M. D., Pratt, T. C., & Holtfreter, K. (2009). Perceived risk of Internet theft victimization. *Criminal Justice and Behavior, 31*, 542–563.

Reiss, A. J. (1951). Delinquency as the failure of personal and social controls. *American Sociological Review, 16*, 196–207.

Sampson, R. J., & Laub, J. H. (1993). *Crime in the making: Pathways and turning points through life*. Cambridge, MA: Harvard University Press.

Schreck, C. J. (1999). Criminal victimization and low self-control: An extension and test of a general theory of crime. *Justice Quarterly, 16*, 633–654.

Sellers, C. (1999). Self-control and intimate violence: An examination of the scope and specification of the general theory of crime. *Criminology, 37*, 375–404.

Shaw, C. R., & McKay, H. D. (1942). *Juvenile delinquency and urban areas*. Chicago: University of Chicago Press.

Stewart, E. A., Simons, R. L., & Conger, R. (2002). Assessing neighborhood and social psychological influences on childhood violence in an African American sample. *Criminology, 40*, 801–830.

Stitt, B., & Giacopassi, A. (1992). Trends in the connectivity of theory and research in criminology. *The Criminologist, 17*(1), 3–6.

Tittle, C. R. (1995). *Control balance: Toward a general theory of deviance*. Boulder, CO: Westview Press.

Toby, J. (1957). Social disorganization and stake in conformity: Complementary factors in the predatory behavior of hoodlums. *Journal of Criminal Law, Criminology, and Police Science, 48*, 12–17.

Uggen, C. (2000). Work as a turning point in the life course of criminals: A duration model of age, employment, and recidivism. *American Sociological Review, 65*, 529–546.

Warr, M. (2002). *Companions in crime: The social aspects of criminal conduct*. Cambridge, UK: Cambridge University Press.

CHAPTER 9

THEORIES OF SOCIAL CONFLICT

Whereas the majority of criminological theories examined so far have focused on individual, group, and environmental factors, an alternative theoretical tradition views *social conflict* as the root source of most social problems, including crime (Vold, 1958). According to this perspective, social order does not reflect a consensus model of what is right and wrong or best for society as a whole. Rather, the criminal justice system's identification and handling of offenders reflects an uneven distribution of power and resources throughout society.

This conflict, or critical perspective, is traceable to the seminal works of Tannenbaum (1938), Lemert (1951, 1967), and Becker (1963), who first proposed that criminal behavior was attributable to the process of **labeling**. Labeling theory contends that the very act of criminalization is itself an arbitrary label given to certain types of behavior. Moreover, when an individual is described or labeled as delinquent or criminal, the accused then internalizes that characterization, tailoring his or her future behavior accordingly.

The rise of American critical criminology transpired during the 1970s, a period characterized by great social upheaval. Current events of the day included the civil rights movement, the Vietnam War, and a general liberalization of the popular culture, as evidenced by the sexual revolution, widespread recreational drug use, and the continuation of the hippie subculture from the 1960s. Theoretical criminology very much reflected the spirit of the times, as society's disenchantment with its traditions and customs prompted challenges to authority and the continuation of a form of social control that many believed was not working.

Some came to view the discipline of criminology as part of the problem due to its traditional research focus on crimes committed by the lower class. When we concentrate on street-level crime, we largely ignore the white-collar crimes of the upper class. From this perspective, criminology serves the interests of the ruling class by distracting attention away from their offenses. A number of criminologists became increasingly opposed to class and racial forms of prejudice and discrimination by the criminal justice system and adopted a social justice orientation to their work. This approach advocated social activism to minimize biases against the poor, women, and racial and ethnic minorities.

THE CONFLICT PERSPECTIVE AND CRIME

Crime, from the conflict perspective, is considered a by-product of social inequality, both the result of efforts by those in power to control groups positioned lower in the social structure and a collective expression of deprivation, alienation, and frustration by those in the working class. This power imbalance orientation to explaining crime is, according to some theorists, grounded in and most evident in the conflict that exists between social classes (Lynch & Groves, 1986). A constant tension between "haves" and "have-nots" is considered a fundamental characteristic of modern social life, and this strain is thought to both push and pull individuals into crime.

The conflict perspective is particularly applicable in highly stratified, pluralistic, and multicultural societies, such as the United States, because there is great diversity in values across social groups (by gender, age, sexual orientation, religion, affluence, race, and ethnicity). This mixture of attitudes is observed in a power struggle for the authority necessary to define behavioral standards, formally through the criminal law and informally through the practice of moral condemnation. Those who gain power naturally define crime and deviance in ways that serve their interests, and their designations determine how society's institutions (schools, religion, and the criminal justice system) will be structured. By structuring society toward their interests, then, particularly in regard to what are considered acceptable and unacceptable (i.e., legal vs. illegal) forms of wealth building and upward social mobility, the "haves" enjoy a created advantage in the competition for economic and social resources.

Those in power are clearly interested in maintaining their advantaged position and use the criminal law as a basis of legitimizing social control, formally exercised through law enforcement and the military. In fact, many conflict theorists contend that the primary function of the criminal law is to protect the property interests of the wealthy (Bonger, 1916/1969; Marx, 1932/1978c; Quinney, 1979, 1980). In so doing, the interests of the "have-nots" are necessarily underrepresented, if at all, thus producing a power imbalance that is accentuated by the fact that the vast majority of people constitute the working rather than the ruling class. Accordingly, theorists are critical of the current system, sometimes calling for radical reform that will effect broader distribution of political power and material resources.

A number of leading critical and radical theories are presented in this chapter and, while they do not specify how power and conflict relate to crime in exactly the same way, they are similar in several respects. They all emphasize, for example, the presence of conflict within society, the importance of social class, and the view of modern capitalist society as the primary source of the inequality that causes or is associated with crime. Scrutiny of capitalism is largely fueled by another commonality, a Marxist heritage.

THE MARXIST HERITAGE

The philosophical underpinnings of the conflict approach are clearly traceable to the writings and revisionist perspective of Karl Marx (1818–1883). Because Marx advocated a mode of government that featured shared ownership of wealth, reference to Marxism typically brings to mind a socialist or communist society. The Marxist view of society includes a number of important related concepts that frame the conflict approach to crime. Marx, in his famous polemical works *Das Kapital* (1867/1978b) and *The Manifesto of the Communist Party* with Friedrich Engels (1948/1978), actually had very little to say about crime. Crime, from the Marxist perspective, is primarily a natural result of the inequality inherent to capitalist societies.

According to Marx (1867/1978b), the economic system of capitalism is the source of most social problems, including crime, because it creates conflict through competition for profit. Profit is considered evil and dehumanizing because it can be realized only by some people taking advantage of others, and it minimizes the cultural, educational, and emotional dimensions of social life in exchange for greater emphasis on the dimension of work.

Marxist Concepts

The capitalistic desire for greater profit is realized through extraction of *surplus value* from the working class (**proletariat**) by the ruling class (**bourgeoisie**). An oversimplified explanation of surplus value is that profit can be realized only through either increasing price or reducing production costs. Through competition, the free market limits profit through price increase, so it is obtained through underpaying laborers, an unfair system that essentially takes advantage of workers.

Profit through surplus value, then, can be realized only through *exploitation* of the proletariat. Because the desire for profit by the bourgeoisie, according to Marx, is insatiable, the degree of exploitation and related forms of dehumanization will lead to *alienation*. Alienation is easy to understand in its tangible forms, such as money and material possession, but the alienation of the working class is a more holistic expression of suffering.

Beyond economic disadvantage, social class distinctions also alienate people in terms of cultural, educational, recreational, and even social deprivation. A good example that illustrates both monetary and social alienation is Greek life on college campuses throughout the United States. Some students (who otherwise would) do not join sororities or fraternities because they simply cannot afford to "go Greek." Because of wealth disparity, then, some students are precluded from this social context—a system that ensures that people from roughly the same economic backgrounds will be segregated into social groups.

Marx predicted that as alienation became obvious and widely recognized throughout the working class, *class consciousness* (an awareness of one's class status) would develop and ultimately unite laborers to revolt against the ruling class and end capitalist-determined society. While various revolutions to end capitalism have not been successful, class consciousness remains a defining aspect of the popular psyche in stratified societies. Definitions of success, marrying well, and social network groups typically factor into the ever-present reality of class consciousness, even if only on a subconscious level.

Orthodox Marxism

Orthodox Marxism, sometimes referred to as **instrumental Marxism**, posits a direct relationship between the interests of the ruling class (profit, power, and prestige) and the functioning of social institutions such as the criminal justice system (Balkan, Berger, & Schmidt, 1980; Quinney, 1979, 1980). In fact, these interests are identifiable in the functioning of the criminal justice system throughout American history.

Workers have not always had a legal right to strike—for example, in protest against unfair working conditions or pay grievances. In the English- and Dutch-owned steel mills in Philadelphia during the 1890s, the first attempts by workers (mostly recent Irish immigrants) to strike were quashed by local police who simply arrested them at the request of the factory owners. Mule-drawn wagons with bars carried the Irish strikers, known as "paddies" (the term *paddy* was a racial pejorative referencing the Irish), away to jail—popularizing into American jargon the term *paddy wagon*. Today, reference to a paddy wagon indicates police vans filled with underage drinkers caught in bar raids, a depiction that is perhaps more than just a coincidence with the original wagons in that heavy drinking was a common practice by Irish workers on the strike line.

Structural Marxism

The acquisition of some political power by the working class over time has forced the ruling class to share some resources (e.g., the minimum wage, worker compensation, and health insurance) with the working class (Lynch & Groves, 1986). However, only a token amount of resources are relinquished toward the goal of placating workers into accepting existing class relations rather than achieving greater equality. By spreading some power and wealth across social groups, the ruling class can successfully redirect working-class frustration by placing blame on the shortcomings of individuals, as opposed to a flawed social structure characterized by inequality.

The controversial issue of minority representation in graduate and law school programs, for example, is minimized if low admission rates are viewed relative to other accepted minorities rather than the aggregate reality. This redirection of blame diffuses class consciousness as a *technique of placation* and enables continuation of the status quo and the capitalist mode. Another example of a technique of placation is the institution of religion, which typically advocates versions of morality that do not condone criminal behavior. Moreover, religion usually promotes humility and respect for authority. Accordingly, people self-regulate their behavior and, in so doing, require less expenditure for formal control. More importantly, the authority and property interests of the ruling class are protected, as religion discourages the conflict necessary for change. Marx, in fact, referred to religion as "the opium of the masses" (1844/1978a), meaning that religion drugged the lower classes into accepting an unfair social system.

Structural Marxism differs from the orthodox approach by acknowledging an indirect relationship between ruling-class interests and the way social institutions operate (Balbus, 1977; Chambliss & Seidman, 1982). Ruling-class interests are often furthered subtly, entrenched in the rules and policies that guide the daily operations of our social institutions. Social institutions normally function so that they typically generate disparate outcomes, which ensures the perpetuation of an elitist hierarchy. While we think of our elected officials, for example, of representing everyone through the democratic political process, the rules governing elections are such that only the wealthy have a realistic chance of being elected. Not surprisingly, the vast majority of our elected representatives are affluent, though the majority of their constituents are not. As a result, these representatives become the upper strata of society responsible for creating laws (i.e., state and federal legislatures).

But what about Marxist thought and crime? Although Marx did not have very much to say about crime, the preceding conceptual line of reasoning has generated several subsequent specific theories of crime, described next. Before examining leading critical and radical statements of crime, it is important to acknowledge the significance of the symbolic interactionist perspective on the conflict perspective, most notably the influence of labeling theory.

LABELING THEORY

The labeling perspective (Becker, 1963; Lemert, 1951, 1967) acknowledges that people first participate in norm violation, either crime or a less serious deviant act, by chance or simply as a part of growing up. The vast majority of youth, for example, engage in some form of delinquent behavior as an expression of rebellion or experimentation that is considered part of the maturation process for all teenagers. The difference between delinquents and nondelinquents may be, in large part, an outcome of who gets caught. Simply getting caught can result in **stigma**, a generic negative depiction of a person based on certain aspects of their behavior. The most commonly cited description of labeling theory comes from Howard Becker's famous book *Outsiders* (1963). Becker contended that "social groups *create* deviance by making rules whose infraction constitutes deviance, and by applying these rules to particular people and labeling them as outsiders. From this point of view, deviance is not a quality of the act the person commits, but rather a consequence of the application by others of rules and sanctions to the 'offender.' The deviant is one to whom that label has been successfully applied; deviant behavior is behavior that people so label" (p. 9). Becker's analysis of deviance illustrated that crime and deviance were largely a creation by rule enforcers who held the power to label.

Initial acts of deviance, termed **primary deviation**, prompt negative reactions from those in authority who devalue delinquent youth, due to a combination of the actual trouble they have already caused and the perception that they will cause further problems. These perceptions of youth as delinquent generate stereotypes that cause a sort of ripple effect, wherein others also come to see the designated youth in a negative light.

Common stereotypes include portrayals of the lower-class criminal, whose criminality stems from little education, blocked opportunities for advancement, and adherence to criminogenic subcultural values. The process of labeling necessarily involves a power dynamic that pronounces the inequality between those who have position to assign labels and those who are labeled. Labeling, through the concept of *master status*, can become a self-fulfilling prophecy. Once a person has engaged in unacceptable behavior and has been identified as a violator, he or she becomes disvalued proportionate to the severity of the offense. Deviant status can come to altogether define a person ("thief," "stoner," "slut"), overshadowing other socially desirable dimensions of his or her behavior.

After individuals have acquired a deviant label, others view and interact with them in such a manner that further misbehavior is expected. Continued participation in delinquency and crime, called **secondary deviation**, reflects both the ironic outcome of the social construction of crime through the labeling process and the importance of self-concept. Symbolic interactionist influence on the labeling approach can be seen in the sociological works of Mead (1934), Cooley (1902), and Becker (1963). Charles Horton Cooley introduced the idea of the *looking-glass self*, suggesting that the self-image reflected in a mirror is a metaphor for perceptions of self determined through the collective eyes of others. A brief example of the looking-glass self might be new clothes for a social event. Do you see an outfit on you as it actually appears or the way you want others to see you? Probably the latter, according to the labeling perspective.

George Herbert Mead (1934), in turn, is credited with a similar concept termed "the generalized other," the idea that our behavior is affected by perceptions and related expectations. By comparing personal behavior and decisions to a perceived appropriate social standard, people create a meaningful reference point. The reference, however, often reflects distinction.

William Chambliss's well-known study "The Saints and the Roughnecks" (1973) depicted the relevance of social class in the labeling process. The Saints were eight delinquent male high school students whose behaviors included heavy drinking, truancy, vandalism, and minor theft. They particularly enjoyed pranks, some of which involved harm, such as changing traffic and warning signs, which caused accidents. As the label "Saints" implies, these middle-class youth from traditional families were seen as "good kids," whose behavior was largely excused by authorities as youthful indiscretion. They were rarely arrested, and many grew up to become professionals such as doctors and lawyers.

The "Roughnecks," on the other hand, were six male high school students from the same town who also engaged in various forms of delinquency. They did tend to fight more than the Saints but engaged in far less vandalism resulting in monetary damage. They were all from lower-class families and had frequent interaction with the police who, along with most of the town, viewed them as troublemakers. This perception was reinforced by their frequent arrests, which officially labeled them and arguably affected their futures. In fact, they ended up either working as wage laborers in low-paying jobs or in prison.

Another study that demonstrated the importance of labeling, more so than actual harm specific to behavior, centered on a shoplifting experiment (Steffensmeier & Terry, 1973). With the permission of a department store's management, students dressed explicitly to depict either a "hippie" or "preppie" appearance and then shoplifted. The study focused on whether reactions to the shoplifting differed between the groups and found that witnesses were far more likely to report the hippies. Even though the students in each group committed the same offense at the same rate, it appeared that simply projecting a lower-class or antiestablishment image elicited a harsher reaction. These and numerous subsequent studies (see Mann, 1993; Tittle & Curran, 1988; Wilbanks, 1987) have confirmed the importance of *extralegal factors*, such as class and race, on the practices of arrests, due process, and sanctioning. The current controversy over racial profiling is a straightforward example of the continued importance of labeling.

Recent research has also explored the short- and long-term consequences of being formally labeled by the criminal or juvenile justice systems. Bernburg, Krohn, and Rivera (2006) examined the short-term impact of formal criminal labeling on involvement in deviant social groups, or networks, and how that involvement increased the likelihood of subsequent delinquency. The authors found that labeling impacts future delinquency because it tends to push adolescents into deviant peer groups. Consistent with differential association theory (see Chapter 6), adolescents who associated with delinquent peer groups were then more likely to engage in further problem behavior.

In one recent innovative study, researchers explored the impact of a felony label on subsequent reoffending (Chiricos, Barrick, Bales, & Bontrager, 2007). A brief overview of the study is worth providing since it illustrates quite well the effects of formal adjudication. In the state of Florida, judges are able to withhold a pronouncement of guilt (i.e., a conviction) for individuals who are convicted of a felony but are sentenced to probation as opposed to incarceration. These individuals lose no civil rights and are able to lawfully state that they have not been convicted of a felony. Reconviction data for nearly 100,000 individuals showed that those who were formally labeled as felons were significantly more likely to reoffend in two years compared to those who were not. This study reveals just how damaging official labeling can be for offenders. These findings also call into question the major tenets of deterrence theory, which suggests that more severe punishments are capable of preventing future criminal behavior.

Braithwaite's theory of **reintegrative shaming** (1989) is the foremost recent contribution to the labeling perspective. Building on the observation of the power of shaming to affect behavior, Braithwaite argued the illogic of stereotyping offenders. Whereas reintegrative shaming sought to punish offenders and bring them back into conventional society, *disintegrative shaming* stigmatized them as deviant through such labels as "ex-con." Blocked from rejoining mainstream society, offenders further develop a self-image of being criminal and ultimately become more entrenched in crime.

This relatively recent formulation is best characterized as an integration of several existing theoretical perspectives, namely labeling, subcultural, control, opportunity, and learning theories. Reintegrative shaming offers a novel approach not only to explaining and predicting those societies and communities that are more susceptible to high rates of crime but also in identifying (at an individual or micro-level) which persons are more likely to reoffend after detection and sanctioning. Braithwaite's theory suggests that those communities incorporating constructive shaming into sanctioning systems will fare better in achieving control over its members as opposed to those that negatively shame, humiliate, and stigmatize its deviants.

As noted above, reintegrative shaming theory rests heavily on the fundamental contentions of the labeling perspective (Becker, 1963; Lemert, 1951, 1974). Criminogenic stigmatization, according to labeling theorists, marginalizes individuals, characterizing them as fundamentally different, negative, and at odds with the larger community. By directing offenders toward the periphery of society, removing the presence of theoretically important social relationships, and detracting from their social embeddedness, labeling can contribute to reoffending. The stigma eventually evolves into an individual's self-concept, creating a self-definition associated with the negative label (Cooley, 1902). Ensuing behavior reflects the criminogenic self-concept, and the cycle of offending commences again.

Braithwaite suggests that stigmatization works to disintegratively shame individuals, pushing them into criminal subcultures (Cloward & Ohlin, 1960; Cohen, 1955). Because such subcultures do provide a certain degree of social support for illegal behavior, once labeling and rejection have occurred, further attempts at admonishing association with the group have no effect. Shaming that is reintegrative, however, is more effective in that disapproval better serves as a deterrent when embedded in relationships normally characterized by social approval and attachment (Braithwaite, 1989, p. 68). In effect, as a result of labeling and disintegration, the opinions of the community come to matter less and efforts to sanction offenders less effective. Only when shaming is executed in a constructive manner by those deemed important to an offender can reintegration and deterrence be achieved (Braithwaite & Mugford, 1994).

While the idea of reintegrating offenders back into society is appealing in theory, it is difficult to achieve due to both social realities and current criminal justice policies. Because the United States is a pluralistic society (heterogeneous, multicultural, and socially stratified), people do not always agree on which behaviors are inappropriate and should be sanctioned. Shaming, as an informal sanctioning mechanism, depends on social consensus, which varies across groups and by particular topics. Americans are divided concerning the legalization of marijuana, prohibition of abortion, regulation of gun ownership, and numerous other issues. Differences of opinion minimize the effectiveness of informal sanctioning, leaving crime problems to the criminal justice system.

The criminal justice system invokes policies involving both disintegrative and reintegrative forms of shaming. Convicted drunk drivers made to wear bright orange vests while picking up trash alongside highways and sex offender notification laws are examples of criminal justice practices employing shame for deterrence (at public and individual levels) and punishment purposes. Offender reentry programs, commonly referred to as "aftercare," seek to facilitate offender transition from incarcerated settings to society. These efforts, often executed in the context of "halfway houses," are consistent with the logic of reintegration. Unfortunately, aftercare is not a high rehabilitation priority, moving many criminologists to observe that policies concerning offender reintegration are largely "image over substance."

Empirical support for reintegrative shaming has been mixed. For example, a recent study (Zhang & Zhang, 2004) examined the relationship between shaming, forgiveness, and predatory delinquency using data from a large national survey and found no effect for either parental or peer reintegrative shaming. Moreover, peer forgiveness actually increased predatory offense involvement, giving rise to criticisms suggesting that serious offenders see reintegrative approaches as a weak response to crime, in effect, "getting off easy." Similarly, an earlier study (Katz, 2002) found that youth involved in aggressive behavior were *least* likely to desist after reintegrative shaming occurs. Findings from a study conducted in Australia showed similar findings as related to predatory delinquency (Losoncz & Tyson, 2007).

Strong support for reintegrative shaming has often been compiled from abroad. In particular, several studies were conducted in China that indicated great success in terms of reduced reoffending (Chen, 2002; Lu, 1999). This research suggested that the collective orientation of Chinese society provides for the interdependency and communitarianism necessary for successful reintegration practices. This may also serve as an explanation as to why this approach has not fared better in the individually oriented United States. Moreover, given that many offenders hail from communities that can be characterized as socially disorganized, the assumption of initial integration may prove ill founded. An exception to this may be with white-collar offenders, who are often socially bonded with strong community ties. In fact, preliminary research into the effectiveness of reintegrative shaming for white-collar offenders has shown positive results (Murphy & Harris, 2007).

In sum, labeling theory contends that through stigmatization, the criminal justice system creates crime and deviance, as offenders come to identify themselves according to the expectations suggested by labels. The point where labeling theory ends and critical theories begin is blurred, but the act of labeling and the power dynamic inherent in the labeling process is a recurring theme throughout critical and radical theories.

MARXIST CRIMINOLOGY

Marxist or radical criminologists use the Marxist conceptual framework to examine the criminal law, crime itself, and the government's practice of social control (policing, prosecution, and sanctioning). The *social origins of the law* are observed as reflecting special interests that are traceable to class interests, be they profit or protection from potential threats by the lower class. The offense of vagrancy, for example, is especially class focused and seems to be a means for legitimizing the displacement of lower-class people (whose appearance or behavior is deemed "undesirable") from public, often affluent, places—apart from any violence or threat posed to person or property (Chambliss, 1964). Marxist criminology interprets vagrancy laws as dehumanizing in that the pursuit of profit is clearly valued more than the human suffering associated with being a vagrant. Marx himself contended that "There must be something rotten in the very core of a social system which increases in wealth without diminishing its misery, and increases in crime even more than its numbers" (Marx, 1867/1978b).

Marxists contend that the criminal law both serves to control the lower classes and provides immunity for crimes of the ruling class. Why, for example, are drug enforcement efforts focused more on crack cocaine? Relatedly, why are the criminal penalties for using and selling crack more severe than for powder cocaine? Marxists reject the argument that crack-related activities warrant greater policing and harsher sentences because crack is more addictive and incites greater violence. Rather, radical criminologists allege *selective enforcement* against social groups (mostly the poor and minorities) that primarily use and sell crack.

The criminal law from the Marxist perspective, then, is seen as a tool of repression by the ruling class. The criminal behavior of the lower class is largely seen as an expression of resistance to economic and social oppression, with some Marxists going so far as to argue that criminals are political activists or revolutionaries whose behavior represents resistance and is oriented toward social change. Criminals, or at least lower-class offenders, are depicted as victims of social inequality. Not surprisingly, mainstream criminologists respond that such a view excuses personal responsibility for criminal behavior.

WHITE-COLLAR AND STATE CRIME

Marxist criminology redirects attention away from the street crime of the lower class to white-collar and political or state crime. **White-collar crime** was first addressed by Edwin Sutherland, who defined it as "a crime committed by a person of respectability and high social status in the course of his occupation (1947). Although this definition suggests individual wrongdoing, the scope of white-collar crime also involves activities engaged in by businesses and corporations.

Some theorists submit that crimes such as consumer fraud and false advertising inflict far greater social harm (by affecting more people and involving far greater amounts of money) than do lower-level personal property crimes, such as burglary and theft (Chambliss, 1988, 1999; Quinney, 1980). In some instances, the white-collar crimes of the upper class can also directly inflict personal injury similar to violent crime. The infamous Ford Pinto case during the 1970s serves as a primary example. In this conspiracy, the automobile company discovered that the casing design around the gas tank in the Pinto model was not sufficient and could lead to fire and explosion in the event of accidents under certain conditions. After calculating the costs of issuing a recall to install appropriate parts to ensure consumer safety versus the amount to settle a projected number of lawsuits (including the loss of lives), the company chose to settle the suits. More recently, executives at Ford Motor Company and Firestone Tires made a similar decision when evidence emerged suggesting that tires used on the popular Ford Explorer sport-utility vehicle would deteriorate when driven at high speeds.

Political crime, or **state crime,** differs from white-collar or corporate crime in terms of its primary objectives—political as opposed to economic. Political objectives are rooted in the state's need to exercise or establish power and authority. State crime is typically dichotomized as crimes of negligence and crimes of omission. The former is defined as the result of a conscious choice on the part of the state not to do something about a potential or observable social harm. Crimes of omission are the result of implicit state support for structural conditions (such as capitalism and patriarchy), which in turn lead to socially harmful consequences. White-collar crime and state crime are often considered in conjunction, as the government enables exploitation through its trade policies and leniency for upper-class violators.

LEFT REALISM

Left realism evolved in response to critical theorists' neglect of inner-city crime, specifically, and the plight of the urban underclass, generally. The English criminologist Jock Young (1987) is among the most prominent theorists associated with left realism, being one of the first to call attention to the intense and multifaceted nature of victimization within inner cities. Inner-city residents are dually victimized by the capitalistic economic system and also at the hands of their immediate neighbors who engage in criminal activity. Left realists also criticize other Marxist criminologists whose primary concern is opposing the criminal justice system rather than providing support for the victims of lower-class crimes. For example, critical theorists' attention to disproportionate involvement in crime by disenfranchised urban African Americans is in the context of institutionalized racism within American society. The focus on why this group is heavily involved in crime, however, ignores that they also suffer disproportionately from high rates of victimization, particularly homicide (LaFree, Drass, & O'Day, 1992).

Left realists suggest that *relative poverty* is a more accurate determinant of crime than *absolute poverty*. After all, poverty has a qualitative dimension that necessitates comparison between groups—that is, poverty can be assessed only in relation to others' wealth, a condition captured by the concept *economic disparity*. Young and others (Dekeseredy & Schwartz, 1991; Lea, 1992; Lowman, 1992; Matthews, 1992) argue that relative deprivation combined with the competitive individualism of capitalism fosters discontent and instigates behavior-labeled criminal.

Left realists are critical of those whom Marx himself described as "armchair sociologists"—criminologists who are content to wait for revolution to create significant changes in the criminal justice system rather than proactively effect change themselves. The prospects for change are thought to be most likely through advocacy of short-term policy revisions that effect economic improvement and increase justice conditions for the lower and working classes. Left realism, then, is one of the most radical conflict theories.

CULTURAL CRIMINOLOGY

Cultural criminology is closely related to the field of cultural studies and is influenced by postmodern insights (Pfohl, 1985; Schwartz & Friedrichs, 1994) that claim that images presented by the mass media are (falsely) seen by many as reality. This perspective, championed most notably by contemporary criminologist Jeff Ferrell (1993; Ferrell & Sanders, 1995), examines *crime control* rather than crime itself and does so by means of *media analysis*. Specifically, cultural criminologists investigate the ways in which the mass media and popular culture influence the general public's understanding of crime in society and, more importantly, how they influence policy development. The central premise of this perspective is that crime is a definitionally subjective term, as is its control. In other words, both the public and policymakers are greatly influenced by what the media presents as socially problematic, and their responses are constructed accordingly.

Cultural criminology is influenced, as well, by alternative qualitative methods (Ferrell & Hamm, 1998; Miller, 1995; Miller & Tewksbury, 2001). It is argued that through the *immediacy of crime,* that is, firsthand observation of offending and victimization, criminologists can come to fully understand the complexity of crime. Cultural criminology is also closely associated with the perspective of **social constructionism,** which is addressed in the following section.

THE SOCIAL CONSTRUCTION OF CRIME, POSTMODERNISM, AND CONSTITUTIVE CRIMINOLOGY

The theories addressed in the preceding chapters have all considered crime from an objectivist viewpoint; however, crime (as well as other social problems) can also be examined from a *subjectivist* perspective. Subjectivists, also known as *constructionists,* contend that crime is a definitionally subjective reality. Accordingly, no act is inherently deviant, criminal, or necessarily a threat to society. Rather, crime is constructed by a process called *claimsmaking.* The claimsmaking process originates from groups or organizations that single out a particular phenomenon, cause, or issue, subsequently drawing or demanding attention to it. Such groups are referred to as *claimsmakers,* and their endeavors are considered a two-stage process. First, a given issue or problem (for our purposes, crime) is identified by primary claimsmakers, thereby drawing attention to a particular problematic condition and demanding a response to it. Second, the condition is discovered and investigated by the media and then presented to a national audience as a pressing social concern. The specified problem is often contended, through exaggeration, to be of epidemic proportions.

Constructionists suggest that those acts labeled criminal and afforded the most attention by the public, media, and agents of social control are not those that necessarily are the most serious, but rather acts that threaten those in power. Constructionists stress the importance of the *discrepancy* between perceived and actual threats, positing that social harm is presented in a manner that draws attention away from the more serious infractions committed by the upper classes. The construction of crime is a diversionary tool, much like the Marxist concept technique of placation, which allows those in power to cover up their own violations by highlighting the deviance of others.

Essential to the social construction of the crime perspective is the identification of *folk devils,* described as unambiguously unfavorable symbols whose real or imagined behavior is a threat to social welfare (Cohen, 1972). Folk devils are necessary because they provide a readily identifiable culprit for the social problem at hand—in our case, crime. An example of using the folk devil construct can be found in the reported church-burning "epidemic" of the mid-1990s (Carter, 1999). In this instance, government officials, special-interest groups, and the media joined forces to perpetuate the claim that a string of church arsons across the southern United States was the result of a nationwide Ku Klux Klan (KKK) conspiracy to terrorize African Americans. Despite official law enforcement investigations that revealed no evidence of such a conspiracy, all interested parties continued to stand behind their accusations. These claims were easily accepted by the general public as truth in part because the KKK was a likely suspect that had engaged in such behavior previously during the civil rights movement and the South's history of racial strife. If claimsmakers had had no one specific to blame, tales of a racial conspiracy might not have been as easily accepted.

Postmodernism is a movement that began in the humanities and transcended to the realm of social science in the 1980s. Postmodernist thought is not particular to criminology alone; rather it is more of a philosophy of knowledge production and accumulation. Criminology, along with other social and natural sciences, traditionally has stressed the use of the positivistic framework in determining causal mechanisms among phenomena. Postmodernist criminology, however, suggests that much of the knowledge related to crime and criminality has been socially constructed and that no real "truth" is readily available for criminologists.

Despite the shortcomings of the traditional criminological approach, postmodernism contends that deconstruction and then a preferable *reconstruction* of the facts is possible. By examining crime and social control in a social, historical, and cultural context, criminologists can then more adequately understand the scope and nature of both criminal offending and criminalization. Postmodernism essentially demands reconsideration of that which we take for granted—that which is assumed as irrefutable empirical "facts."

Constitutive criminology is a wide-ranging critical theory whose roots are traceable to Marxism and postmodernism. Among the most prominent theorists associated with this tradition are Henry and Milovanovic (1991, 1996), both of whom stress the importance of how humans shape their social worlds. Constitutive criminologists argue that the roots of crime are traceable to unequal power relations that shape society's impressions of and responses to criminal behavior. Constitutive criminology focuses, then, on the processes by which crime is "constructed" rather than caused.

FEMINIST CRIMINOLOGY

There are many varieties of feminist criminology: liberal, radical, and Marxist or socialist. While slightly different, these perspectives have common assumptions. First, although biological differences are acknowledged, gender is seen as a socially constructed reality shaped by cultural, historical, and social factors (Gelsthorpe & Morris, 1990). Feminists reject that behavior is attributable to being male or female; rather it is the result of the prevailing cultural values concerning gender roles and relations. Also, social order and interaction are seen as a function of male dominance. A patriarchal society influences females, according to feminist criminology, in such a way that they have a unique perspective on class, race, and gender interrelationships.

Feminist criminologists have traditionally examined the role of extralegal factors and how they result in more lenient treatment for women than men (Chesney-Lind, 1997; Chesney-Lind & Shelden, 1992; Gelsthorpe & Morris, 1990). It is a matter of some controversy whether the criminal justice system's leniency for women is a matter of less-serious female crime, a lower rate of criminal charges, or other social factors. The two most frequently considered social factors are *chivalry* and *paternalism*. Chivalry refers to traditional gender relations, with women placed on a pedestal and needing protection. Paternalism is, in feminist criminological thought, a condescending concept that devalues women by perpetuating a view of them as feeble and even childlike.

Feminist criminology is characterized by intuitive, tentative, and sometimes circular theorizing. Traditional criminological theorizing, in comparison, is more objective and linear—stated in a format suitable for testing by the logic of variable analysis more so than feminist theories. Feminist criminologists have argued that traditional methods of evaluating theory are not applicable, largely because the objectives are not to confirm hypotheses but to effect change through social movement.

Feminist criminologists take issue with criminology's neglect of women offenders and how they are misrepresented through stereotyping. This perspective addresses two general problems: the gender ratio and the issue of generalizability. The *gender ratio* refers to the relative level of criminal involvement by males and females. A fundamental question addresses why women are less likely, and men more likely, to commit crime. The *generalizability* problem refers to whether the traditional criminological theories, largely framed by male criminologists focusing on male offenders, can adequately account for female crime.

A general assumption of feminism is that the production of knowledge (the process of theorizing and research) reflects a male perspective on the natural and social world. Virtually everything—social life, social order, and social institutions—is *gendered*. Feminism is consistent with the conflict perspective in its observation that a gendered society generates inequality. Male superiority and dominance in politics, economics, and social life ensures gender discrimination. The nature and intensity of this inequality varies across versions of feminist theory.

Liberal feminism is a cultural orientation to gender differences, such as separate socialization experiences for boys and girls. Traditional attitudes about gender roles, particularly female participation in the labor market, are blamed for power imbalances. By promoting policies that eliminate, or at least soften, traditional dimensions of power, it is thought that greater social harmony and less gender inequality will result.

Freda Adler (1975) and Rita Simon (1975) were early feminist theorists who sought to explain what they observed as the shrinking gender ratio between male and female crime. The central thrust of their argument, referred to as the *liberation perspective,* is that as women gain more equality in a range of life spheres, including education, occupation, and the family, equality will spill over into criminality. Despite the logic of this argument, empirical support for this theory is scant (Chesney-Lind, 1997; Steffensmeier & Streifel, 1992) and has been generally rejected by many feminist theorists as not being feminist enough, or at all.

Radical feminism is a more aggressive approach to gender relations in that men are viewed in a negative light for taking advantage of women, primarily through sexuality. A key concept of radical feminist thought is **patriarchy,** which is used to describe a social order dominated in all respects by males. This domination extends into both criminality and official responses to it (i.e., the criminal justice system). Formal control mechanisms reflect the patriarchal social order in that laws benefit and enable male domination. Women's biological dependence during childbearing years and fundamental physical strength differences subjugate women and situate them in a disfavorable gender-based power dynamic. Also, the male-based social origins of law are thought to be a root source of the objectification of women. In short, radical feminism sees the criminal law and its enforcement as serving the interests of men at the expense of women.

Women who comply with the gendered social system are considered to have been effectively co-opted by male society through material and social rewards that only reinforce the status quo. Additionally, the labeling of various female behaviors, especially sexual deviance, is thought to be a form of dominance that, ironically, furthers similar deviant behavior.

John Hagan's *power-control theory* (1989), though not a radical feminist theory per se, attempts to empirically validate claims that the patriarchal social order is related to criminal offending in terms of gender. Specifically, Hagan hypothesizes that females who are raised under more egalitarian familial structures (families where there is more equality between husbands and wives in terms of occupational prestige and income) will engage in higher incidence of criminal behavior than their counterparts hailing from traditional, male-dominated families. Although Hagan's own findings have supported this premise, other research (Jensen & Thompson, 1990; Morash & Chesney-Lind, 1991) has failed to adequately confirm his predictions.

A third feminist perspective, *Marxist* or *socialist feminism*, attributes gender oppression to the inequality inherent in capitalistic economies. Derived from Marxist principles, socialist feminism argues that capitalism, through a gendered labor market structure, allows men to assert economic dominance over women. This economic dominance, in turn, influences all other aspects of social life, including the extent and nature of female criminality. Socialist feminists support the creation of egalitarian societies that would be free from both class and gender divisions.

Feminist criminology has become increasingly influential in recent years. Traditional projections of masculinity (toughness, heterosexuality, and breadwinner status) in subcultural settings have been found instrumental to explaining violence. Beyond attention to female criminality and the treatment of female offenders, attention to the social origins of gender has furthered understanding of crime in general. James W. Messerschmidt has been a prominent voice in calling attention to the gendered nature of behavior. Messerschmidt, in his book *Masculinities and Crime* (1993), argues that the prevalence of male offending is due primarily to socialization processes that emphasize male success and domination. Both street and white-collar crime are dominated by men, then, in an attempt to assert their strength and supremacy.

PEACEMAKING CRIMINOLOGY AND RESTORATIVE JUSTICE

Peacemaking criminology (Pepinsky & Quinney, 1991), like most conflict perspectives, does not address why people commit crime. Like similar theories, this view acknowledges the importance of the labeling process that splits people into either a criminal or a noncriminal group. The theory's name references the government's "war" language in the context of crime (such as "the War on Drugs"). Peacemaking criminologists are concerned about minimizing social inequality, but also place responsibility for victimization and harm with offenders.

Another perspective very similar to peacemaking criminology is **restorative justice** (Strang & Braithwaite, 2001), in which crime is seen as an outcome of damaged social relationships, and the solution is thought to be in bringing people together through community and individual interaction. The foremost assumption is that the criminal justice system's approach of deterrence and punishment is faulty and should be replaced with less-formal approaches emphasizing reconciliation and the restoration of strained relationships. Accordingly, informal solutions to disputes, such as arbitration and juvenile alternatives to court, are advocated because they divert people from the justice system and prevent formal criminal labeling.

Restorative justice advocates attention to victims' rights, offender accountability, and public safety. Consequently, proponents of this perspective stress the need for interpersonal reconciliation as opposed to traditional state-sponsored responses to crime wherein victims have little or no say in the justice process. Additionally, restorative justice mandates offender accountability such that perpetrators must face their victims and publicly acknowledge responsibility for their actions. Restorative justice, then, is a systems-based approach to an alternative means of achieving social justice. A recent example of restorative justice in practice is the advent of the national youth court movement, which adjudicates juvenile crime through informal, community-based processes that divert youth from entanglement in the juvenile justice system.

SUMMARY

The conflict perspective views the fundamental causes of crime as the economic and social forces operating within society, especially the influence of capitalism. The criminal law and criminal justice system are thought to function on behalf of the ruling social class. The ruling class defines the criminal law with its own interests in mind, and criminal justice policy both controls the poor and perpetuates existing class relations. The working class is economically exploited but also socially alienated, as ruling-class standards of morality are represented in criminal and deviant labels imposed on them.

The criminal justice system's focus on the lower class distracts attention away from crimes of the ruling class, such as white-collar crime and state crime. High levels of property crime and violence in the urban underclass and impoverished rural areas are seen as expressions of deprivation and frustration. Morality crimes, such as sex, drug, and gambling offenses, are considered control mechanisms that punish those whose income is not taxed to the benefit of capitalistic government.

The Marxian heritage has heavily influenced various critical and radical theories. While these theories differ by specifying different aspects of the criminogenic effects of inequality, they all are discontent with the current social system and consider it an underlying basis for many social problems. The terms *critical* and *radical* suggest criticism of the criminal law and its role in contributing to social inequality, and the need for radical action to effect change in the criminal justice system. Critical criminologists believe that they can help effect this change through demystification of equitable social relations as shaped by the forces of capitalism.

KEY TERMS

bourgeoisie the Marxist conception of the ruling or capitalist class, which controls the means of production and exploits the proletariat

labeling a process by which a negative attribute (i.e., delinquent or criminal) is assigned to an individual, resulting in internalization of that identity

orthodox/instrumental Marxism a perspective that posits a direct relationship between the interests of the ruling class and the functioning of social institutions

patriarchy a social order dominated in all respects by males

political/state crime crime committed on behalf of governments toward political objectives

postmodernism a philosophy that questions traditional means of inquiry and knowledge production and accumulation

primary deviation the initial incidence of deviant behavior occurring in the natural course of adolescence or young adulthood

proletariat the Marxist conception of the lower or working class that is exploited by the bourgeoisie

reintegrative shaming a process by which a community admonishes and shames individuals with the purpose of bringing them back into conventional society; popularized by the Australian criminologist John Braithwaite

restorative justice a perspective that views crime as a function of damaged social relationships and calls for a reparation of those bonds

secondary deviation continued participation in delinquency or crime due to an internalized self-concept reflective of negative labeling

social constructionism a perspective that addresses the subjectivity of crime and its control

stigma a generic negative depiction of an individual based on certain aspects of his or her behavior

structural Marxism a perspective that acknowledges an indirect relationship between ruling-class interests and social institutions

white-collar crime crimes committed by people of high status in the course of their occupation

DISCUSSION QUESTIONS

1. What are the key differences between orthodox/instrumental Marxism and structural Marxism?

2. How do the main assumptions of the conflict perspective differ from positivistic theories of crime?

3. Do you believe that affirmative action will decrease social inequality, consequently lowering the overall crime rate?

4. What is patriarchy, and what is its impact on the criminal justice system?

5. Do you think restorative justice programs will really make a difference, or is this movement more likely to be viewed by offenders as just a way of "getting off" easy?

REFERENCES

Adler, F. (1975). *Sisters in crime: The rise of the new female criminal.* New York: McGraw-Hill.

Balbus, I. D. (1977). Commodity form and legal form: An essay on the "relative autonomy" of the state. *Law and Society Review, 11,* 571–588.

Balkan, S., Berger, R. J., & Schmidt, J. (1980). *Crime and deviance in America: A critical approach.* Belmont, CA: Wadsworth.

Becker, H. S. (1963). *Outsiders: Studies in the sociology of deviance.* New York: Free Press.

Bernburg, J. G., Krohn, M. D., & Rivera, C. J. (2006). Official labeling, criminal embeddedness, and subsequent delinquency: A longitudinal test of labeling theory. *Journal of Research in Crime and Delinquency, 43*(1), 67–88.

Bonger, W. (1969). *Crime and economic conditions.* Bloomington: Indiana University Press. (Original work published 1916.)

Braithwaite, J. (1989). *Crime, shame and reintegration.* Cambridge, UK: Cambridge University Press.

Braithwaite, J., & Mugford, S. (1994). Conditions of successful reintegration ceremonies: Dealing with juvenile offenders. *British Journal of Criminology, 34,* 139–171.

Carter, C. S. (1999). Church burning in African American communities: Implications for empowerment practice. *Social Work, 44,* 62–68.

Chambliss, W. J. (1964). A sociological analysis of the law of vagrancy. *Social Problems, 12,* 67–77.

Chambliss, W.J. (1973). The Saints and the Roughnecks. *Society, 11,* 24-31.

Chambliss, W. J. (1988). *On the take* (2nd ed.). Indianapolis: Indiana University Press.

Chambliss, W. J. (1999). *Power, politics, and crime.* Boulder, CO: Westview Press.

Chambliss, W. J., & Seidman, R. B. (1982). *Law, order and power* (2nd ed.). Reading, MA: Addison-Wesley.

Chen, X. (2002). Social control in China: Applications of labeling theory and the reintegrative shaming theory. *International Journal of Offender Therapy and Comparative Criminology, 46,* 45–63.

Chesney-Lind, M. (1997). *The female offender: Girls, women, and crime.* Thousand Oaks, CA: Sage.

Chesney-Lind, M., & Shelden, R. G. (1992). *Girls, delinquency, and juvenile justice.* Pacific Grove, CA: Brooks/Cole.

Chiricos, T., Barrick, K., Bales, W., & Bontrager, S. (2007). The labeling of convicted felons and its ocnsequences for recidivism. *Criminology, 45*(3), 547–581.

Cloward, R. A., & Ohlin, L. (1960). *Delinquency and opportunity: A theory of delinquent gangs.* New York: Free Press.

Cohen, A. K. (1955). *Delinquent boys: The culture of the gang.* New York: Free Press.

Cohen, S. (1972). *Folk devils and moral panics: The creation of the Mods and Rockers.* New York: St. Martin's Press.

Cooley, C. H. (1902). *Human nature and the social order.* New York: Scribner.

Dekeseredy, W. S., & Schwartz, M. D. (1991). British and U.S. left realism: A critical comparison. *International Journal of Offender Therapy and Comparative Criminology, 35,* 248–262.

Ferrell, J. (1993). *Crimes of style: Urban graffiti and the politics of criminality.* New York: Garland.

Ferrell, J., & Hamm, M. S. (1998). *Ethnography on the edge.* Boston: Northeastern University Press.

Ferrell, J., & Sanders, C. R. (Eds.). (1995). *Cultural criminology*. Boston: Northeastern University Press.

Gelsthorpe, L., & Morris, A. (Eds.). (1990). *Feminist perspectives in criminology*. Philadelphia: Open University Press.

Hagan, J. (1989). Micro and macro structures of delinquency causation and a power control theory of gender and delinquency. In S.F. Messner, M.D. Krohn, & A.E. Liska (Eds.), *Theoretical integration in the study of deviance and crime: Problems and prospects*. Albany: State University of New York Press.

Henry, S., & Milovanovic, D. (1991). Constitutive criminology: The maturation of critical theory. *Criminology, 29*, 293.

Henry, S., & Milovanovic, D. (1996). *Constitutive criminology: Beyond postmodernism*. London: Sage.

Jensen, G., & Thompson, K. (1990). What's class got to do with it? A further examination of power control theory. *American Journal of Sociology, 95*, 1009–1023.

Katz, R. (2002). Reexamining the integrative social capital theory of crime. *Western Criminology Review, 4*, 30–54.

LaFree, G., Drass, K. A., & O'Day, P. (1992). Race and crime in post-war America: Determinants of African-American and white rates, 1957–1988. *Criminology, 30*, 157–188.

Lea, J. (1992). The analysis of crime. In J. Young & R. Matthews (Eds.), *Rethinking criminology: The realist debate* (pp. 69–94). London: Sage.

Lemert, E. M. (1951). *Social pathology*. New York: McGraw-Hill.

Lemert, E. M. (1967). *Human deviance, social problems, and social control*. Upper Saddle River, NJ: Prentice Hall.

Lemert, E.M. (1974). Beyond mead: The social reaction to deviance. *Social Problems, 21*, 457–468.

Losoncz, I., & Tyson, G. (2007). Parental shaming and adolescent delinquency: A partial test of reintegrative shaming theory. *Australian & New Zealand Journal of Criminology, 40*(2), 161–178.

Lowman, J. (1992). Rediscovering crime. In J. Young & R. Matthews (Eds.), *Rethinking criminology: The realist debate* (p. 141). London: Sage.

Lu, H. (1999). Bang Jiao and reintegrative shaming in China's urban neighborhoods. *International Journal of Comparative and Applied Criminal Justice, 23*, 115–125.

Lynch, M. J., & Groves, W. B. (1986). *A primer in radical criminology*. New York: Harrow & Heston.

Mann, C. R. (1993). *Unequal justice: A question of culture*. Bloomington: Indiana University Press.

Marx, K. (1978a). Contribution to the critique of Hegel's *Philosophy of right*: Introduction. In R. C. Tucker (Ed.), *The Marx-Engels reader* (2nd ed.). New York: Norton. (Original work published 1844.)

Marx, K. (1978b). Das Kapital. In R. C. Tucker (Ed.), *The Marx-Engels reader* (2nd ed.). New York: Norton. (Original work published 1867.)

Marx, K. (1978c). The German ideology: Part I. In R. C. Tucker (Ed.), *The Marx-Engels reader* (2nd ed.). New York: Norton. (Original work published 1932.)

Marx, K., & Engels, F. (1978). Manifesto of the Communist Party. In R. C. Tucker (Ed.), *The Marx-Engels reader* (2nd ed.). New York: Norton. (Original work published 1948.)

Matthews, R. (1992). Reflections on realism. In J. Young & R. Matthews (Eds.), *Rethinking criminology: The realist debate* (pp. 1–24). London: Sage.

Mead, G. H. (1934). *Mind, self, and society*. Chicago: University of Chicago Press.

Messerschmidt, J. W. (1993). *Masculinities and crime*. Lanham, MD: Rowman & Littlefield.

Miller, J. M. (1995). Covert participant observation: Reconsidering the least used method. *Journal of Contemporary Criminal Justice, 11*, 97–105.

Miller, J. M., & Tewksbury, R. A. (Eds.). (2001). *Extreme methods: Innovative approaches to social science research*. Boston: Allyn & Bacon.

Morash, M., & Chesney-Lind, M. (1991). A reformulation and partial test of the power control theory of delinquency. *Justice Quarterly, 8*, 347–378.

Murphy, K., & Harris, N. (2007). Shaming, shame, and recodovism: A test of reintegrative shaming theory in the white-collar crime context. *The British Journal of Criminology, 47*(6), 900–917.

Pepinsky, H. E., & Quinney, R. (Eds.). (1991). *Criminology as peacemaking.* Bloomington: Indiana University Press.

Pfohl, S. J. (1985). *Images of deviance and social control: A sociological history.* New York: McGraw-Hill.

Quinney, R. (1979). The production of criminology. *Criminology, 16,* 445–458.

Quinney, R. (1980). *Class, state and crime* (2nd ed.). New York: Longman.

Schwartz, M. D., & Friedrichs, D. O. (1994). Postmodern thought and criminological discontent: New metaphors for understanding violence. *Criminology, 32,* 221.

Simon, R. (1975). *Women and crime.* Lexington, MA: Lexington Books.

Steffensmeier, D. J., & Streifel, C. (1992). Trends in female crime: 1960–1990. In C. Culliver (Ed.), *Female criminality: The state of the art.* New York: Garland.

Steffensmeier, D. J., & Terry, R. M. (1973). Deviance and respectability: An obser-

vational study of reactions to shoplifting. *Social Forces, 51,* 417–426.

Strang, H., & Braithwaite, J. (Eds.). (2001). *Restorative justice and civil society.* Cambridge, UK: Cambridge University Press.

Sutherland, E.H. (1947). *Principles of Criminology.* Philadelphia: Lippincott.

Tannenbaum, F. (1938). *Crime and the community.* Boston: Ginn.

Tittle, C. R., & Curran, D. (1988). Contingencies for dispositional disparities in juvenile justice. *Social Forces, 67,* 23–58.

Vold, G. B. (1958). *Theoretical criminology.* New York: Oxford University Press.

Wilbanks, W. (1987). *The myth of a racist criminal justice system.* Monterey, CA: Brooks/Cole.

Young, J. (1987). The tasks facing a realist criminology. *Contemporary Crises, 11,* 337–356.

Zhang, L., & Zhang, S. (2004). Reintegrative shaming and predatory delinquency. *Journal of Research in Crime and Delinquency, 41,* 433–453.

CHAPTER 10

EVALUATING AND INTEGRATING THEORY

Our understanding of the causes of crime, how its occurrence is unevenly dispersed throughout society in a fairly systematic manner, and how various policy responses might fare is certainly greater than it would be without the benefit of theoretical insight. In general, theories provide conceptual frameworks in which a vast range of crime topics are systematically analyzed. The findings from analyses, in turn, provide insight into and recommendations for addressing crime problems. To the extent that theories enhance the scientific study, they are significant to preventing and reducing crime.

Theoretical criminology is complex and involves multiple levels of analysis and may vary in degree of abstract thought. Criminology entails both macro and micro levels of analysis of both rational and irrational behavior; it engages both structure and process; it offers diverse conceptions of society through consensus and conflict perspectives; and it debates the relative influences of free will and determinism. While each of the separate theories presented in the preceding chapters advances our understanding of crime, no single theory adequately explains or can predict *all* of the crime in society. Most theories are more capable to better our understanding of some offenses, more so than others. This basic shortcoming has moved criminologists to evaluate theories, both individually and collectively, toward the goal of developing more thorough explanations. The development of new theories and the refinement of existing ones are typically referred to as **theory construction**—a process wherein factors that are known to be correlated with crime are connected to new ideas. The basic idea is that something new can be explained or existing explanations can be improved through the identification of previously unidentified concepts. New concepts come from a more abstract definition of a reality that involves ideas, images, and often a new way of expressing a phenomenon through more precise or descriptive language. By reducing concepts to cause and effect elements (i.e., variables) through operationalization (i.e., measurement), social scientists can assess the rigor and value of theory.

Most theories tend to better address certain types of offenses by featuring explanations that more effectively account for either violent or property crime.

Other theories are more specific to juvenile delinquency than adult criminality or otherwise account for the criminal behavior of some social groups more so than others, as specified by, for example, social class or age group. While all of the individual theories we examined emphasize certain causal factors (the various separate empirical realities that are known to be correlated with crime), none of them successfully incorporate all of the many identified causes. This basic shortcoming gives rise to specific questions concerning theoretical criminology, particularly, "Which theories are right?" and, conversely, "Which theories are wrong?" Unfortunately, the answers to these questions aren't obvious and entail consideration of several relevant issues. Below, we will take a brief look at how theories are evaluated and how these evaluations shape the direction of theoretical development.

EVALUATING THEORY

To begin a discussion of comparing the relative value and "correctness" of individual theories, we must first consider both the *diversity* and *complexity* of the many statements that combine to constitute theoretical criminology. Neither of these characteristics should be surprising. After all, the body of criminological theory has been developed over several decades (and centuries when considering the Classical School), and we can observe how individual theorists' conceptualizations of social problems reflects the spirit and values of their respective times. The prominence of subcultural theories during the 1950s and early 1960s, for example, reflects the identification of value systems that did not coincide with middle-class standards of the day and, consequently, became a reference point for what was widely believed to be moral decay. As values associated with subcultures became increasingly popularized and the national political pendulum shifted in a general liberal direction, subcultural theories became less popular and were replaced by alternative perspectives. Going further back in time, the classical perspective was viewed as extremely liberal and progressive during the 1700s, but its descendants, deterrence and rational choice theories are classified today as conservative.

Similarly, research methodologies have become increasingly sophisticated with the evolution of the social and behavioral sciences. The ability to realize greater precision in determining causal inference due to advances in statistical analytic techniques, for example, has enabled reconsideration of previously accepted relationships and complicated certain assumptions about the causes of crime—particularly in regard to how various crime correlates combine to generate additive and interactive effects. Theories have thus become increasingly complex, as today's theorists are more cognizant of the importance of the theory–methods symmetry and the need to construct theory that can be empirically assessed with up-to-date methods.

A considerable proportion of environmental criminology, for example, is derived from the Chicago school social ecological approach to crime. This school of thought was developed during the first half of the twentieth century and was predominantly theoretical in nature, as access to large-scale crime and delinquency surveys was limited and statistical techniques were relatively new. Much of the empirical knowledge base regarding ecological criminology was generated through multiple regression analyses conducted during the 1980s and 1990s, reflecting greater scientific rigor than generally reflected in prior research. Today, many of these studies have been brought into question as scholars acknowledge that the nonrandom nature of crime (and thus the data related to it) violates basic assumptions requisite for utilizing many of the regression analyses that were conducted in these studies. Criminologists have thus moved to reconsidering the crime–environment relationship with newer statistical techniques capable of accounting for the limitations inherent to statistically examining criminal behavior and events.

In order to sort out these concerns, criminologists compare and evaluate theories in three general ways. Theories can be developed and assessed singularly, through theoretical competition, or by theoretical integration. **Singular theory assessment** is the simplest approach to evaluating theory—an approach that simply seeks to identify the level of empirical support that exists for a theory. In short, data are gathered in order to examine whether formally stated propositions that specify causal relationships between theoretical concepts (often in the form of hypotheses) can be accepted—a process known as **theory testing.** If sampling is adequate toward the social science axiom of generalizability, operationalizations of key variables are precise so as to minimize the chance of measurement error, and statistical or qualitative analysis reveals causal relationships, a theory is confirmed. Of course, lack of empirical support for the formally stated propositions that constitute individual theories leads to rejection of hypotheses and the search for alternative explanations.

It is important to understand that theories are not easily confirmed or disconfirmed. Theories are tested by multiple researchers who may, and often do, find contradictory and different levels of support. Theory testing also entails both spatial (place) and temporal (time) variation. That is, a particular theory may be confirmed by a study in one country but not another and, likewise, by past but not present research. Perhaps the value system or social structure is different across countries, or the social demographics of an area change over time due to in and out migration patterns. Last, there is also the basic concern of generalizability—that is, the scope of the applicability of findings. As we have seen in the preceding chapters, some theories work quite well for certain social groups but not others. Accordingly, it is usually not the case that a theory is absolutely confirmed or rejected by any single test. Rather, specific theories are confirmed with noted limitations. Nonetheless, criminologists observe the general relative value of theories according to the amount of empirical support found for each theory and the generality or scope (i.e., the extent of the crime problem addressed) that each theory offers.

Moreover, a theory may receive both partial confirmation and partial rejection within and across separate tests. A simple way to grasp this idea is to consider theory as partly true and correct. Usually, theory tests prove that at least some of the propositions or major statements of a theory are true. On the other hand, most theory tests fail to prove that all of a theory's propositions are valid and generally applicable to different types of crimes or groups of offenders. A specific theory test might confirm, for example, that the involvement and attachment elements of the social bond (the focal point of social control theory) are correlated with specific types of juvenile delinquency, but that the commitment and belief elements are not.

Most theory tests focus on single theories by subjecting data representative of a theory's primary concepts to empirical scrutiny. These tests enable us to accept and reject various theories according to a systematic scientific standard. Singular theory testing, however, does not permit *comparison* of multiple theories simultaneously to determine both relative levels of empirical support and the comparative scope of explanation offered. Such comparison is made through a process known as theory competition as discussed below.

Theory Competition

Theory competition involves direct and systematic comparison of two or more theories. The "competition" lies in rank ordering individual theories according to (1) the amount of empirical support (confirming evidence) and (2) the scope of coverage, that is, the breadth of explanation offered. While these two criteria are used to examine individual theories as described previously, assessing several theories at once enables a general appreciation of which theories best explain various aspects of the crime problem. Reference to the level of empirical support demonstrated typically, but not always, means whether variable analysis reveals an acceptable threshold of statistical significance (as discussed in Chapter 1). As we mentioned before, statistical evidence confirming causal inference is certainly not the sole standard for accepting, rejecting, and comparing theory. Scholars also regularly engage theoretical comparison in pure conceptual and logical contexts, especially conflict and cultural theorists whose respective explanations are presented in a language that is not particularly well suited for testing through variable analysis.

Theory competition is important in two respects. First, comparing theories in a competitive sense enables us to look for better explanations and disregard (or use cautiously) others that have received only minimal or no support. Inasmuch as theory informs and guides criminal and juvenile justice programs and policies, competitive theory testing has serious implications for real-world program development and continuation. The national youth court movement (sometimes referred to as "teen court"), for example, is directly derived from restorative justice and reintegrative shaming theories. Youth courts and similar other community-based justice programs have been rapidly implemented across the country, but only a few of them have been evaluated. Most youth courts and similar programs are funded by grants that require evaluation, which, in turn, is important for theory construction. As evaluations of initiatives that are based on theoretical propositions occur, research simultaneously informs policymakers about both the effectiveness of specific criminal justice efforts and whether additional programs should be modeled according to similar or alternative theories. The youth court movement is but one of many examples of how theories shape and improve the world of criminal justice.

A second important consequence of competitive theory testing is the generation of knowledge necessary for theory construction and evolution. There is a healthy sense of intellectual competition among theoretical criminologists, whose advocacy of certain perspectives often entails critical attention to the shortcomings and new assertions of rival explanations. Accordingly, theory competition involves close empirical scrutiny of theoretical statements, both in the hope of evidencing newly contended relationships (i.e., confirming discoveries) and demonstrating lack of empirical evidence toward discontinuation of invalid perspectives. Through this ongoing process of theory competition the field of criminology moves forward and remains current in both the assessment of society's crime problems and informing responses by the criminal justice system.

Theory is generally furthered in one of three ways: (1) the emergence of original theory, (2) theoretical elaboration, and (3) theoretical integration. Original theory is the emergence of a set of propositions explaining a phenomenon (in our case either crime or criminality) that is generally thought to identify a novel cause or source. Many of the theories presented in this text, such as those framed by Sutherland (1947), Cohen (1955), Miller (1958), and Shaw and McKay (1942), are deemed original because they identify and emphasize distinct causes of crime—social learning, anomie, subcultures, and social disorganization, respectively. Totally new and unique theories focusing on previously unidentified causes and correlates of crime are very rare, largely due to the breadth and pluralistic nature of the many existing theories. Instead, theory is more often developed through elaboration and integration.

Empirical Support for Competing Theories

Before moving on to the topics of theoretical elaboration and integration, let's look at the levels of support for some of the different theories we've been examining throughout this text. The theories we've examined view crime as a function of many separate causes—that is, they situate the reasons (and responsibility) for crime across a broad range of personal and social factors. Accordingly, individual theories endorse a range of sometimes competing and ideologically opposed policy responses. At the most basic level, some theories suggest that rehabilitation, prosocial value development, and peer- or community-based programs will best alleviate crime rates, while other theories lend credence to a deterrence-based form of justice. So which theories have received the most empirical support when subjected to competitive theory testing?

In reporting the relative empirical support for criminological theories it is important to call attention to one qualifying concern. While theories are compared in terms of strength (empirical evidence) and scope (generalizability), not all of the theories or even all of the leading theories can be examined simultaneously. Attempting to do so would simply be illogical. Comparing all of the theories at once wouldn't be meaningful because the individual theories attempt to explain different dimensions of crime. As we've seen, some explain how the criminal law is formed or constructed according to power struggles (conflict theory) or according to normative consensus (classical criminology), others attempt to account for the criminality of social demographically identified groups (original strain theory, subcultural and social learning theories), and still others speak to the crime rate through social ecology. This diversity of coverage, then, makes direct comparison of all theories a lot like comparing apples and oranges. Instead, theories are more commonly grouped by type, as they were clustered for presentation in the first nine chapters of this text, and support is discussed in terms of which perspectives seem most fitting for criminological research questions specific to criminality, crime rate, or legal origin.

Perhaps the easiest way to quickly decipher which theories are receiving empirical support is to observe the ones that are currently guiding criminological research and criminal justice practice. Ideally, invalid theories are phased out over time as they cannot withstand empirical scrutiny and the specific juvenile and criminal justice programs modeled after them prove ineffective. Clearly, outdated biological theories of criminality, such as Lombroso's criminal body-typing approach, have been invalidated and are rarely taken seriously anymore. Newer and more elaborate biological theories, however, aren't necessarily seen as taboo anymore and have received a modicum of empirical support that has somewhat revived the biological perspective (Wright & Miller, 1998). Psychological theories that emphasize impulsivity, personality tendencies, and emotional factors, for example, have not received widespread support and seem able to explain the criminality of a fairly narrow group of offenders.

In general, sociological explanations tend to receive more support than either biological or psychological theories, but this claim is partly a matter of classification. Traditional strain theory and similar theories that emphasize the importance of anomie are often considered sociological theories but certainly contain psychological elements. Regardless of whether traditional strain theory is seen as sociological or social-psychological, there is limited empirical support—certainly far less than exists for revised versions such as reverse strain theory. Other sociological or structural theories, such as social disorganization theory, while infrequently tested, are comparatively strong and suggest a consequential correlation between neighborhood cohesiveness and stability and level of crime. Although a dominant perspective for much of the last three decades, social control theory receives only moderate support today.

Newer conflict theories fare better than older Marxist and critical perspectives, but again the statement must be qualified and put into context. Most critical perspectives, be they Marxist, labeling, or conflict theories, address the inconsistencies within and inadequacies of the criminal justice system, but with only minimal empirical support. Critical theories focusing on law formation, however, have received greater empirical support.

Subcultural theories are often considered obsolete and, accordingly, almost never tested. Theories emphasizing values and subcultural influence were largely dismissed as tautological during the 1970s but, in all fairness, have received almost no testing due to criminologists' inability to effectively operationalize the key variable of subculture. Recent cultural explanations of crime, such as Nisbett and Cohen's culture of honor hypothesis, contend that value systems have causal effect but are confirmed through mixed methods that do not rise to commonly accepted standards of theory validation. Nonetheless, subculture remains an important, though relegated, concept in criminology whose import is too readily and simplistically explained away as an exogenous variable. The mere fact that criminologists continue to look to subcultures, more so now as a context for than cause of crime, suggests both a lingering importance and that theorists may be too dismissive of a subculture's criminogenic nature. Recent events such as the mass removal of children in El Dorado, Texas, from the Fundamental Latter Day Saints (FLDS) compound, Yearning for Zion, and evidence of immigrant human trafficking rings indicate the relevance of group affiliations in terms of ethnicity and religion along a culture-to-cult continuum.

Interest in theory testing most often centers on the well-known deterrence-versus-rehabilitation debate, particularly in response to high-profile crimes involving celebrities or particularly ruthless acts for which the death penalty might be imposed. Rehabilitation advocates essentially believe that society has the ability, through social programs, individual counseling, and education and skills enhancement, to rework the attitudes and belief systems of offenders. Bolstering an offender's level of social bondedness, for example, would presumably vest that person in conventional behavior, yet there is only limited support for social control theory. Supporters of rehabilitation approaches to crime find greater support in tests of social learning and, most frequently, restorative justice theories that seek to rework offenders' psyches and de-escalate conflict with the criminal justice system, respectively.

On the other hand, there is frequent public outcry when a hardened criminal released on parole commits additional crime, particularly when extreme violence is involved. The public often questions why such people are released in the first place and whether society needs harsher punishments to deter repeat offenses. Sociological criminologists have typically found little support for deterrence theory, but again, the matter must be put into context. As we saw in Chapter 2, deterrence is both perceptual and literal and is intended for both individuals and the general public. There is little evidence in support of deterrence, especially for the most serious crimes that society would ideally wish to deter the most. Serious violent crime, however, is often emotive in nature (people become so angry at times that they are not rational), thus negating a meaningful criminal calculus. Accordingly, there is little reason to believe that increasing the severity of punishment will automatically force or motivate people to choose noncriminal courses of action. Nonetheless, it is altogether certain that individual-level deterrence is absolutely effective in regard to capital punishment. On a less extreme level, emerging evidence shows that deterrence can be effective in situationally specific contexts, such as drug testing for offenders. Despite the presence of limited evidence supporting deterrence theory, the deterrence model remains the single most consequential theoretical perspective in terms of criminal justice practice and policy. In fact, the vast majority of what transpires within and across the three prongs of the criminal justice system is rooted in deterrence principles. The notion of crime prevention (especially efforts at general and perceptual deterrence) and the U.S. Sentencing Guidelines (emphasizing proportionality of punishment), for example, are reflections of a determining deterrence logic.

THEORETICAL ELABORATION

Theory testing and theory competition both effect theory construction as a sort of metaphorical compass pointing the direction for new theory building. As mentioned previously, completely original theory is fairly uncommon—most of the major causes and a great many secondary causes of crime have already been discovered and examined. Theory nonetheless continues to advance in other ways, one of which is **theoretical elaboration.** Theoretical elaboration requires neither the introduction of totally new ideas nor the resolution of differences across theories. Rather, this approach entails building on existing theory by considering what new variables might be added to realize more complete explanations.

A good example of theoretical elaboration is Haynie's (2001) attention to delinquent peer groups. Drawing on concepts from social control and differential association theory, properties of social networks are identified that link these theoretical perspectives and enable elaboration. The delinquent peer explanation recognizes that differential association conditions peer groups and that, at the individual level, the nature of social bonding is predictive of delinquency. By fleshing out the structural properties of peer groups, however, the nature of group delinquency can be better understood. Specifically, the delinquent peer effect specifies that delinquency is a function of the influence exerted by friendship groups whose effect can be observed through the network characteristics of centrality (where someone is located, such as at home or a part-time job, which provides or limits interaction with others), density (how many people are in the group and how frequently they interact), and popularity (the level of acceptance, involvement, and desirability a person realizes within the group). The delinquent peer elaboration on the major differential association and social control theories reaffirms these perspectives but also furthers knowledge about how groups affect behavior. Through this elaboration, new specific research questions can be identified and studied. Popularity, for example, presents interesting queries. On the topic of popularity and teenage sexual victimization, for example, we can hypothesize two opposite trajectories. On one hand, it is plausible that popularity protects people (in this example, typically teenage girls), because most people within a youth culture are familiar with who is, in fact, popular. The assumption to be tested here is whether popularity translates into protection from harm as more people desire to look out for those who are well liked. On the other hand, popularity might work the other way—that is, it might actually increase the risk of sexual victimization. Popular youth logically are invited to a greater number of social events, go on more dates, and are thus exposed to a greater number of potential risks. So whether popularity offsets these risks or contributes to victimization is a specific research question stemming from theoretical elaboration.

An argument might be made that virtually all of the theories we've examined are a result of theoretical elaboration, but this is true only in the broadest sense. Cohen's attention to subculture certainly incorporates and builds on Merton's anomie perspective, and Aker's social learning theory clearly extends Sutherland's conceptualization of differential association. Similarly, Braithwaite's reintegrative shaming theory builds on earlier consensus and labeling perspectives. These theories are largely considered original, however, because they introduce and emphasize causal and contributing factors previously ignored or neglected. Theoretical elaboration, then, is better understood as a process of extending existing perspectives to address crime in ways that further our overall knowledge base.

THEORETICAL INTEGRATION

An alternative approach to the shortcomings of single theories and elaboration is **theoretical integration.** Theoretical integration is also referred to as *theoretical subsumption.* This refers to more focused or specific concepts being regrouped or absorbed under a larger concept, such as Hirschi's original social bond being reconfigured as a precursor to self-control in his revised theory with Gottfredson (Gottfredson & Hirschi, 1990). Theoretical integration basically enables two main objectives: (1) the construction of models that offer greater accountability for unexplained crime—that is, fuller explanations can be realized by combining complementary and distinct components of separate theories into a single explanation—and (2) the creation of general theory. Criminological theories are considered middle-range theories because they seek to account for systematic patterns in human behavior and the social structure predictive of criminality and crime rates. It is accurate to classify virtually all of the theories we covered in this book in Chapters 2 through 8 as middle-range or specialized theories. This is because, unlike the more general social perspectives described in Chapter 1 (functionalism, symbolic interactionism, and conflict)—which ask "What makes society possible?"—criminological theory is limited to a focused attention on a dimension of society (crime and its control). Theoretical integration in criminology, while not as ambitious as the general social functionalist and other perspectives, marks the development toward a more comprehensive framework wherein a broader range of crime and deviance can be related to fundamental causal components. General theories are grand perspectives that purport to account for all types of crime and deviance, often across time and space, consistent with the label of being "general." While most criminologists have focused on coupling the central elements of middle-range theories as discussed directly below, some sociologists argue the utility of explaining crime through general or grand theories (i.e., functionalism, symbolic interactionism, and conflict stratification). Chris (2007), for example, contends that both Hirschi's original social control theory and Gottfredson and Hirschi's subsequent self-control theories are derived and subsumed from Talcott Parson's structural version of functionalism.

There are two main ways that theoretical integration occurs. The first, **sequential integration,** is fairly easy to understand and is more common. This type of integration, also known as **propositional integration,** involves identifying and combining complementary but conceptually distinct concepts from separate theories toward realizing greater predictability for some crime phenomenon. The term *sequential* is important because the propositions from one theory are simply linked to the propositions of another to form a more elaborate explanation. Consider, for example, how variation in one element of the social bond (attachment) can affect the nature of social learning. According to social control theory, youth form attachments to realize a sense of place and belonging with their primary group, most often parents and immediate family members. Presumably, youth who are poorly bonded with their family—that is, individuals who are not strongly attached—will likely attach to others in their immediate environment. Primary attachments to other youth and adults in the community (social control theory) help us understand how youth develop attitudes and a general outlook that likely approximates the worldview and behavior of the people with whom they interact and whom they emulate (social learning theory). Such a process may result in either a socially desirable or undesirable outcome, depending on the balance of conventional and deviant practices of either parents or neighborhood role models.

Numerous sequential or propositional theoretical integrations during the last two decades have demonstrated the value of combining different schools of thought. Prominent examples include Tittle's control balance theory (1995), Thornberry and colleagues' interactional theory (1991), Krohn's network analysis (1986), and Elliot's integrated delinquency theory (1985). Elliot's theory provides a straightforward example of linking propositions from separate theories to realize greater predictability and explanation. This particular delinquency explanation incorporates dimensions of strain, social control, and social learning theories into a single linear statement. In short, the theory contends that anomic strain (the inability to realize achievements stemming from a means–end discrepancy, for example) negatively conditions social bonds (i.e., strain detracts from prosocial bonds), which, in turn, leads to greater exposure to and involvement with similarly situated delinquent others. Through heightened exposure to a delinquent peer group, youth receive social reinforcement (a primary component of social learning theory) for the delinquency and crime to which they are exposed on a regular basis (as confirmed by self-reported delinquency studies).

Krohn's (1986) integrated theory of crime is rooted in the key assumptions and propositions of both social learning and social bonding theories. However, unlike the original versions, his theory is situated in a social network context. A social network is simply a set of individuals or groups associated by friendship or some other type of relationship. Krohn contends that a social network is capable of exerting influence over individual behavior (social control), and similar to Elliot's integrated theory, he rejects the idea that social control is necessarily related to positive, prosocial, or law-abiding behavior. Rather, through incorporation of social learning principles, this theory suggests that if the social network within which one is situated is characterized by delinquency or deviance, exposure to such negative behavior and, presumably, attitudes favorable toward that behavior can encourage delinquent or criminal activity.

Krohn proposes that the strength of the social network's effect is attributable to the network's structural characteristics, specifically its *multiplexity* and *density*. Multiplexity refers to the number of relationships that two or more individuals have in common, such as school, neighborhood, or extracurricular activities. According to Krohn, multiplexity denotes "what individuals' associates do (differential association) and the kind of activities in which they are mutually involved (commitment and/or involvement)" (Krohn, 1986). Density is defined as the ratio of actual social relationships to the total number of possible relationships in a network. Network density is negatively related to crime and delinquency—that is, the higher the density, the lower the delinquency within a social network.

Another example of prepositional integration is found in Thornberry and colleagues' interactional theory (1991). This theory, derived from social structural, social bonding, and social learning theories, suggests that the underlying causal mechanism of delinquency is the weakening of the social bond. This weakening, however, only serves to make it *more likely* that one will engage in delinquent or criminal behavior. Compatible with social learning theory, Thornberry contends that only through association, reinforcement, and definitions (favorable to delinquent behavior) will delinquency become a behavioral pattern. According to this theory, the social learning process itself is affected by structural variables such as race, social class, and community and neighborhood characteristics. Noting that most causes of crime are interrelated and thus have reciprocal effects, Thornberry identified numerous correlations that cut across theories. For example, delinquency can affect (usually in a negative or undesirable way) many of its causes. Low parental attachment increases associations with delinquent peers—an example reflecting both social control and learning theory elements.

The second main type of theoretical integration, **conceptual fusion,** is a little more complex. Whereas sequential integration links complementary concepts in a linear logic model, conceptual integration seeks to merge similar ideas that, while stated differently and presented as distinct variables, actually constitute theoretical overlap. Theoretical overlap refers to concepts and variables across individual theories that account for the same variation in the same or similar dependent variables. Additionally, integration can cross levels of analysis, meaning that fused concepts (or the previously described approach of linking propositions) are drawn from theories that are at a micro level or macro level of analysis. When integration links or combines theories from the same level of analysis, regardless of whether it is at a small-group or societal level, it is considered to be "within-level." Some theoretical integrations are more ambitious and attempt to link the processes of group behavior with structural factors (i.e., combining both micro and macro levels of analysis into a single statement), an approach that is labeled "cross-level."

There are fewer examples of conceptual integration than there are for sequential integration. Akers's notion of conceptual absorption (another way of saying conceptual fusion) is important to the topic of theoretical integration, generally, and illustrates how similar ideas expressed in distinct theories can be effectively merged to explain specific behaviors. Akers (1985, 1989) contends that social control theory components, as expressed through the elements of the social bond, are subsumed and fused to assume similar but somewhat unique meaning. Whereas commitment usually refers to the degree of investment in conventional or criminal activity as indicated by the extent to which the other is sacrificed, commitment is "absorbed" in Akers's theory by social learning. Akers contends that the social learning theory concept of differential reinforcement both subsumes and is preferable to commitment. Whereas commitment only denotes sacrifices, differential reinforcement refers to the balance of rewards to punishments. Through attention to punishments (sacrifices), then, differential reinforcement "covers" what is offered by social control theory—at least the commitment component—but also includes consideration of positive influences on behavior and is thus a more complete theory. Similarly, the other social bond elements are arguably subsumed, such as belief being covered by learned definitions of crime as favorable or not.

SUMMARY

After defining the types of theoretical integration and discussing some of the major characteristics, it is important to note that integrated theory has not received the level of support that one might think. The idea of theoretical integration is to realize greater levels of explanation and predictability of crime through linking and fusing the most salient features of independent theories. Once identified, these leading concepts are reassembled into a new and ideally more complete statement. While the practice of combining the strengths of separate theories sounds promising as a thought experiment, in practice integrated theories are not often tested, and the ones that have been tested typically receive about the same or only slightly greater empirical support than in single theory tests. Despite a lack of overwhelming success to date, contemporary criminologists seem to remain enthusiastic about theoretical integration, which is likely to continue as a primary means of theory building for years to come. As Osgood (1998) noted a decade ago, criminologists should freely "steal" the viable concepts and elements from relevant theory in related disciplines toward realizing more thorough and comprehensive explanations of crime. This sentiment of clear advocacy for an increased interdisciplinary orientation to theory construction is becoming ever more normative and apt to characterize theoretical criminology over the next few decades.

KEY TERMS

conceptual fusion   a type of theoretical integration involving the merging of similar ideas into a broader conceptual framework

sequential integration   a type of theoretical integration that involves identifying and combining complementary but conceptually distinct ideas from two or more theories

singular theory assessment   an approach to evaluating theory that seeks to identify the level of empirical support that exists for a theory

theoretical elaboration   an approach to theory building that entails extending existing theory by considering what

new variables might be added for a more complete explanation

theoretical integration   an approach to theory building that incorporates key elements of two or more existing theories

theory competition   an approach to evaluating theory involving the direct and systematic comparison of two or more theories

theory construction   a process wherein factors that are known correlates of crime are connected to new ideas

theory testing   a process wherein data are gathered in order to examine the empirical validity of a theory's propositions

DISCUSSION QUESTIONS

1. How is theory testing related to theory building?

2. What are the similarities and differences between singular theory testing and theoretical competition?

3. How does theoretical elaboration differ from theoretical integration?

4. Identify and discuss the two main types of theoretical integration.

5. What theories do you think could be integrated to develop a general theory of crime?

REFERENCES

Akers, R. L. (1985). *Deviant behavior: A social learning approach* (3rd ed.). Belmont, CA: Wadsworth.

Akers, R. L. (1989). A social behaviorist's perspective on integration of theories of crime and deviance. In S. Messner, M. D. Krohn, & A. Liska (Eds.), *Theoretical integration in the study of crime and deviance: Problems and prospects* (pp. 23–36). Albany: State University of New York Press.

Chris, J. J. (2007). The functions of the social bond. *The Sociological Quarterly, 48*, 689–712.

Cohen, A. K. (1955). *Delinquent boys: The culture of the gang.* Glencoe, IL: Free Press.

Elliot, D. S. (1985). The assumption that theories can be combined with increased explanatory power: Theoretical integrations. In R. F. Meier (Ed.), *Theoretical methods in criminology.* Beverly Hills, CA: Sage.

Gottfredson, M., & Hirschi, T. (1990). *A General Theory of Crime.* Palo Alto, CA: Standford University Press.

Haynie, D. L. (2001). Delinquent peers revisited: Does network structure matter? *American Journal of Sociology, 106*, 1013.

Krohn, D. M. (1986). The web of conformity: A network approach to the explanation of delinquent behavior. *Social Problems, 33,* 19–29.

Miller, W. B. (1958). Lower-class culture as a generating milieu of gang delinquency. *Journal of Social Issues, 14*(3), 5–19.

Osgood, D. W. (1998). Interdisciplinary integration: Building criminology by stealing from our friends. *The Criminologist, 23*(4), 1.

Shaw, C. R., & McKay, H. D. (1942). *Juvenile delinquency and urban areas.* Chicago: University of Chicago Press.

Sutherland, E. H. (1947). *Principles of criminology* (4th ed.). Philadelphia: Lippincott.

Thornberry, T. P., Lizotte, A. J., Krohn, M. D., Farnsworth, M., & Jang, S. J. (1991). Testing interactional theory: An examination of reciprocal causal relationships among family, school, and delinquency. *Journal of Criminal Law and Criminology, 82,* 3–33.

Tittle, C. R. (1995). *Control balance: Toward a general theory of deviance.* Boulder, CO: Westview Press.

Wright, R. A., & Miller, J. M. (1998). Taboo until today? The coverage of biological arguments in criminology textbooks, 1961 to 1970 and 1987 to 1996. *Journal of Criminal Justice, 26*(1), 1–19.

INDEX

■ ■ ■ ■ ■ ▬▬▬▬▬▬▬▬▬▬▬▬▬▬▬▬▬▬▬▬▬▬▬▬▬▬▬▬▬

Note: Page numbers in bold indicate location of key terms.